Praise for *The Relationship Fix*

"Anyone who wants to improve their relationship should read this book. Dr. Jenn shares the roadmap to resolving the most common issues couples struggle with, using her no-holds-barred style and lots of entertaining stories. She backs up her suggestions with clinical experience and the latest research."
John M. Gottman, Ph.D., author of *The Seven Principles for Making Marriage Work*

"Dr. Jenn Mann has written a truly insightful book! It looks at the spiritual and psychological reasons relationships run into trouble and gives clear advice on what to do about them. A must-read."
—Tracy McMillan, author of *Why You're Not Married . . . Yet: The Straight Talk You Need to Get the Relationship You Deserve*

"In this book, Dr. Jenn gives couples the tools to revolutionize their relationship. She talks about the things most therapists don't talk about and gives clear instructions that most therapists won't give you. This book puts the power to change your relationship in your own hands where it belongs."
—Phil Stutz, co-author, *The Tools: Transform Your Problems into Courage, Confidence, and Creativity*

"*The Relationship Fix* is like having Dr. Jenn walking beside you, sharing her twenty plus years of time-tested proven ideas, exercises, techniques, and therapies. Sexuality is one of the toughest areas for couples to talk about, and Dr. Jenn gives direction and ways to expand connection, communication, and confidence, whether you've been together for two weeks or two decades."
—Lou Paget, bestselling author of *How to Be A Great Lover: Girlfriend-to-Girlfriend Totally Explicit Techniques that Will Blow His Mind*

"I couldn't put it down! We all need *The Relationship Fix* and Dr. Jenn shows us exactly how to do it. This empowering book teaches us how to make lasting changes to transform our relationships. Using research, moving stories, and decades of real world clinical experience, Dr. Jenn has created a book that couples and singles need, right now, so that we can connect, fight fair, and jazz up our sex lives. Thank you Dr. Jenn!"
—Lisa Bloom, civil rights attorney and author of *Think: Straight Talk for Women to Stay Smart in a Dumbed-Down World*

"I've witnessed Dr. Jenn work magic with couples. *The Relationship Fix* will help you move mountains in yours."
—Dr. Mike Dow, *New York Times* bestselling author of *The Brain Fog Fix: Reclaim Your Focus, Memory, and Joy in Just 3 Weeks*

"Chock full of the latest research, mixed with years of clinical experience and great common sense, *The Relationship Fix* has the power to transform your relationship and your life. With clarity and moving examples, Dr. Jenn Mann leads couples through everything from why it's good for you to be nice to how to spark up your sex life. Practical, accessible, and enjoyable—a terrific book for couples."

—Terrence Real, author of *The New Rules of Marriage: What You Need to Know to Make Love Work*

"My way is 'do good to feel good.' Dr. Jenn's *The Relationship Fix* will help you 'feel good to do good.'"

—Dr. Patricia Allen, author of *Getting to "I Do": The Secret to Doing Relationships Right!*

"Dr. Jenn is truly a gifted teacher on love and romance, and once you've digested her wisdom, you can pretty much navigate any situation in your relationship. She's a trusted guide who shares foundational insights, so your relationship—with yourself and your partner—can thrive. Oh, and it's also a really juicy read!"

—Kathy Freston, *New York Times* bestselling author of *The One: Finding Soul Mate Love and Making it Last*

"This is the book I have been waiting for to recommend to the moms in my parenting groups! In *The Relationship Fix*, Dr. Jenn teaches parents everything they need to know to have a better relationship and be a relationship role model for their kids."

—Jill Spivack, LCSW, Parenting Expert, Bravo's *There Goes the Motherhood*, and bestselling author of The *Sleepeasy Solution: The Exhausted Parent's Guide to Getting Your Child to Sleep–from Birth to Age 5*

"In this fun readable book, Dr. Jenn shares her unique gift for helping couples better their relationship. She will give you new insight, topnotch communication skills, and help you transform your relationship."

—Laurie Ann Levin, PsyD, ACSGC, author of *Life in Life: Live Longer, Strengthen Your Relationships, and Create a Healthier Life*

"All parents and parents-to-be must read this book! Dr. Jenn teaches readers techniques that will make all relationships and families stronger, more peaceful, and loving. Just what every parent needs to raise healthy and happy kids, and enjoy being a couple along the way!"

—Tanya Altmann, MD, FAAP, author of *What to Feed Your Baby: A Pediatrician's Guide to the 11 Essential Foods to Guarantee Veggie-Loving, No-Fuss, Healthy-Eating Kids*

"Dr. Jenn Mann gives practical advice that (when followed) works! Her prescription for a healthy relationship is doled out with compassion, humor, and candor."

—Jenny Hutt, host of *Just Jenny* on SiriusXM

R*the*elationship *fix*

*Dr. Jenn's 6-Step Guide
to Improving Communiction,
Connection & Intimacy*

DR. JENN MANN

Host VH1 *Couples Therapy with Dr. Jenn* and Bestselling Author

STERLING
New York

STERLING
New York

An Imprint of Sterling Publishing Co., Inc.
1166 Avenue of the Americas
New York, NY 10036

ISBN 978-1-4549-1526-3

Distributed in Canada by Sterling Publishing Co., Inc.
c/o Canadian Manda Group, 664 Annette Street
Toronto, Ontario, Canada M6S 2C8
Distributed in the United Kingdom by GMC Distribution Services
Castle Place, 166 High Street, Lewes, East Sussex, England BN7 1XU
Distributed in Australia by NewSouth Books
45 Beach Street, Coogee, NSW 2034, Australia

For information about custom editions, special sales,
and premium and corporate purchases, please contact Sterling Special Sales at
800-805-5489 or specialsales@sterlingpublishing.com.

Manufactured in the United States of America

2 4 6 8 10 9 7 5 3 1

www.sterlingpublishing.com

Interior design by Renato Stanisic

This book is dedicated to Eric Schiffer, the love of my life.
You inspire me to be a better partner, a better therapist,
and a better woman.

I appreciate all you do to help me grow and heal.
Thank you for appreciating who I am, what I do,
and the core of my being.

You are my bear, my white tiger,
my soul mate, my everything.

This book is my love letter to you.

Contents

Foreword

Couples have been around for thousands of years, but help for couples in the form of books and manuals that offered professional advice began to appear only around 1940. In this therapy literature, couples were viewed as individuals trying to have a good relationship, but failing. Viewed alternately as neurotic, immature, or lacking communication and problem-solving skills, they were seen by separate therapists in separate offices, who administered the cure. If you were deemed neurotic, you would generally be treated by a depth psychotherapist to uncover lost memories and hidden feelings. If you were deemed immature or relationally uneducated, therapy consisted of cognitively learning how to communicate, negotiate, and resolve conflict.

In the 1950s, with the divorce rate rising after World War II, therapy for couples began to boom and books for couples proliferated, but the effectiveness rate hovered around 25 percent. The major contribution to this low impact on relationship satisfaction of couples in therapy was the psychological paradigm operative in all forms of therapy. In this paradigm, with its roots in 18th-century Enlightenment philosophy and Freudian psychology, human beings were viewed as entities who were separate, independent, and self-sufficient, with inner worlds that were intrinsically isolated from each other.

Until the last decade of the twentieth century, therapists viewed couples through that lens. Since marriages were born in the fires of romantic love, and those fires had been extinguished, the wish for most couples was the restoration of the flame and the goal of most therapists was to remove the impediments to that wish so couples could achieve it. The therapeutic technology included a depth understanding of the childhood contribution to conflict and the employment conflict resolution skills to regulate interpersonal behavior and get emotional needs met.

By the end of the twentieth century, a paradigm shift that replaced the individual with the relationship became operative in the therapeutic world. The first move toward viewing relationship as the effective variable in healing was made in the early 1950's by Carl Rogers, who posited that empathy between the client and therapist was the effective variable in healing. This theme expanded from a trickle to a stream in child psychology and new forms of therapy in the second quarter of the twentieth century. It entered couple's therapy in the last quarter of the century with our introduction of Imago Relationship Therapy in *Getting the Love You Want*.

Couples therapy in the relational paradigm shifts perspective from the individuals in the relationship to the space between them, from the self as isolated to the self as relational, and sees safety as the non-negotiable quality of the space between as the precondition for connecting. Dialogue as the relational technology helps couples transform conflict into co-creation and replaces conflict resolution and mutual need gratification with connecting, joy, and wonder. Safe connecting interactions create "presence," which is the panacea that meets all the needs of every couple. This shifts the location of change from inside the individuals to the space between them. This is a new breed of couple's therapy that improves the success rate to 80 percent.

The Relationship Fix is an expression of this new approach. The fact that the title includes "Relationship" and that "fix" is the goal is a clue that Dr. Mann operates intellectually and clinically in the relationship paradigm. Another clue is that her first chapter is "Create Connection" and first subtitle is "Connection is King." In addition, the off-ramp into her richly populated book is the assertion that infidelity and other relationship ills are a function of the absence of emotional connection. As Dr. Mann indicates, "To feel seen, heard, understood, and adored is magic to our hearts, minds, and souls." And, we add, that is the sole agenda, not only of couple-hood, but of the human race. To arrive there is to return to where we began before we were thrown out of the Eden of childhood: connecting, joy, and wonder. That is our nature, and committed couple-hood is the least traveled but most powerful road to the promised land. That is the new and only agenda of relationship therapy.

Dr. Mann says there are only six steps on the road to connection and intimacy, and communication is the way to get there. She provides an encyclopedia list of concepts, exercises, and practices for the journey. These are spread throughout chapters that focus on connection, fighting fair, negotiating, resolving childhood issues, forgiving and making amends, and igniting your sex life. Any couple who reads this book carefully will feel empowered by the sheer amount of information and guidance the author provides. And couples who use the information cannot help but fix their relationship, nay, transform it, because the process is so clear and direct. Such a book is sorely needed. We hope it gets a broad readership. And we recommend it to every couple. Whether you need it or not, your relationship will improve by just knowing the options available. We are honored to endorse it.

Harville Hendrix, PhD and Helen LaKelly Hunt, PhD,
Making Marriage Simple and *Getting the Love You Want.*

Introduction

If you picked up this book, you are probably hoping to improve your relationship. Hey, who doesn't want a better, stronger relationship? If you are on the verge of a divorce or breakup, in a great relationship but want to take it to the next level, or you're single and want to make sure your next relationship is better, this book is for you.

I promise that if you and your partner do the things I recommend, it will change your relationship for the better. As an author, I always work to give my readers specific, doable actions that they can implement. I want this book to revolutionize the way you think and behave in your relationship. My recommendations are based on almost three decades of clinical experience as a licensed Marriage and Family Therapist in private practice; my work as a relationship expert on television and radio; the most important relationship research in the field; and my own personal experiences. When you read about my own struggles, I hope you'll relate to them, and that some of them will even make you laugh! There are no perfect people and, therefore, no perfect relationships. Mine included.

That said, by following my recommendations, you can have a spectacular, fun, soulful, connected, sexy relationship. Communication, connection, and intimacy (physical and emotional) are the foundations of any romantic partnership. Connection is oxygen to relationships; without it, they die. Most couples don't know how to create and nurture connection, or how to get it back when it fades. This book will change that. All couples experience conflict in their relationships. Because of this, my chapters on fighting fair, negotiating, forgiving, and making amends are particularly important. You can't avoid conflict, but you can learn how to handle it.

Your childhood has a profound impact on how you function in your relationships. The childhood trauma therapy group I do every season on my show, VH1 *Couples Therapy with Dr. Jenn*, is always one of the most important and poignant sessions we do all year. It helps people understand themselves and their partners better, and to have more compassion for each other. Whether you have had trauma or not, your childhood becomes the roadmap for your adult relationships. We tend to pick people who trigger our old wounds and are stunned by the intensity of our pain and anger when our loved ones hurt us.

Last, but not least, I talk about sex. Sexual intimacy is the glue that holds many relationships together. It is the difference between being roommates and being romantic partners. No matter how good (or bad) your sex life is, this chapter will help you take it up a few notches. You will improve your comfort level, sexual communication, technique, and understanding of your own and your partner's needs. I recommend doing the sexual inventory in Appendix B once a year to help you continue to grow sexually as a couple.

A long time ago, in 1993 to be exact, I was an outspoken psychology student in graduate school. One of my professors was appearing on a segment of Channel 2 *Action News*. She was looking for other psychological experts to come on the show and speak—and she asked me to join her. I had already spent years counseling people one on one in an office setting, and working for the Los Angeles Commission on Assaults Against Women (LACAAW), as a rape and domestic violence counselor. When I watched the show air, I realized that instead of affecting one person at a time in my office, I could potentially affect millions. I have not been the same since.

This country, this world, does not teach people how to have healthy relationships. Fortunately, though, I do! I see people in my private practice in Beverly Hills. I counsel celebrities on VH1 *Couples Therapy with Dr. Jenn* and VH1 *Family Therapy with Dr. Jenn.* I appear as a relationship expert and counsel people on many other shows, as well. Hundreds of people reach out to me every night on my call-in advice radio show. I am bombarded with emails and messages on social media asking me to help. For all of you who can't travel to see me, can't afford therapy, or are afraid your voice might be recognized on the radio, this book is for you. Opening it is like opening the doors to my treatment room, where I tell you everything I know to help you make your relationship better.

Relationships take work. There is no way around that. To have a long-term relationship or marriage requires grit, determination, courage, and stamina. It's like running a marathon. You wouldn't expect to do that without hard work and training. Relationships are no different. I offer you *The Relationship Fix* as your training bible.

Recently, I was speaking at a conference about this book. A woman asked a great question: "Can I read this book without my husband knowing and make my relationship better?" The answer is "yes" and "no." It only takes one person to create a chain reaction that alters the system. Role modeling good behavior, communicating better, and making your partner feel adored and appreciated always have an impact. The best way to get your partner to change is to lead and inspire. "Don't wait for him to change," I told her. "You be the one to change the dynamics." We always do best in our relationships when we lead and inspire instead of nag and criticize. It isn't always easy to do that, though.

Now, for the "no." As I always say in the first session I lead with the couples on VH1 *Couples Therapy with Dr. Jenn,* "not every relationship is meant to be saved." Sometimes it is my job as a therapist to help people leave a relationship respectfully. If the person you are with is completely unwilling to change or meet your minimum requests, your relationship is unlikely to work. If, after reading and implementing the strategies in this book, you find that your relationship is not meant to be, I hope you will bring your new insight and behavior to the next one. No relationship is a waste of time, except the ones we don't learn from.

So here, in *The Relationship Fix,* is everything I have learned professionally and personally, for your reading pleasure.

At the end of the day, I am still the same grad student who wants the opportunity to help as many people as possible. I believe this book is that opportunity. May it help you and your relationship grow.

Dr. Jenn Mann

Feel free to reach out to me on social media @DrJennMann and let me know what you think of the book. Please use the hashtag #RelationshipFix so I can find you.

Create Connection

A few years back I read a study that completely revolutionized the way I think about affair prevention, both as a therapist and as a woman. Highly respected therapist, rabbi, and researcher M. Gary Neuman asked two hundred men—one hundred cheaters and one hundred noncheaters—to complete questionnaires and participate in interviews, in order to create a comprehensive study of what makes men cheat. The results were shocking—even to him.

Here's what he learned: While society paints men—especially men who cheat—as pants-dropping, testosterone-driven horn dogs who can't control their sexual urges, it was *not* sex that drove the cheaters to cheat. Only 8 percent of the men who cheated said that an unsatisfying sexual relationship with their wife was the cause of their infidelity. The number one reason these men cheated was emotional dissatisfaction. In fact, 48 percent of the men reported that this was the primary issue that made them cheat, and 88 percent said that the cheating was about significant dissatisfaction in marriage.

Interestingly, only 12 percent of the cheating men said that their mistress was more attractive than their wife. Apparently, the number one way that a mistress differed from the cheater's wife was that she made him feel wanted, loved, and appreciated. What this speaks to is that the majority of men who cheat are not looking for someone who is necessarily "hotter" than their wife. According to this research, most men are not on the lookout for new, acrobatic sex with other women; they are *looking for emotional connection.*

Years later, when M. Gary Neuman did a similar study with cheating and noncheating women, he discovered that—much as he did with the men he'd researched—only 7 percent of the cheating women claimed that sexual dissatisfaction was the primary factor that prompted them to cheat. When asked about emotional issues in their marriage, the number one problem women reported was not having enough time with their husbands, closely followed by feeling underappreciated.

Connection Is King

Connection is the greatest vaccination against infidelity that you can bring to your relationship. There will always be someone who is younger, hotter, thinner, perkier, fitter, or better endowed than you are. But if you are nurturing a sense of connection with your partner— striving to make him feel loved and adored, and providing something unique that no one else can provide overnight, or provide it the way you do—you have the home court advantage.

When, for whatever reasons, you don't pay attention to the needs, desires, or dreams of your partner, you miss the opportunity to connect. To feel seen, heard, understood, and adored is magic to our hearts, minds, and souls. Tuning in and paying attention to your partner are the keys to helping her feel connected to you. In season 4 of VH1 *Couples Therapy with Dr. Jenn*, Whitney Mixter of *The Real L Word* captured this so beautifully when she made the following promise to her wife Sada Bettencourt, also of the *The Real L Word*: "I will try to be more aware and more nurturing and more giving to your needs. All I need from you is for when I'm not 100 percent there yet for you to tell me what you need, if I don't do it automatically. That's all I ask."

It isn't always easy to do, but this chapter will provide you with all the tools you'll need to make that vital connection happen in your relationship.

Thirty-Six Questions That Will Make Your Partner Fall in Love with You

Over twenty years ago, researcher and psychologist Arthur Aron performed an experiment in closeness and intimacy that was so effective that two of his research subjects fell in love and got married, and when college professor Mandy Len Catron re-created the study for herself and a male professor in a bar, they fell in love, too. She wrote about the experience in an article for the *New York Times*, titled "To Fall in Love with Anyone, Do This."

Here's how the experiment works and how you can use it in your own relationship to increase connection, regardless of gender or sexual orientation: A single heterosexual man and woman are paired together and given thirty-six questions that have been broken into three sets of increasingly personal questions to ask each other (see Appendix A for a list of those questions). At the end of the conversation, the subjects sit silently and stare into each other's eyes for four minutes.

According to the study, a key pattern associated with development of a close relationship is "sustained, escalating, reciprocal personal self-disclosure." In other words, to become and remain close, we must be open and forthcoming with our partner about our inner world. Intimacy occurs on multiple levels. According to researchers Harry Reis and Phillip Shaver, intimacy is a process where both partners feel that their innermost self is validated, understood, and cared for by the other.

In describing her experience, Catron likened it to a boiling frog that does not feel the water getting hotter until it is too late. She said, "I didn't notice we had entered intimate territory until we were already there," which speaks to the intimate nature of personal self-disclosure and how seductive it is.

Men who are great seducers don't need pick-up lines or hot cars. They have an innate awareness that getting a woman to open up to them creates a sense of closeness, vulnerability, and connection that sets the stage for sexual seduction: You want to know me? You care about me? You care about my inner life? Here are my panties.

Similarly, women who know how to make men feel special understand that showing interest and getting them to open up is crucial. Case in point: Brian was a married man who loved his wife, Nicole, a fitness trainer, who was working extra hours at the gym to win a spot as a manager and impress her boss. At the same time, Brian and Nicole were in the process of trying to have their first child and were on the verge of meeting with fertility doctors to find out why Nicole wasn't getting pregnant. Brian felt discouraged about his inability to impregnate his wife—but the stress was getting to Nicole as well, and both threw themselves into their work as a way to reduce that stress. Nicole wasn't at all concerned when Brian hired a new assistant because she was not as attractive as Nicole—not nearly.

Paula, the new assistant, was very focused on her new boss and wanted to do a great job. She looked up to Brian, which made him feel strong and powerful. In Paula's eyes, Brian could do no wrong. They found themselves having long lunches together, and when Paula complained to Brian about her boyfriend, he gave her advice and tried to help. This personal talk opened the door for a more intimate relationship and soon they were talking about the problems in Brian's marriage, their beliefs about relationships, their philosophy of life, and their hopes and dreams. All of this opened the door even further for a more emotionally intimate relationship that eventually led to an affair.

What we can learn from the thirty-six-question experiment is that opening your inner world to another person and letting him share his with you is truly the key to intimacy. Choosing to create that kind of intimacy, as Brian did, with a person outside of your relationship is playing with fire. On the flip side, when you do that with your partner, you are building a bridge to intimacy that will benefit your relationship for many years to come.

The thirty-six-question experiment demonstrates that love is an action. You can choose to open up to your partner and you can choose to help her open up to you. No matter how long it has been since you have had a meaningful conversation, you can initiate one now. The thirty-six questions in Appendix A are a good place to start.

Attachment Needs from Cradle to Grave

The point of Mandy Len Catron's article in the *New York Times* was, as she put it in the title, you *can* make anyone fall in love with you. While that statement may sound extreme, here is what we know from the experiment:

1. **Love requires intimacy.** Without meaningful conversations, showing your partner you care about her inner life, and asking questions, love shrivels up and dies like a plant without sunlight.
2. **Face-to-face conversations are crucial.** The focused attention required by a face-to-face conversation nurtures the connection between two people. Stop looking at the TV screen or your phone and start looking at your partner.
3. **Eye contact goes a long way.** The four-minute eye gaze at the end of the experiment serves a purpose. To gaze into another person's

eyes is to connect. It shows where your attention is directed and bolsters the relationship. There are also physiological benefits. Looking directly into your lover's eyes releases adrenaline; prompts activity in the amygdala, which processes emotion; helps produce the "feel good" drug dopamine; and releases oxytocin, which is the hormone associated with bonding.

4. **Talk is a means of reviving a relationship.** The Arthur Aron study shows the magic of asking questions, showing interest, and opening up. If those behaviors are missing from your relationship, you can choose to bring them back and add life to your relationship.

5. **Be careful who you encourage to open up to you, and who you open up to.** Sharing, asking questions, and opening up are the gateway drugs to an emotional affair and more. Protect your relationship by being conservative about opening that gateway.

The need to love and be loved is one of our most basic and primal needs. It starts in infancy. In the first hours of life we seek to make contact with the eyes and faces of those around us, and find comfort in the arms of a parent. Our brains are prewired to connect and form attachments. Those mutual attachments secure our well-being: If I am attached to mommy and mommy is attached to me, she will feed me, change me, take care of me, and I will survive. Mutual attachments also provide us with comfort in a big, scary world. Early on, they create a road map, for better or worse, for our adult attachments.

When a baby comes into this world, he is constantly learning if the world is a safe place to be. Will his needs be met? Will he be cared for? Will he be safe? Much of this learning takes place with a child's primary caregiver, usually the mother. When his cries are met with attention and a parent who is looking to respond to those needs—hunger, a diaper change, relief from discomfort—he learns that the world is a safe place, where he can count on his needs being met. He learns that he can count on people and those who love him will look after his needs.

John Bowlby, a celebrated psychologist and child development theorist who laid much of the groundwork for today's attachment theory, said that the quality of the connection and the experience of emotional deprivation in our early childhood create our personality and attachment style. These patterns and experiences form our habitual ways of connecting with others and create a template.

A child who feels loved and secure can trust that feeling and, therefore, have faith in love relationships in adulthood. She anticipates that her needs will be met and is able to believe in her partners. A child who grows up in a home with unpredictable parents—who are volatile, violent, and struggle with substance abuse; are verbally abusive, neglectful, or struggle with mental illness—is likely to experience tremendous ambivalence or fear about attachment, connection, and intimacy.

The perfect example of this is rapper DMX from season 1 of VH1 *Couples Therapy with Dr. Jenn.* During the childhood trauma session he talked about the repeated beatings he received from his mother. He described her braiding electrical cords while he slept and waking him up by standing on his back, whipping him. He talked about her beating him so badly with a broomstick that she knocked out two of his teeth. "She used to beat me 'til she was tired," he recalled. But the turning point was when he was seven. Without telling him in advance, his mother brought him to an institution and left him there. "That's when the problem was born," he told me. "That's when I pretty much said, 'You know what? F**k everything and everybody.' But it hurt. It hurt. I was saying, 'Dang, you just gonna leave me like that?'" At an early age he learned that women could not be trusted, they would hurt him, and he should not get too attached to them because they might, like his mother, leave him at any moment.

The Culture of Autonomy

In assessing attachment issues in children, Bowlby and developmental psychologist Mary Ainsworth identified four factors that, they believed, form the basis of attachment:

1. Monitoring and maintaining closeness with a loved one.
2. Reaching out to a loved one for comfort and support when you're feeling unsure or upset.
3. Missing a loved one when you're apart.
4. Counting on a loved one when you go out into the world and have experiences.

If you stop and think about it, the attachment experiences observed in children with caregivers are the same ones we as adults experience in our love relationships. But we live in a culture that pressures us to suppress and deny our dependency needs behind a mask of strength and autonomy. We are taught to feel shame about our dependence on others and encouraged to count on no one but ourselves.

To follow this cultural directive is to take the easy way out. It is also a great way to prevent yourself from fully experiencing love with your partner. Dan was a fifty-year-old writer. He met Christopher while interviewing him for an article he was writing on creativity. They hit it off immediately and formed a fast friendship that ultimately became romantic. Despite their multihour phone conversations and daily texting, they did not spend very much time together. Dan loved

Christopher, but always made excuses about why they couldn't be together in person. He kept Christopher at arm's length. A year into the relationship, Dan experienced a major medical emergency, but he didn't even tell Christopher that he had been in the hospital until a few days later. When Christopher told him that he wanted to be there for him when he had a series of subsequent medical tests, Dan refused to let him come with him, telling him, "I am a rock, I am an island, and I don't need anyone."

Dan's resistance had nothing to do with being a strong man. His inability to be vulnerable and allow Christopher to be close went back to his violent, volatile upbringing. It also stemmed from his subsequent poor choices of disloyal and vindictive partners. All these experiences left him unable to trust, tolerate closeness, or be willing to let anyone in. Dan's autonomy doesn't reflect strength or true independence, but rather a fear of dependency and closeness. It is actually a sign of weakness.

To truly allow yourself to love and be loved is an act of courage. It means giving your partner the power to crush your soul—trusting, all the while, that he won't. If you grew up in a home that did not provide you with secure attachments, however, that kind of trust and vulnerability can be terrifying.

Attachment Threats

Once we get past the honeymoon stage of a relationship, filled with hope, fantasy, projection, and dopamine, our attachment fears tend to bubble to the surface. They create anxiety, anger, fear, and aggression. In his book *Wired for Love*, psychologist Stan Tatkin described it best: "Fears and expectations that date back to earlier experiences of dependency, but that didn't arise during courtship or dating, are activated as commitment to the relationship increases. As a result, partners start to anticipate the worst, not the best, from their relationship. Anticipation of the worst is not logically purposeful, nor does it necessarily surface in conscious awareness, because this type of anticipation resides in the deep and wordless part of the brain."

According to Sue Johnson, the creator of *Emotionally Focused Couples Therapy*, which is based on attachment theory, most fights couples have are protests over emotional disconnection. These fights occur when partners are feeling emotionally unsafe or disconnected. Underneath the conflicts, what they really want to know is this: Can I count on this person to be there for me and respond when she's needed? Will she make me feel that I matter, that I'm valued and accepted? The criticism and accusations that spin out of these conflicts are just a cry to reestablish connection.

When we have conflicts with our partners, all of us experience some fear. For those who don't have a history of safe and secure attachments, this experience can be overwhelming. It can drive us into what neuroscientist Jaak Panksepp refers to as "primal panic," which causes us to either become clingy and needy, in an attempt to get reassurance and comfort, or to become withdrawn and detached in order to soothe and protect ourselves. Without understanding what is really happening, couples push each other away. They react to the details of the fight, instead of the underlying need for connection and reassurance.

When Karen's husband, Jack, was away on business for a week, they stayed in close contact, via phone calls, face time, texts, and emails. But on the last night of the trip Jack had to attend a company party. Jack's company was known for its extravagant late-night parties, which involved a lot of drinking. Karen had always been uncomfortable with these parties, and the fact that Jack had cheated on his first wife while he was away on a business trip didn't help matters, either. Jack always tried to be sensitive to Karen's anxiety by staying in close touch whenever he traveled. If Karen didn't hear from Jack for a couple of hours, she would begin to worry. When Karen called Jack on the night of the party and his phone went straight to voice mail she began to panic. Jack didn't realize that his phone had died until he was on his way back to his hotel room, four hours later. By the time he recharged it and turned it on, he had multiple voice mails, missed calls, and texts from Karen, who had worked herself into a frenzy. In her fear, she became aggressive and accusatory when they finally spoke. Jack, feeling attacked, became defensive and aggressive in response. He had been on good behavior—no drinking or hanging out with female employees—and he felt resentful and angry that after all these years Karen still didn't trust him. For her part, Karen felt hurt and angry that Jack wasn't more sensitive to her needs. The intense emotions of the phone call, made at a late hour, morphed into a highly emotional fight that culminated with Karen hanging up on Jack—and the start of couples therapy with me.

It is hard to respond to the underlying attachment needs of others when our brains and our hearts are wired to look for problems, instead of ways to connect with our partners. If Jack had been able to respond to Karen's needs, he might have reminded her how much he loves her and spent some time reassuring her by saying, "I am so sorry for worrying you. That must have been really scary. I didn't realize that my battery had died. You have nothing to worry about. I love you and you are the most important woman in my life. If you are up for it, I would love to tell you about my evening and hear about yours."

If Karen had been able to rein in her anxiety, she wouldn't have started out her conversation from an accusatory, aggressive stance. Instead, she would have shared her fears and admitted her vulnerabilities. She might have talked about how hard it is for her to be apart from Jack, and how anxiety-provoking it is for her whenever he is far away from home.

WHAT ARE YOUR ATTACHMENT TRIGGERS?

Knowing what is likely to trigger your attachment anxiety can help you and your partner avoid future problems. Becoming aware of your triggers and sharing that information is a great way to prevent future problems together. Rate the following on a scale of zero to five—with zero being not at all triggering and five being the most triggering—how triggering the following things are for you.

Your partner being away on a business trip.   0 1 2 3 4 5

Going to sleep.   0 1 2 3 4 5

Waking up.   0 1 2 3 4 5

One or both of you going to work.   0 1 2 3 4 5

Not getting a response to a text
message for three hours.   0 1 2 3 4 5

Seeing your partner being flirtatious
with someone else.   0 1 2 3 4 5

Your partner being angry at you.   0 1 2 3 4 5

Your partner feeling sad or depressed.   0 1 2 3 4 5

Your partner turning down your
sexual advances.   0 1 2 3 4 5

Your partner staring at
someone or commenting on
that person's attractiveness.   0 1 2 3 4 5

Your partner talking favorably about an ex.   0 1 2 3 4 5

Your partner ignoring your
bid for connection.   0 1 2 3 4 5

Your partner turning down plans
to do something together.   0 1 2 3 4 5

Your partner going out with
friends without you.   0 1 2 3 4 5

Your partner participating in a
hobby (painting, horseback riding,
fixing cars, etc.) without you.   0 1 2 3 4 5

Danger, Will Robinson

The brain specializes in threat perception and response. It looks for signs—real or imagined—that might indicate a break in attachment. When we feel threatened, we constantly assess facial expressions, body language, tone of voice, and words. We *look* for problems.

When attachment fears surface, we go to a very primitive place where we can no longer accurately assess what is really going on, because our perceptions become fact in our own minds. When we're in this state, we often spend an inordinate amount of time debating the details and reconstructing what happened when what is needed instead are connection and reassurance. An alarm goes off in the amygdala, the part of our brain that controls fear, and before we know it we are swept up in emotion and saying or doing things without thinking clearly. It is easy to do a lot of damage to a relationship when this happens. Being aware of this vulnerability is the first step in preventing a slide into that destructive mind-set.

It is important to know which situations in our lives trigger attachment fears—and when they are most likely to arise. Both Jack and Karen were aware that Jack being away on a business trip was a trigger for Karen. Many people, especially those with shaky attachments, have trouble with launchings and landings, like going to work or school. Trips that cause a separation between partners often prompt separation anxiety. Many of us have trouble with mornings and bedtimes because they are mini separations. Awareness of the causes of our own separation anxiety, and being sensitive to the causes of our partner's separation anxiety, can help. Creating rituals around high anxiety times can be effective and promote bonding. Planning a regular morning routine that includes holding hands and sharing goals for the day or a nightly phone call before bed, if your partner is traveling, may reduce anxiety.

Benefits of Attachment

When you are dependable, consistent, and able to reassure your partner during difficult times, you make him feel secure. You become the safe place that allows him to flourish emotionally and handle stress much better. The benefits are both emotional and physical and work for both partners.

A strong emotional bond with your partner makes you both feel safe and protected from life's difficulties. The emotional benefits of connection, attachment, and a good relationship are multilayered. In a *Journal of Personality and Social Psychology* piece titled "Attachment Style and the Mental Representation of the Self," researcher Mario Mikulincer found that people with secure attachments have a more positive view of themselves, a more balanced identity, and a more coherent sense of self-concept. In other words, those who are able to form solid attachments have a better sense of self and self-esteem.

In another study, Mikulincer found that people with secure attachments handle anger significantly better than those who do not. Securely attached people are less prone to anger, are more constructive in dealing with their anger, and have more adaptive responses. In other words, they are able to calm themselves down, roll with the punches, and use the conflict to communicate their needs in the relationship. People with healthy attachments experience more regular positive moods, attribute less hostile intent to others, and anticipate more positive outcomes in their interactions with people. Those with more avoidant or ambivalent attachment styles have less control over their anger, are more hostile, use more escapist responses, and are less aware of their own signs of anger. Additionally, in a Carnegie Mellon University study by psychologist Brooke Feeney, researchers found that couples with a secure bond and who felt supported by their partners, had better self-esteem and felt more optimistic about achieving their goals.

The health benefits of secure attachments are numerous. The physiological connections between two romantic partners are so significant that psychologist and researcher Jim Coan refers to them as the "hidden regulators of our bodily processes and emotional lives." In a study Coan conducted, women held the hands of their partners while receiving an electrical shock. When they held their lover's hands, the women experienced less stress and less pain. The women who rated their relationship as "happy" received the most profound analgesic effect.

Over and over, research proves that healthy attachments and connected relationships help the immune system and our physical health. According to research done at the Center for Cognitive and Social Neuroscience at the University of Chicago, loneliness raises blood pressure so significantly that the risk of heart attack and stroke is doubled. And in an Ohio State

University study by Janice Kiecolt-Glaser, researchers found that the more belligerent and contemptuous couples are, the higher the level of stress hormone and the more compromised the immune system. Another study by the same researcher gave women small blisters on their hands and had them fight with their husbands. The more contentious the fight, the longer it took for the women's skin to heal.

Developing and Maintaining Trust

To gain all the benefits of healthy attachments and connected relationships, you must establish an environment of trust and safety in the relationship. Trust is the admission ticket to connection. When I talk about trust, I am not just talking about fidelity, which tends to be the first thing most people think of when the word comes up. Trust is also about the following:

- Can I trust you to be there for me?
- Can I trust you to have my back?
- Can I trust you to keep my secrets?
- Can I trust you not to make fun of me or hurt me when I share something that makes me feel vulnerable?
- Can I trust you in the bedroom to make me feel safe enough to make weird noises, share sexual fantasies, or try things that may feel scary?

Trust is very complex. It can only be built up over time with good, consistent behavior. While no one is perfect, patterns of behavior speak volumes.

Here are a few things you can do to nurture trust in your relationship:

1. **Don't be judgmental.** Seek to understand your partner and be open to her thoughts, fantasies, and opinions, even if you don't understand or agree with her. Create an anticipation of acceptance. When you have shown yourself to be a consistently open-minded partner, who does not judge, your spouse will grow to expect the best from you and believe that you are likely to accept her, warts and all.

2. **Create a "couple bubble."** In a couple bubble, you come first for each other. Your partner is the first person with whom you share information; you don't share private details about your life together with others; you protect your relationship from others who might try to harm it in any way; and you make each other a priority.

INCOMING MISSILES

Every season on VH1 *Couples Therapy with Dr. Jenn* I do a group therapy session with the couples about what I call "incoming missiles." These are the threats, usually from outside sources, that come at your relationship. Here are a dozen of the most common ones that I have seen over the years. Rate them, from one to twelve, in order of most to least threatening to your relationship.

☐ In-laws

☐ Parents

☐ Children

☐ Friends

☐ Social media

☐ Alcohol/drugs/other compulsive behaviors

☐ Ex-boyfriends or -girlfriends

☐ Other men or women

☐ Pornography

☐ Work

☐ People pleasing

☐ Untreated anxiety, depression, or other mental health issues

It is important to make an effort to work together to protect your relationship from these potential threats.

3. **Maintain the sexual agreements you have made.** If you are in a monogamous relationship, stick to that. If you are in an open relationship, stick to the rules you have made within that agreement.

4. **Don't disappear, stonewall, or go MIA.** Abandonment creates anxiety and mistrust. Blocking out your partner prevents you from working through conflict as a couple, a crucial connection-building skill.

5. **Don't make threats.** Do not threaten to leave, hook up with other people, "take a break," get back with an ex, withhold sex, or abandon your partner.

6. **Be consistently loving and kind.** This goes a long way toward creating a strong connection between two people.

> ## THE SILENT TREATMENT
>
> In a meta-analysis of seventy-four different studies on the demand-withdrawal pattern known as the "silent treatment," researchers found that couples who engage in this behavior experienced lower relationship satisfaction, less intimacy, and poorer communication. They also found a high correlation with anxiety and aggression as well as physiological problems such as urinary, bowel, or erectile dysfunction. They concluded that this very common pattern of conflict does "tremendous damage."

Take the High Road

Being a good mate and an emotionally mature partner means taking the high road. You must work hard to be your highest self, your best self. This means bringing a level of maturity to the relationship that helps keep you from being reactive, impulsive, or aggressive *regardless of your partner's behavior.* This is the stuff of an advanced relationship.

In my work, learning to take the high road was a theme for one of my clients, Tory, whose boyfriend knew how to push her buttons. He would say or do things that upset her, sparking her totally justified anger, but then she would become so emotionally reactive that she looked like the one who was out of control. She would scream, yell, name-call, and slam doors. Not only did this make her look bad, it also prevented her boyfriend from talking with her. Their conflicts typically would spiral out of control. I spent a lot of time teaching Tory about taking the high road, which was ultimately a game changer for them.

Six Ways to Take the High Road and Bring Your Relationship to the Next Level

1. **Give to your partner.** Give to your partner, not because you want something back, but just because you love your partner and want to make him happy. Know that the act of unilateral giving helps you to become a more spiritual person. Don't wait for love to inspire you to give. Giving will inspire you to love.

2. **Bring your highest self to the relationship.** Work on yourself in order to bring calm and peace to the dyad. Figure out what helps you to be your best self, whether it's therapy, meditation, exercise, religion, whatever—and do it weekly.

3. **Be the spiritual leader.** Don't wait for your partner to step up to the plate. According to Susan Page, author of *Why Talking Is Not Enough*, a leader agrees to watch over not only her own needs, but also those of the group. A good leader also promotes the goals of the group, not just her own, and wants the whole group to succeed. Leadership is not about fairness. A good leader often has to do more work than others, but gets the satisfaction of leading the group to victory.

4. **Challenge yourself to love your partner better.** Look for ways you can be a better mate. Where can you improve? How can you love your partner better? Ask yourself these questions daily and act on them.

5. **Practice compassion.** If your partner is upset, even if you are the cause of the upset, work to help and understand him. This is always hardest when your partner is mad at you or his actions have triggered your own anger. For example, if your partner is angry with you for buying an expensive pair of shoes, ask yourself why this is so upsetting to him. Perhaps he is worried that he isn't going

to make his annual bonus and now feels tremendous pressure. Maybe he came from a home where money was scarce, and your purchase of an expensive pair of shoes has triggered his anxieties about money. If you are taking the high road, your response will be empathetic, not defensive, and will be about showing compassion for your partner, not defending your own behavior.

6. **Focus on yourself.** To be a great partner, you must be ruthlessly honest with yourself about your own shortcomings. You can't control the person you love, but you can control the work you do on yourself—which ultimately benefits both of you. When you find yourself having big reactions, look inward. Ask yourself questions like these: What is it that is triggering me? Where does this emotional reaction come from? What can I learn about myself from this experience? How does it connect to my childhood?

Become an Expert on Your Partner

When your partner feels that you are an expert in knowing him, he will be more open to your feedback. Feeling seen, heard, understood, and appreciated are crucial experiences for building connection. Knowing that you care enough about him to be fully aware of his likes, dislikes, inspirations, dreams, fantasies, and quirks makes him feel loved and cared about. Understanding buys us influence. We don't take advice from people unless we feel totally understood.

Becoming an expert on your partner strengthens the bond with him, makes him feel loved, and protects your relationship from outside threats. Here's how to do it:

1. **Study your spouse.** Observe her. Try to figure out the most effective ways to encourage, inspire, and affirm her. Learn what makes

her tick. Don't assume that what you want more of in your relationship is what she wants more of. Get in her head and work to understand her.

2. **Be a great listener.** Listen to the specific details of the story your partner is sharing with you and become attuned to what she is experiencing emotionally when she shares that story with you. Too often we rush to fix a problem or make our loved ones feel better because of our own difficulties watching them struggle. Give your partner the chance to express herself, uninterrupted, and let her have her feelings.

3. **Get to know your partner's friends.** If these people are important to him, you should know them. What does he like about them? What draws him to them? The more a couple's friends and family intermingle, the happier spouses are, according to research that examined the social circles of 347 couples.

4. **Be involved with your partner's work, hobbies, and interests.** Involvement with your spouse creates a connection between the two of you. Part of loving another person means listening to things you never thought you'd care about. Listening to a spouse talk about politics or world events gives you a window into her thought process, her values, and her concerns. Developing new interests and being exposed to new things only makes you more well-rounded. Not to mention, if you are not there to connect with, he will bring that excitement and energy to someone else. M. Gary Neuman, whose research on cheating has given us so many fascinating insights, found that 72 percent of cheating men met the "other woman" at work or during an activity of personal interest.

KNOW YOUR PARTNER'S LOVE LANGUAGE

Everyone expresses and receives love in different ways, according to Gary Chapman and Ross Campbell, authors of *The Five Love Languages*. Seldom do spouses have the same love language, but in order for couples to feel loved and understood, they must learn each other's languages.

There are five ways we speak and understand emotional love:

- **Words of affirmation**. Verbal compliments, words of appreciation, and encouraging words are the tools of this love language.

- **Quality time**. This love language comes in the form of undivided attention, eye contact, and quality conversation, which means discussions where both people share their experiences, thoughts, feelings, and desires in a positive manner.

- **Gifts**. If gifts are your partner's love language, they serve as visual symbols of love. The cost doesn't matter, unless it is consistently out of line with the giver's financial abilities. The partner of a millionaire who gives $1 gifts over and over will not feel validation of love and worth, but the partner of the struggling student who spends a dollar on a gift is likely to feel special.

- **Acts of service**. This means doing things you know your partner would like you to do to please her. You are showing her your love by serving her. These acts can be anything from the mundane, like cleaning out the cat's litter box, to romantic, like serving breakfast in bed, depending on your partner. These kinds of acts require thought, planning, time, effort, and energy.

- **Physical touch**. This goes way beyond sex. Holding hands, kissing, hugging, massages, spooning, and affectionate gestures are just a few of the ways you can connect with your partner if this is his love language.

5. **Take pride in being a good partner.** Being a good partner takes skill, sensitivity, discipline, and maturity. Taking pride in knowing how to respond to your spouse's unique preferences and needs shows that you are invested in the relationship and sends him a message that you care.

Ten Ways to Foster Connection in Your Relationship

The littlest things make the biggest difference.
—Nik Richie, praising his wife, Shayne Lamas, Season 2,
VH1 *Couples Therapy with Dr. Jenn*

We live in a very disconnected society, which teaches us almost nothing about how to create connection, embrace intimacy, and have healthy relationships. Technology, demanding work schedules, and kids make it easy for lovers to avoid closeness and escape from the discomfort of vulnerability that is required for a truly intimate relationship.

For some reason we seem to assume that the rules that apply to other areas of our lives don't apply to our relationship. We expect to put in time at the gym to be fit. We expect to work hard to succeed professionally. But many couples think that their relationship should work without devoting time, attention, or hard work to it. But the truth is, relationships do require an investment of your time, energy, and resources. As I always say on VH1 *Couples Therapy with Dr. Jenn*, "Relationships are hard work and this is where the work begins."

Here are ten things you can do to nurture connection in your relationship:

1. **Connect throughout the day.** Text your partner every day to let her know you are thinking about her and that you love her. In a study called "Using Technology to Connect in

Romantic Relationships," researchers found that texting to express affection was associated with higher reported partner attachment for both men and women.

In addition to daily texts, make sure to spend a *minimum* of thirty minutes a day talking face-to-face without any distractions, like phones, televisions, or computers. In Neuman's study of faithful versus cheating wives, he found that happy faithful wives spend, on average, more than thirty minutes a day talking with their husbands.

2. **Make a lot of eye contact.** "Only actual eye contact fully activates those parts of the brain that allow us to more acutely and accurately process another person's feelings and intentions," says Kate Murphy in a *New York Times* article, titled "Psst. Look Over Here": "Think of it as a cognitive jump-start that occurs whenever you lock eyes with another person." Eye contact shows where your attention is directed and lays the foundation for intimacy. Remember that four-minute eye gaze at the end of the Aron intimacy study (page 3)? It served a purpose. Eye contact has been called the foundation of the dance of intimacy.

3. **Look for opportunities to show support.** Celebrating each other's victories has been found to be a crucial factor in strengthening a couple's bond. A study published in the *Journal of Personality and Social Psychology* found that the way a person responds to his partner's successes is even more important than how he responds in a crisis. In questionnaires and interviews, seventy-nine heterosexual couples, who had been dating at least six months, were asked to characterize their partner's typical reaction to positive news. The couples rated their relationship satisfaction at the start of the study and again two months later. Researchers found that it was a partner's reactions to his loved

one's achievements that most strongly predicted the strength of the relationship. So next time your husband wins a tennis game or your wife gets a promotion, break out the champagne!

4. **Show gratitude.** Studies by Sara Algoe and Amie Gordon found that couples who show gratitude for each other are more satisfied in their relationships, feel closer to each other, and are more likely to be in their relationship nine months later. In another study, Gordon found that gratitude in a relationship creates a positive cycle of generosity. One partner's gratitude for the other prompts both partners to think and act in ways that show gratitude, and promotes a desire to hold on to their relationship. In addition to being more committed, study participants who were more grateful for each other also appeared to care more for their partners and listened to them more attentively than others. It appears that gratitude creates a positive cycle.

In another study of appreciation in relationships, Amie Gordon asked couples to fill out appreciation journals. The researchers found that on days when one partner reported feeling more appreciated, she tended to appreciate her partner more the next day. This created a positive cycle of appreciation, which correlated with couples staying together. The second part of the study found that more highly appreciative couples tend to have more positive body language with their spouse and touch each other more. Looking at your partner's positive qualities and strengths can help you feel more grateful for the relationship. Choose to create a positive cycle of appreciation in your relationship.

Along those lines, Neuman also talks about the importance of creating a culture of appreciation in your relationship. He notes that the most common cause of emotional dissatisfaction reported by male cheaters is "I felt underappreciated by my wife. She was not significantly thoughtful and caring toward me." We all need to be appreciated. We tend to take for granted the things we expect our partner to do. When was the last time you thanked your partner for waking up in the middle of the night for a sick child, earning a living, cleaning out the litter box, or throwing dirty clothes in the laundry? Because we expect these things, we rarely acknowledge them. But we all want recognition for what we are doing right.

GRATITUDE TIPS

Study after study shows that gratitude is a key factor in relationship longevity and satisfaction. Couples who are not used to practicing gratitude frequently tell me that they don't even know where to start. Here are some things you can do to show gratitude in your relationship:

- Say "thank you."
- Do something for him that he doesn't like doing, without being asked.
- Give her an unexpected gift or card.
- Give a compliment.
- Tell him why you appreciate his acts of kindness.
- Appreciate her time and thoughtfulness, not just the results.
- Let him know how important he is to you and why.
- Praise her in private and in front of others.
- Find creative ways to express your gratitude.
- Pay attention to subtle hints that indicate something she would like you to do, and do it.
- Do one of your partner's household chores, just to make her day easier.

- When you have a success, recognize him for his support or anything he may have contributed to your accomplishment.

- Be there to help her when she is not feeling well.

- Recognize his additional efforts.

- Let her know you are happy she is home when you first see her at the end of the workday.

- Be affectionate.

- Say "I love you" and let him know why you feel that way.

- Tell him how handsome he is or how beautiful she is.

- Let your partner know how sexy he is and why he turns you on.

- Let her know she is important to you.

- Focus on what he is doing right, instead of the negatives.

- Make time for her.

- Make a gratitude list about your partner.

5. **Set your partner up to succeed.** I can't tell you how many calls I get on my radio show from people, usually women, who expect their partner to be a mind reader. It is crucial for you to clearly express your needs and desires to your partner. Whether it is asking for more help around the house, a desire for some flowers, or a request for oral sex, if you want it, you have to ask for it, no matter how difficult it may be for you.

"But I shouldn't have to ask!" you say. Wrong! We have a responsibility to teach our partner how to meet our needs. It is not fair to expect your husband to be a mind reader or even to take a subtle hint. Men are not wired that way. If you go to a female friend's house and say, "Do you have a sweater I could borrow?" she is likely to pick up on the fact that you are cold and to offer to turn on the heat. A man is far more likely to solve the immediate problem by handing you the sweater. If you are cold, you are far better off being direct with a man by saying, "Honey, I am cold. Would you mind turning on the heat?"

The good news is that good men want to please their partner. They take pride in "being good" and providing for their partner. They tend to be very sensitive to disappointing the woman they love. If you find him getting angry or defensive, you may want to look at your delivery—the way you're expressing yourself.

When requesting behavior changes, always start with the positive, build on good behavior, and let him know how meaningful an experience has been ("On my birthday last year you cleaned out the cat's litter box. I know it may sound silly, but this meant so much to me that I am still thinking about it. It made me feel really cared about and taken care of."). Be specific ("Would you be willing to do that once a week?"). Being vague, like saying you need more help around the house, is a setup for failure. Make sure you are specific about the task you are hoping he will do. Do not lace the request with criticisms or resentments ("You never help around the house, but I am hoping you will do this anyway"). If he agrees, be sweet and gracious ("Thank you so much for being such a supportive husband. I feel really lucky."), never sarcastic or passive-aggressive ("Now let's see if you really do it").

6. **Have fun together.** During the early courting stage, couples spend a lot of time doing fun new activities together and exposing each other to new experiences. After a few years of marriage, life becomes filled with work obligations, household chores, kids

who need attention, and other mundane tasks. Studies show that couples who continue to play together, well into their relationship, increase bonding, communication, conflict resolution, and relationship satisfaction.

An Arthur Aron study, published in the *Journal of Personality and Social Psychology*, found that sharing new and exciting activities is consistently associated with better relationships. This "novelty habit," as Aron calls it, releases dopamine, a neurotransmitter that controls the brain's reward and pleasure centers. Watching a new television show together isn't going to do that. The good news is that you don't have go skydiving to create a "novelty habit." It can be as simple as trying a new restaurant together, riding a roller coaster at an amusement park, going to hear a lecture together, or taking a walk in a different part of town.

7. **Be affectionate and emotionally responsive.** Ted Huston, PhD, a professor of psychology and human ecology at the University of Texas at Austin, can predict divorce with amazing accuracy. Professor Huston launched PAIR, the Processes of Adaptation in Intimate Relationships project, which followed 168 couples through the first thirteen years of marriage. He found that the most significant interpersonal dynamic that predicted divorce was the loss of love and affection. The couples who remained married throughout the course of the duration of the study experienced very few changes over the first two years of marriage in their feelings of love for their spouse, the amount of affection they expressed toward their spouse, and the extent to which they perceived their spouse as responsive to their needs.

Being responsive to what relationship researcher Dr. John Gottman calls "bids for connection" is vital if you are going to be an emotionally receptive partner. "Bids" are attempts to get our partner's attention and connect with him. All couples make bids, and they come in many forms—a question, a statement, a look, a sound, a smile. Such bids are all attempts to get attention. Some are subtle and others are blatant. But responding is a crucial ingredient in this recipe of relationship success. By recognizing your partner's bids and being responsive to them, you create connection and love. Regularly turning away from your partner's bids will eventually cause her to stop trying to reach out to you. According to Gottman, the author of *The Science of Trust*, rebids only occur 20 percent of the time. Most people are too hurt and discouraged to try again. The less people turn toward each other, the less satisfied they are in the relationship.

Warmth and affection are necessary for a loving marriage. Grabbing your wife's ass while she is brushing her teeth at the sink is not likely to be perceived as an act of love and affection, especially if the relationship is already tense. Putting your arms around her, however, and kissing her cheek, after telling her how much you love her is far more likely to be appreciated as affection. Look for these opportunities.

8. **Practice restraint.** Being a great partner requires maturity, emotional discipline, and restraint. Waiting for the right moment to have a conversation or share some constructive criticism and working on not being reactive when you have been hurt, as well as being aware of your triggers, are skills all couples need. It is especially tough to have the discipline to wait to have a difficult conversation when you are already worked up.

Here are six common circumstances where it is best to table a conversation and save it for another time:

- **One of you is hungry.** All of us get cranky when we're hungry. We can't think clearly and tend to be short-tempered when what we really need is something to eat.
- **Someone is exhausted.** When you haven't had enough sleep, you are more likely to be aggressive with your loved ones.
- **You have been triggered.** You are having a big reaction and emotions are running high. Nothing will get accomplished at this time.
- **Your kids are in the room.** It is great for kids to see adults work through conflict effectively, but it is not good for them to see screaming, yelling arguments.
- **You are running late.** You are late to a family dinner, special event, the theater. The stress of the ticking clock will only make things worse.
- **One of you is intoxicated.** You are not thinking clearly. Your inhibitions are down and you are likely to say things you will regret. Don't do it! Save a difficult discussion for a calm, clearheaded time, when you can give it the attention it deserves.

9. **Help your partner grow.** You have a responsibility to yourself and your partner to work on yourself as well as the relationship. New research takes this a step further: If you want a deeper level of satisfaction and commitment, you need to help your partner grow on multiple levels and she needs to help you.

According to Gary W. Lewandowski, a researcher on relationship satisfaction, "People have a fundamental motivation to improve the self and add to who they are as a person." We are constantly seeking to "increase our store of ideas, experiences, skills, interests, and resources in order to accomplish an ever evolving set of goals."

Lewandowski and Arthur Aron studied how people use their relationship to accumulate knowledge and experiences, a process they refer to as "self-expansion." One way to expedite this process of self-growth is to engage in a romantic relationship. When we fall in love, we are exposed to our partner's resources, experiences, ideas, skills, and strengths.

Every shared conversation and event becomes an opportunity for expansion, which creates positive feelings. Research shows that the more our partner helps us grow and exposes us to new ideas and experiences, the more committed and satisfied we are in the relationship, and vice versa.

10. **Have sex.** It has often been said that in a long-term relationship, men need to have sex to feel loved and women need to feel loved to have sex. The confluence of love and sex is a powerful glue that bonds romantic partners.

In modern-day society, it is too easy to neglect one's sex life. Work, kids, paying the bills, and all the daily pressures we have take precedence over learning new sexual techniques, exploring sexual fantasies, and finding the time and energy to connect sexually.

But sex is an important ingredient in connection. The bond it creates doesn't just take place on an emotional level, but on a physiological level as well. When we have sex, our body releases oxytocin, the "cuddle hormone" or the "love hormone." Oxytocin is also released when a mother breast-feeds her baby, and it helps her to bond with her baby. Both men and women release oxytocin during sex. As Susan Kuchinskas says in *The Chemistry of Connection*, ". . . when the intoxicating neurochemicals of romance have ebbed, the oxytocin released during sex reinforces the bond and helps us weather the inevitable annoyances and hardships of living with someone and raising a family."

Connection Deal Breakers

Some behaviors are so serious that they prevent a couple from being able to develop a close relationship and a safe connection, no matter how many things they may have done to make it possible. These are total deal breakers:

1. **Emotional unavailability.** You can't have a relationship with someone who is unable to be giving, loving, and present in the relationship, and who constantly pushes you away.

2. **Addiction or compulsive behavior.** Wherever there is addiction or compulsivity, emotional intimacy cannot exist. This kind of behavior puts a wall between you and your beloved. Enabling addiction and other dangerous, compulsive behavior helps one person to self-destruct and causes the other to harbor toxic resentment.

3. **Mental illness.** There are certain mental illnesses that just make a person incapable of having an adult relationship.

4. **Unwillingness to get help.** If your partner has developed a serious problem that is now hurting the relationship, she has to get help. For example, if she is depressed and unwilling to seek out help, nothing is going to improve without treatment, and you should not be expected to stand by and watch her self-destruct.

5. **Abuse.** Any abuse—whether it is physical, emotional, or sexual— is totally unacceptable in a relationship. If your partner has hit you once, there is always the possibility that he will do it again, and you will never be free to be totally honest with him again.

6. **Habitual cheating.** People make mistakes and while cheating is *never* okay, there is a big difference between someone who screws up once and someone who is a habitual cheater. The latter shows a pattern of hurtful behavior, poor impulse control, and a lack of honor.

7. **Lack of character.** You can teach relationship skills to your partner, but you cannot teach character . What you see is what you get.

8. **Compulsive lying.** Whether it is a sign of a lack of conscience or a full-blown antisocial personality disorder, this is a deal breaker. If you can't trust your partner to tell the truth, your relationship is doomed.

Invest Time and Energy in Your Relationship

The more time, energy, and commitment you put into your relationship, the stronger it will be. We become more devoted to the things we invest in. My friend Tom once bought an old used Porsche as an investment. He read everything he could find on fixing up cars. He saved up to get the best parts. He found the perfect color to repaint the car and the top-of-the-line people to do the job. He researched the ideal sound system for that type and size of car, and managed to negotiate a great deal for one. He read, he researched, he saved, and he worked on that car day and night. This automotive obsession took place over the course of a year. He had originally planned to sell the car, but after a year of investing his own blood, sweat, and tears in it, he was so in love with the car that he couldn't part with it. He felt an enormous sense of pride in his hard work, and all the time and energy he invested in it made him feel connected to that car.

Relationships are no different. We value the people in whom we have invested our time, energy, and affection. When Neuman asked happily married women why they thought they had not cheated, the number one answer for 75 percent of them was that they worked hard on their marriages and felt close to their husbands. The chances of things working out increase dramatically when both people in a relationship tend to it with equal care. You want to constantly challenge yourself and look at where you can do more to better yourself, support your partner, and be a better partner. Always look to see where you can *give* more, *not* where you could be *getting* more. As the insightful DMX once said, "It is only by unselfishly giving that you can truly receive something."

PRESCRIPTION TO CONNECTION

TOPIC	FREQUENCY MINIMUM	DESCRIPTION
Appreciation	Twice daily	Let your partner know something you appreciate about him as a person or about something he has done. Do this through a face-to-face conversation, an email, a text message, a phone call solely for this purpose, Skype, a love letter, a sticky note, or any other form of communication. Set an alarm in your phone if you need a reminder until it becomes second nature.
Face-to-face time	Thirty minutes a day	Have sacred time together, when you are not on your phones, computers, iPads, or watching television. Ask about each other's day and take time to connect and take each other's emotional temperature.
Rituals	Weekly	Create rituals that you share together. They can be daily, like praying together before going to sleep, or weekly, like a special Friday night drink you share to celebrate the end of the week.
Therapy	Weekly	I recommend that all individuals undergo one year of weekly therapy on their own. I also recommend that couples have at least six months of weekly couples therapy, even if nothing is wrong in their relationship. It is a good idea to establish a relationship with a therapist so you have a built-in support system for your relationship.

Business Meeting	Twenty minutes, weekly	Couples should have a once-a-week business meeting, where they have a forum to discuss household chores, finances, schedules, and any other family business. Try to keep this meeting on the same day, at the same time each week, and limit it to no more than thirty minutes.
Date Night	Once a week	Get out of the house and have a face-to-face date night, just the two of you. Book babysitters in advance. I recommend that all couples have three babysitters they trust and can call when they're needed. While on a date night, don't talk about kids, money, or business.
Romantic Vacation	Twice a year, minimum two nights and three days each	Take the time to have a romantic retreat together. It does not have to be expensive, and it should not include kids or other adults. This is just about the two of you.
Bucket List	Annual	Make a bucket list of things you would like to do together and check things off as you do them, adding new ideas as they occur to you. The first of the year is a good time to do this together.
Sexual Inventory	Annual	Once a year, couples should have an in-depth conversation about what things they like, don't like, want more of, preferences that have changed, new things they would like to try, and anything else that's relevant to sexual satisfaction and connection.

Fight Fair

I called him a fat f**k.
—Courtney Stodden talking about a fight with her husband,
Doug Hutchison, Season 2, VH1 *Couples Therapy with Dr. Jenn*

Shut up!
—Shayne Lamas to her husband Nik Richie, while on a date,
Season 2, VH1 *Couples Therapy with Dr. Jenn*

It escalated and . . . and then I told him I wanted a divorce.
Alex McCord, describing an argument with her husband,
Simon van Kempen, Season 2, VH1 *Couples Therapy with Dr. Jenn*

"Man the f**k up and say something you p***y!"
Liz Jannetta to then boyfriend Jon Gosselin, Season 4 of VH1 *Couples Therapy with Dr. Jenn*

Conflict in a relationship is inevitable. How this conflict is handled, however, often determines whether or not a relationship lasts or goes down in flames. All of us have said things we regret while in a fight with our partner. When we get hurt, angered, triggered, or scared, we are most likely to lash out. The goal is to learn to recognize those moments and to have the impulse control to stop yourself so you can turn a difficult moment into a productive discussion, instead of escalating it, and control the destiny of your relationship.

All couples have disagreements, which must be negotiated, but not everybody knows how to fight fairly. This is a crucial skill. Your ability to have a healthy relationship depends on how well you know how to fight. When I say "fighting well," I don't mean "winning" fights; rather, the goal is for you and your partner to walk away from the discussion with a sense of resolution, understanding, and connectedness. In the heat of an argument, when buttons have been pushed, maintaining your cool and knowing what to say are key relationship-saving skills.

Studies have shown that 69 percent of conflicts between couples never get fully resolved. This only further confirms the importance of the interactions between couples *during* a conflict. At the end of the day, you may not be able to resolve the conflict, but it gives you an opportunity to use the interaction around the conflict to let your partner feel heard and acknowledged, instead of leaving her feeling hurt and disrespected. Creating a respectful process that allows both people to feel heard is important for the long-term health of your relationship.

Interestingly, studies show that couples who start out their marriages with less conflict report more happiness in the beginning, but three years later are more likely to be headed toward divorce, if they hadn't already divorced. On the other hand, couples who start out with more conflict and work through their problems are more likely to be in a stable relationship after three years of marriage. Researchers believe that early conflict in a relationship allows couples to work through the kinks and give their marriage a better chance of surviving over the long run.

HOW FIGHTING IS HELPFUL TO YOUR RELATIONSHIP

Fighting:

- Brings problems to light so they can be processed.
- Helps you learn what is important to your partner.
- Gives you insight into your own issues and triggers.
- Teaches you how to anticipate and resolve future issues.
- Can release tension in the relationship.
- Allows you to express your emotions to your partner.
- Helps you recognize the ways in which you are different.
- Shows how invested you are in the relationship and how much you care to get resolution.
- Demonstrates that you both feel safe enough in the relationship to voice your different opinions.
- Sheds light on weaknesses in your relationship so they can be strengthened.
- Deepens the bond and creates more closeness when you are able to manage the conflict well.

The Four Core Relationship Needs

We all want to feel seen, heard, understood, and appreciated by our romantic partner. When personal disclosure is met with acceptance, it is a healing experience. It mirrors the unconditional positive regard that children are supposed to receive from their parents. When those core needs are not met—when we feel judged, criticized, or misunderstood by our partner—it can set off primitive alarm bells in our psyche.

Unlike our relationship with our caregivers as children, adult love relationships are reciprocal. There is something incredibly healing about having a relationship with a person who "gets you" and is there for you. Not only do you get to receive love, but also you get to *give* it. When we step out of our own narcissistic needs, and think about the needs of others, we are connecting at a higher level.

The Honeymoon Is Over

It is easy to get along in the honeymoon phase of a relationship. During the early stages, when we are falling in love, all we see is how alike we are and how wonderful our new partner is. We see our commonalities ("You like peas? I like peas, too!"), not our differences. We are merged. We feel like one person, not unlike the way an infant feels with his mother.

The first time we see our differences, it may feel like a huge betrayal ("What do you mean you voted for *him*?"), because it marks the moment when we are thrown back into the reality of being two separate people with different thoughts and beliefs. This realization can be jolting. It is not uncommon for this experience to be the trigger for a couple's first fight.

Ten Reasons Why You *Think* You Are Fighting

Working with couples, in my private practice and call-in-advice radio and television shows, I've noticed that certain issues come up over and over again. And while these issues may be real, they are superficial—not the core reasons that couples fight:

1. **Money.** Statistically speaking, money conflicts are one of biggest harbingers of doom in a relationship. According to a Utah State University study by Jeffrey Drew, couples who reported disagreeing about finances once a week were over 30 percent more likely to get a divorce than those who reported disagreeing about money matters a few times a month. A neutral mediator, such as a financial expert—an accountant, a business manager, or, if that is not financially possible, a jointly created budget that both parties agree upon—can go a long way toward keeping the peace.

2. **Household Chores.** A Pew Research poll found that 62 percent of men and women report that sharing household chores is very important to marital success. While all the studies show that men are doing more household chores than ever before, they are still way behind women in their contribution to housekeeping. In a Chicago Sloan study of working families called "The 500 Family Study," it was found that men did 33 percent of the household tasks, compared to 67 percent of those tasks being performed by women. The way couples negotiate the division of household chores in the first two years of marriage is particularly important, because this usually establishes a pattern that persists over time and can lead to increased conflict. The importance of an equitable division of household chores goes up exponentially after children arrive, which is when partners, especially women, become more resentful of the burden of housekeeping falling disproportionately on their shoulders.

WEEKLY HOUSEHOLD MEETINGS

I recommend that all couples have a weekly twenty-minute meeting to discuss household issues. Having this platform is important for couples to discuss issues and develop a workable system to manage them. The agenda for this meeting should include division of chores, activity planning, going over schedules for the week, financials, parenting issues, and any other important upcoming tasks. Couples should limit these meetings to no more than thirty minutes so they don't become arduous, dread-filled meetings. Some recommendations:

- Make a list of all household chores. Go back and forth, taking turns picking who will do what for the week.

- Go over the to-do list from the previous week. Discuss what worked and what didn't.

- Talk about any major parenting issues and observations about the kids.

- Coordinate calendars and make sure everyone has all the information for the week.

- Discuss any major purchases, financial planning, or incoming money that is out of the ordinary.

- Go over any upcoming vacations, business trips, or events.

- Always try to start and end the meeting on a positive note.

3. **Parenting.** According to data from the Relationship Research Institute of Seattle, about two-thirds of couples see the quality of their relationship drop within three years after the birth of a child. Sleepless nights and hormonal shifts, combined with less time for adult conversation, sex, and connection can be brutal for

couples. Not to mention that many couples find that their parenting styles are dramatically different than what their partner expected, and they struggle to find common ground. I always recommend that couples create a parenting philosophy—and put it in writing—*before* having children. Afterwards, when you are having a conflict, you can refer to your written philosophy and discuss which choice it supports, to help you make a decision as a couple.

4. **In-laws.** When two people get married, or are in a serious long-term relationship, they should be the "number one" person for each other. Your partner's interests should come before those of anyone else. The most common in-law–related call I get on my radio show is when a spouse sides with her parent instead of her partner, or allows her partner to be mistreated by members of her family of origin. This is unacceptable. Putting a parent's needs above your husband or wife's is a betrayal, and allowing your parents to mistreat your spouse is totally disrespectful. In order to be a good partner, you have to separate from your parents and put your relationship first.

5. **Jealousy.** Jealousy is a reaction to a real or perceived threat to a valued relationship. A nationwide survey of marriage counselors found that jealousy is a problem for one-third of all couples who come in for marriage therapy. Sometimes jealousy is born of insecurity, broken trust in childhood, feelings of inadequacy, or poor self-esteem. Other times it is the result of a partner's poor boundaries, inability to make his partner feel loved, lies, criticism, sexualizing others, or cheating. The greatest antidotes to jealousy are making your partner feel she is the most important person in your life, having good boundaries, keeping your word, and creating connection. If jealousy problems are coming from your or your partner's history, or unresolved issues, therapy is necessary.

6. **Leisure.** The "free time" fight is a common one among couples, especially those with children. The four most typical conflicts are: (1) how much time couples spend together versus apart; (2) whose time is more valuable; (3) who makes the final decision about how leisure time will be spent; and (4) how much of a priority the relationship is versus individual wants, needs, and desires. Finding a balance is particularly hard in this day and age of high-demand careers, financial stress, and expectations of gender equality. Research by sociologist Suzanne Bianchi found that, even as men have taken on many more household chores than in the past, wives spend about five hours more time doing housework per week, and enjoy six hours less free time per week, than their husbands. This often leads to resentment and fighting. Both partners in a couple, regardless of whether or not they work outside the home, need some time for self-care: to go to the gym, play a game of golf, catch a ball game with a friend, get a manicure, and the like, in order to have balance in the relationship and not burn out. I recommend that each couple reserve one night where one partner watches the kids and the other enjoys a self-care activity for a few hours (and, no, strip clubs don't count as a self-care activity). The ability to refill our emotional gas tank once a week is often all it takes to avoid relationship burnout.

7. **Appearance.** We have a responsibility to ourselves and to our partner to look good. While we all age, fight gravity, and have to face wrinkles, we do have a responsibility to work on ourselves and look our best in a relationship. We also need to put ourselves together when it comes to dress, working out, eating, and grooming. We have a fantasy that our partners are supposed to love and be

attracted to us no matter what. That is unrealistic. Life doesn't work that way. Our desire is cued by what we see and when we let ourselves go, it impacts our partner's attraction to us and breeds resentment.

8. **Sex.** While there are many different reasons that couples fight about sex, the single most common conflict I see is disparity in desire. No couple wants the exact same amount of sex at the exact same time over the course of many years. This disparity often leads to feelings of hurt, rejection, and anger. Sex is a sensitive and complex issue in a relationship. Typically, in long-term heterosexual relationships, men need to have sex to feel loved, whereas women need to feel loved to have sex. While there are exceptions to this rule, they are rare, in my experience. Sex is the glue that keeps couples together. Without sexual contact, romantic partners are reduced to being roommates or just pals. When you make a commitment to be in a monogamous, committed relationship, you are committing to be the sexual provider for your mate. To withhold sex is to do damage to the bond you share and leaves the relationship vulnerable to an affair. Understand that I am not suggesting that you have to provide sex for your partner at all times. There is a big difference between an occasional "Honey, not tonight" and an ongoing pattern of sexual withholding. Sex is necessary to feed the connection between partners. In my clinical experience, couples who are sexually connected work through conflict better.

9. **Drinking or Using.** Alcohol is a tricky topic in marriages. Any time you drink (or use drugs for that matter), you are not totally present in your relationship. This "checked out" quality does

harm to the relationship when it occurs on a regular basis. Even one drink can lower inhibitions enough to make people say things they later regret. It is not uncommon in young couples who start out partying together and then settle down for one person to mature and stop drinking or taking drugs, while the other person doesn't. This inevitably creates conflict. A nine-year study of couples and alcohol consumption by Gregory Homish and Philip Smith found that nearly 50 percent of couples, where only one person drank heavily (six or more drinks or drinking until intoxication), were divorced nine years later, compared to 30 percent of other couples. The divorce rates were even higher when it was the wife who was the heavy drinker.

In a marriage, it is a deal breaker when one person is an alcoholic or a drug addict and is unwilling to get treatment. As I've often said on my radio show: "Where addiction or compulsivity lies, emotional intimacy cannot." Addiction creates an invisible wall between partners and makes it impossible to have a healthy relationship. The bottle or the drug becomes the primary partner and the priority in the relationship. This is the nature of addiction.

10. **Social Media.** According to a study of two thousand married couples, 25 percent reported having at least one argument a week about social media, 17 percent say it happens every day, and one in seven have contemplated divorce because of how their spouse uses social media. The American Academy of Matrimonial Lawyers reports that 81 percent of their attorneys found an increase in divorce cases as a result of social networking. Social media opens the door to sending inappropriate messages to other people, tracking down former flames, posting nasty comments about a partner, friending or following inappropriate people, having affairs, and compulsive use, resulting in partner neglect. In study

after study, researchers report a link between increased social media use and decrease in marital satisfaction. It is important for couples to agree on using social media appropriately; show each other respect (regarding with whom they interact and how); avoid neglecting their partner as a result of overusing social media; and respect their partner by being mindful of social media boundaries. Your partner's comfort and emotional safety should always come first when making decisions about how you use social media.

My boyfriend Eric and I are both public figures and each of us has personal and professional social media accounts. When we first started dating, Eric was coming off many years as a single guy, dating and meeting hordes of women. His personal Facebook page reflected this. There were literally hundreds, if not thousands of bikini-clad, duck-faced, half-naked, provocative women who had friended him, and he had friended them back. They were a combination of ex-girlfriends, women he had dated, women who wanted to sleep with or date him, female friends with ulterior motives, random women he had met at events, and female fans just hoping to get a little closer to the handsome guy they saw on TV. All of this was appropriate when Eric was a single guy on the prowl, but he wasn't any more. I am a very secure person and do not have a history of being jealous in relationships, but this made me very uncomfortable. When we first started talking about the issue, Eric had a hard time understanding why I had a problem with it. He was not interested in these women, had never cheated in a relationship, and didn't see them as a threat. It was a painful, ongoing conversation. For Eric, my request to unfriend these women felt like it was all about my controlling him, especially since, in his eyes, they did not pose a threat to our relationship. But to his credit, Eric's desire to be a great partner overrode everything. He began to eliminate the wannabe seductresses on his social media. Eric made our relationship and my emotional safety the priority. Eventually, he just handed me his phone and said, "Unfriend anyone you want. Our relationship is more important." This took our relationship to a new level. I don't mind if Eric is connected with long-term ex-girlfriends who are respectful of our relationship, people he went to school with, or old pals. I am perfectly fine with all the scantily clad, cleavage showing, ass-bearing, selfie-taking ladies who want to follow him on his professional page. I hope millions of them follow him and support his work. They just don't get to cross over to his personal Facebook page or into his life. Finding common ground was a process, but one that has paid off and made our relationship stronger.

SOCIAL MEDIA TIPS FOR COUPLES

- Put the relationship first.
- Share passwords on social media accounts.
- Have a relationship status that shows that you are both in a relationship.
- Have separate business and personal social media accounts.
- Do not friend or follow people who make your partner uncomfortable.
- Answer questions about new people you have friended or followed without getting defensive or angry.
- Agree upon your philosophy about contact with exes on social media and stick to it.
- If you get a private message from someone that might make your partner uncomfortable, share the information within twenty-four hours and make a plan together about how or if you will respond.

- Do not be flirtatious, comment on people's appearances, or be overly friendly online.
- Do not private-message anything you would not want your partner to read.
- Unfriend or unfollow anyone who crosses established boundaries.
- Always think before you type, especially if you are angry at your spouse.
- Do not post pictures of your partner without prior approval.
- Do not post pictures of yourself that make your partner uncomfortable.
- Do post pix of you and your partner together that show you are in a relationship.
- Do not share your fights, conflicts, or problems on social media.
- Go out of your way to say nice things about your partner on social media.
- Limit your social media time so you do not neglect your relationship.
- Never create additional social media accounts that your spouse doesn't know about.

The Ten Real Reasons Why You Are Fighting

All couples fight. As a matter of fact, according to a UK study of three thousand couples, the average couple argues 312 times a year. You may think that those arguments revolve around the previously mentioned issues, and oftentimes they do. Even when they appear to be about those issues, the truth of the argument usually goes much deeper.

To put it simply, couples don't fight about what they think they are fighting about.

So what's really going on when couples are going at each other? These are ten of the most common problems:

1. **You're in the negotiation stage.** In the early stages of a relationship, you see an idealized version of your new partner through rose-colored glasses, but sometime after the honeymoon stage is over, you start to get a more accurate picture of who your partner really is, flaws and all. When you let go of the fantasy, you start to see the reality of the other person and realize what your differences are. Some of those differences are small ("How can you not like sushi?"), and some are big ("What do you mean you want to raise your children Jewish?"). But in order for a relationship to work, it must be negotiated. During the negotiation stage, couples establish their core beliefs as a unit, as well as their spoken and unspoken relationship rules. Negotiation is not about one person winning and the other person losing; more often than not, it is about finding a middle ground that both of you can live with.

   Typically, negotiation is anxiety-provoking for both parties. It is a time when your differences are highlighted, which can trigger a fear of being abandoned. The idea that you and your partner are different, and may not agree on important issues, may feel like a betrayal. This often creates feelings of anger and frustration.

2. **You're missing connections.** In our relationships, we constantly reach out to our partners to get their attention. Sometimes these attempts are subtle ("Did you see that lightning?") and other times they are overt ("Come over here, Sexy. I want to wrap my

arms around you!"), but they are always efforts to connect. Not responding to these experiences is likely to leave your partner feeling neglected or unseen in the relationship, and can lead to conflict.

Dr. John Gottman, relationship researcher and author of *The Science of Trust*, calls these attempts "bids for connection." He found that newlyweds who ended up divorced six years after marriage only reacted to their spouse's bids 33 percent of the time, whereas couples who remained together six years after marriage responded to each other a whopping 86 percent of the time.

3. **Someone is trying to change the rules.** When two people come together to form a relationship, they create rules. Some of them are spoken ("You take out the trash and I'll take care of the laundry," "Let's make this a monogamous relationship"), and others are unspoken ("When you drink too much, I'll cover for you," "You'll be the strict parent and I'll be the lenient one"). Whether they know it or not, all couples are guided by these kinds of rules. These relationship laws help couples function more easily because everyone knows what to expect.

Problems occur, however, when one person in the relationship wants to change the rules. Even when a change is good, it disrupts the gentle homeostasis of a relationship. When one person in a relationship starts to get healthy—that is, gets sober, recovers from an eating disorder, overcomes depression, or becomes a more capable spouse—the other partner often either sabotages her progress or starts to feel a lot of big feelings. Both people's feelings need to be processed as the dynamic changes. It is normal to resist change even when it is good, but in order to grow and progress, relationships need to constantly shift and evolve.

4. **You're in the middle of a power struggle.** All couples experience power struggles in their relationship. These usually occur as soon as you get past the honeymoon phase. Sometimes they are small and easily resolved, but other times they are bigger and can last for years. When two people have particularly strong personalities, or if they are very stubborn, these struggles can become explosive and long-lasting. Season 4 of VH1 *Couples Therapy with Dr. Jenn* captured this dynamic when Whitney Mixter, star of the reality show *The Real L Word*, described the conflict between her wife Sada Bettencourt and herself, when she said, "We are two very strong, fiery personalities. And when you put two very strong personalities together there can only be one king of the jungle. We are still trying to figure out who that is."

Linda and Mary were both used to being the king of the jungle. They faced their first big power struggle when they moved in together. It all began in the kitchen when they were unpacking dishes and groceries. Mary began to put the wineglasses on the top shelf in a cabinet, which turned out to be exactly where Linda had planned to store the cereal boxes. Both of them were deeply invested in getting their own way and, as a result, things escalated into a screaming match. Neither could hear the other person's point of view, and both were too entrenched in their position to be willing to give in to the other.

You know you are in the midst of a power struggle when you are more invested in winning than you are in having a peaceful, loving relationship. Your relationship suffers when you go to that place. Power struggles create distance and resentment, instead of connection and trust. When you are in the midst of a power struggle, the focus is on being "right," or getting your way, which keeps you from hearing the other person's perspective. This prevents couples from utilizing good communication skills and, over time, erodes the sense of safety and security that is necessary for a strong relationship. The more you are able to let go of your attachment to being right, the more open you are to your partner and the stronger your relationship will become.

POWER STRUGGLES AND EMOTIONS

In the study called "Perception of Partner's Emotions Impacts Lovers' Quarrels," Keith Sanford of Baylor University and his research team found that people perceived a threat to their control, power, and status in the relationship when they observed an increase in their partner's hard emotions (i.e., anger, frustration, etc.). This created a belief that their partner was being hostile, critical, blaming, or controlling. The same study found that people perceived their partner as being neglectful when they observed an increase in their partner's soft emotions (i.e., sadness, hurt, etc.). In other words, when their partner was sad or hurt, they interpreted that behavior as meaning their partner was less invested in the relationship. This creates a perception that the other person is not as committed or into the relationship. How you perceive your partner's emotions during a fight—accurate or not—greatly influences your thoughts, feelings, and reactions. The next time you are having a conflict, ask yourself if you are responding to what is really happening, or if you are just responding to your partner's emotional state.

5. **One of you is in "Part X."** Originally coined by Dr. Phil Stutz, author of *The Tools: Transform Your Problems into Courage, Confidence, and Creativity*, the term "Part X" refers to a state of mind that is very primitive. Everybody has a "Part X," but it

may look different, depending on who you are. "Part X" is like pornography; you know it when you see it. Generally speaking, though, when someone is in this state of mind it is not possible to reason with him or have a constructive discussion. In that moment, you have to abandon all hope of a rational, productive conversation.

"Part X" is stubborn and aggressive. It is usually born of fear—fear of abandonment, rejection, criticism, and failure are especially common. "Part X" is incredibly convincing and generally invested in tearing you down and making you feel bad. It is insistent, stubborn, and must always have its way. It is not interested in a relationship, compromise, or even working things out, much like a toddler in the throes of the "terrible twos." "Part X" prevents you from really hearing your partner and working through conflicts.

A perfect example of the "Part X" phenomenon occurred during season 5 of VH1 *Couples Therapy with Dr. Jenn* when Treach, the lead singer of the rap group Naughty By Nature, and his long-term girlfriend Cicely had a huge blowup about the babysitter who was watching their kids while they were doing the show. Apparently, the babysitter had allowed an unauthorized friend—someone the couple did not trust—to stay with her at the house. Treach and Cicely were both angry about it, and during the conflict Treach got really intense. He was in Cicely's face, yelling and threatening, and demanded that she get the woman out of the house. Cicely was angry because she felt that Treach was throwing all his new tools for coping with conflict out the door as soon as the first crisis came up in their relationship. In her anger, Cicely said something along the lines of "When things get bad, you are out the door." Treach, who had been abandoned by his own father, was completely triggered by what he believed to be a threat from Cicely to kick him out of the house. His anger triggered hers and, in return, he was completely set off by the perceived threat of abandonment from her. They were so deep in "Part X" that they couldn't even hear that they were both on the same side, so the fight escalated. Had they both been able to step out of "Part X," they would have seen that they both saw their babysitter's friend as a threat, were both furious that she was in the house, and both wanted her gone. They were 100 percent on the same page, but "Part X" prevented them from seeing that. We have all been there.

When you are in "Part X," you can't clearly hear what your partner is saying, you see her as the enemy (even if you are on the same page), you are typically aggressive in your discussion style, rigid in your views, and unable to have a rational conversation (even though you probably think you are being totally rational). You are unable to view the conflict through the lens of the positive history the two of you share. This state of mind is poison to your relationship. Everybody goes there sometimes, but partners must work to keep their "Part X" on a leash so it does not attack the relationship like a rabid dog. This state of mind has caused many couples to lose a perfectly good relationship.

6. **The stress is getting to you.** In today's economy, couples are facing more stress than ever. David and Laurie, who came to see me in private practice, had been married for two years when the company David worked for made some cuts and he was one of the unfortunate casualties. When the layoff happened, David and Laurie's daughter was one year old, and Laurie, who had been hoping to transition into being a stay-at-home mom, was two months' pregnant. Four months later, Laurie's father passed away and her mother, who was suffering from Alzheimer's disease, had to move in with the couple because she could no longer take care of herself. At that point, David had not found a job and Laurie was very resentful, which, in turn, made David withdraw,

creating more tension between the two. David became depressed, which made him less involved in taking care of the house and upset Laurie even more. By the time they came to see me, they were fighting constantly and probably would have already gotten a divorce, if they could have afforded it.

Not surprisingly, studies show a strong correlation between stress and relationship problems. A study of "stress spillover" (stressful experiences that are external to marriage, such as work or money problems) in marriage by April Buck and Lisa Neff found that on the most stressful days, partners reported more negative behaviors toward their spouses and less relationship satisfaction. In another study, "Stress and Reactivity to Daily Relationship Experiences," by Lisa Neff and Benjamin Karney, researchers found that spouses, especially wives, who experienced high levels of stress reacted more strongly to the normal daily ups and downs of the relationship, regardless of "attachment style" (that is, the way you form and maintain a bond in a relationship) or level of self-esteem. The same study found that the greater the stress, the more reactive people are to the normal ups and downs of their relationship. They also discovered that when partners are under increased stress, they perceive slights more acutely and are more likely to "read them" in each other's vocal tone. Even people with high-level relationship skills can be thrown off by life stress. Relationship skills are not static over time, they don't occur in a vacuum, and they are inevitably affected by stress.

It is easy to be a happy couple when everything is going well. It is how we handle crisis and stress that ultimately defines our relationship and determines our future. There is an old *Twilight Zone* episode, called "The Monsters Are Due on Maple Street." Strange things begin to happen in this quaint neighborhood. The lights, cars, and power stop working on Maple Street, and the residents, young and old, begin to panic and form a mob. When one man's car starts on its own, people immediately suspect him of being to blame for the chaos and accuse him of being the "monster" responsible for what is happening. Lights begin flashing on and off in houses throughout the neighborhood; lawn mowers and cars start up for no apparent reason. The mob becomes hysterical, and terrified residents smash windows and pull out weapons. Things devolve into an all-out riot. The camera pulls back from the hysteria and we see two aliens looking down on Maple Street. One comments to the other that they don't need to start a war; all they have to do is create enough chaos and people will turn against and destroy one another. "They pick the most dangerous enemy they can find and it is themselves," one of them says.

It is no different for couples. In times of chaos and crisis, we have a choice. We can turn against each other and create hysteria and hostility, or we can cling to one another and work together. The latter choice allows couples to survive the crisis and come out stronger and more connected. We can choose to move away from our partner or move toward him, creating camaraderie and closeness. When Laurie and David stopped treating each other with resentment and hostility, everything changed. They decided that David would stay home for a year and take care of the children while Laurie focused on her career. Together they researched options for Laurie's mother who, as it turned out, was eligible for in-home nursing care. Now that she was confident that her kids were being well cared for at home, Laurie did such a great job at work that six months after giving birth she was given a huge bonus, which made up for the time David had been out of work.

7. **You have unrealistic expectations.** We typically idealize and romanticize the concept of committed relationships, like marriage. We think of candlelight dinners and picket fences, not conflict resolution and compromise. I often get calls on my radio

show, usually from women, who thought marriage was going to change their man for the better; turn a man with a wandering eye into a faithful husband; transform an unmotivated couch potato into an ambitious career-oriented guy; or change a bar-hopper into a family man. Inevitably, these callers are gravely disappointed. Relationships are hard work, and time tends to water down the good behavior that we initially see during the honeymoon phase of the relationship. Couples who don't make a conscious choice and commitment to continue to better themselves and work hard on the relationship usually slip into complacency.

The way you conceptualize your relationship has a lot to do with your commitment to working through problems. Studies show that people who believe in the concept of soul mates struggle more when their relationship faces conflict. In the study, titled "Framing Love: When It Hurts to Think We Are Made for Each Other," researchers found that those who viewed love as a perfect unity between two halves that are made for each other, as opposed to a shared journey filled with ups and downs, had big decreases in relationship satisfaction when conflicts arose. It appears that the concept of soul mates makes people think that nothing will go wrong in a relationship, and when it does, these idealists are not prepared for the wear and tear that normal relationships undergo. They view conflict as a sign that the other person is not their soul mate, and are more likely to give up on the relationship.

Relationships are not perfect and neither are people. It was Leo F. Buscaglia who said, "Never idealize others. They will never live up to your expectations." When we don't see our partner for who he is, we set ourselves up for disappointment. The flip side of that coin is when we devalue our partner's strengths because they don't meet our preconceived notions of a good mate. Sarah called my *Dr. Jenn* radio show because she was upset about her less-than-ambitious husband. She described him as being a loving, nurturing, kind man who made her laugh, but he was not as driven as she was. Nothing about him had changed. He was the same guy he'd been when they first met years ago. Sarah's expectations that he would be different caused her to resent her loving husband. It prevented her from appreciating his many wonderful qualities. Because he wasn't the driven provider she had imagined, she couldn't appreciate all the great things he did for her and their family. In order to avoid resentments, we have to see and appreciate the person we are with.

8. **Your unresolved childhood issues are getting in the way.** The unconscious mind doesn't know the difference between past, present, and future, and it is always trying to heal old wounds now. The father of Amber, a client in my private practice, had divorced her mother when Amber was very young, and virtually disappeared. Because children are egocentric, they think that everything is about them. This is a developmentally appropriate reaction, but, as a result of this early abandonment, Amber thought her dad was never around because there was something terribly wrong with her. She thought if she had just been a better student, a prettier girl, better behaved, or just more lovable, he would have stuck around. Amber internalized that message and became a grown woman who always thought, deep down inside, that she wasn't that lovable.

When Amber met Steve, a handsome, successful investment banker, it was love at first sight. Something about him felt familiar, as if she had known him forever. Her unconscious mind was drawn

> ## QUESTIONS TO ASK YOURSELF DURING A FIGHT TO CREATE SELF-AWARENESS
>
> - How might my past be *influencing* my reaction to this conflict?
> - Do I sound like my mother or father when I make these remarks? Does my partner? How might this trigger me?
> - What is motivating me to say this?
> - If I say this, what will my partner's reaction likely be? How is this likely to play out?
> - Is my reaction in line with the situation?
> - Is it possible that I am having a strong reaction because of something from my own history?
> - What might I be playing out from my own childhood in this fight?

to him because it desperately wanted to resolve old wounds from her childhood. The chemistry between the two of them was off the charts and Amber fell fast and hard. She moved in with Steve six months later. Her fantasy of the life she thought they would have together came to a screeching halt when she was faced with the realities of his day-to-day work schedule. Instead of curling up with Steve in front of his fireplace, she often found herself home alone, resentment building. When Steve was home, he was distracted by his cell phone and laptop. Amber felt frustrated, disappointed, and rejected, just as she'd felt when she was a little girl.

Desperate to get his attention, Amber dressed up in sexy outfits and attempted to seduce Steve. The more she tried to entice him, the more she seemed to repel him. When seduction didn't work, she tried to talk to him about her feelings, but she was so hurt and angry that she just ended up yelling. "If only you could make him pay attention to you," her unconscious mind declared, it would be proof that Dad was wrong and she really was lovable. But when you are invested in changing someone as a way to heal your past, change is unlikely to happen. Your reactions tend to be out of proportion to the crimes your partner commits and your desperation to change him tends to drive him away. The combination of the two creates more conflict.

9. **You each want different levels of intimacy in the relationship.** It is a basic psychological assumption that all people want closeness. At the core, people seek to feel a sense of belonging. They want to know they are cared about and accepted, despite their flaws. But oftentimes, childhood wounds or fears about being hurt prevent people from tolerating the closeness necessary to achieve true intimacy. For many, it is easier to run than to stand still and tolerate the feelings that come up.

Intimacy requires us to be transparent, vulnerable, and present. It demands open dialogue and reciprocity. Each disclosure moves us one step closer. But we all have our limits, and when our limit for intimacy is reached, we turn away. It is healthy to catch your breath, so to speak. But sometimes, once the limit is reached, people push away from the relationship by distancing themselves from it, running away from it, or acting out. Acting out can happen through addictive or compulsive behavior. This is not to say that addiction is caused by too much intimacy. Rather, someone with addiction issues is likely to have a low tolerance for intimacy and use her substance of choice to avoid it. But you don't have to be an addict to avoid intimacy.

All relationships are a dance between two people, where they move closer together and farther apart. As much as this dance causes the partners pain, it maintains the status quo.

When one member of a couple feels the other one turning away, it can cause anxiety and tension in the relationship. Distancing can feel like rejection and easily trigger old wounds. It is unusual for two people to be in the exact same place at the same time throughout their relationship. Sometimes one person will want more closeness, and at other times it can be the other partner. Finding the right balance for both members of the couple can be challenging.

10. **Trust has been broken**. When you hear "broken trust," your mind probably jumps to issues of fidelity. But trust is about more than monogamy. We constantly test our partners throughout our relationships, both consciously and unconsciously. It starts with small tests like, "Will you show up for our date?" "Will you do what you said you were going to do?" and, "How are you going to act toward me when we are with your friends?" As time goes on, trust becomes about bigger issues like, "Are you going to support my dreams?" "Will you commit to me?" "Do you want to have children together?" and, of course, "Are you going to cheat on me?" We are constantly assessing our partner's trustworthiness. When we are disappointed in this area, it can be particularly devastating.

It is impossible to have a meaningful romantic relationship with someone you cannot trust. Intimacy is based on the ability to be open and vulnerable, and when that doesn't occur, a relationship inevitably hits a roadblock. When trust has existed, but then is broken, the outcome generally depends on four factors:

1. **How much "emotional capital" the couple has in the bank.** Couples who have a long history of positive interactions, mutual respect, kindness, and understanding are far more likely to survive a

betrayal because they have this important history to draw upon.

2. **How motivated the couple is to work through the problem.** Incentive can come from many sources—the desire to stay together for the sake of children, not wanting to break up a family business, religious beliefs, the hope for a better relationship—but there must be something motivating the couple to try. This inspiration often serves as the driving force during difficult times of relationship reconstruction.

3. **The ability to make amends.** In order for there to be forgiveness and healing, the person who broke the trust must make effective heartfelt amends. For more information about that, see chapter 5.

4. **Whether or not the couple is able to use the incident to rebuild the relationship.** After a betrayal, especially an infidelity, the relationship must be reconstructed. For the most part, affairs are a symptom of a problem in the relationship that must be addressed. While it is easy to turn an infidelity into an issue of victim and villain, good and bad, moral or immoral, this prevents the next, crucial step from taking place: To recover, the relationship must be renegotiated and redesigned, and both partners must address the issues that were problematic before the affair.

Why Fight Fair?

Every couple has low points in their relationship. Everyone makes mistakes and even the healthiest couples argue. While you shouldn't fight about every little thing, you can't sweep issues under the rug, either. You have to work through them. What is most important when arguing is the way you treat one another. In other words, it is not *if* you fight but *how* you fight that will determine the health and future of your union.

The ability to fight fairly not only predicts the likelihood of a breakup but also a couple's future health. According to marital researchers at the University of Utah, 93 percent of couples who fight dirty will be divorced in ten years. If you are belligerent, disrespectful, defensive, or aggressive during your fights, you may win your argument, but you are likely to lose your relationship. Relationship researcher John Gottman, who is best known for his ability to predict divorce with 94 percent accuracy, has identified four common predictors of divorce: criticism, contempt, defensiveness, and stonewalling.

Gottman explains that couples who discuss their grievances in a relationship seem to be able to work through conflict, while those who criticize or attack the other person's character do not. Showing contempt for your partner—which Gottman defines as an interaction that contains sarcasm, cynicism, name-calling, eye rolling, sneering, mockery, or hostile humor—causes tremendous damage to a relationship. In fact, in one study, Gottman found that wives who make sour facial expressions during conversations, which Gottman views as an example of contempt, are likely to be separated from their husbands within four years. When a relationship has devolved to the point where a couple is regularly demonstrating contempt, they are no longer trying to get along but are communicating their disgust toward one another. Defensiveness is a predictor of divorce because it quickly and quietly erodes a marriage. When partners are defensive, they blame each other without taking responsibility for their own actions. This stalemate makes it impossible to work through conflicts at all. Stonewalling, similar to defensiveness, is equally damaging, although it can take more time for the full effects to become apparent. When even one member of a couple is guilty of stonewalling, it makes any sort of dialogue impossible, which results in an inability to communicate and work through problems.

In addition to killing your relationship, this type of fighting can also destroy your health. According to a University of Utah study, after 150 healthy couples discussed a contentious topic, such as family, money, or chores for six minutes, those who were on the receiving end of a domineering, one-sided argument experienced significant hardening of their coronary arteries. This is not surprising, since we know that being faced with conflict often elicits a "fight or flight" response. This primitive automatic reaction prepares the body to fight or flee from a perceived attack or threat to our survival. The response actually originates in our hypothalamus, which initiates a series of nerve cell firings and chemical releases that prepare our body to run or fight. A surge of adrenalin accompanies it, along with an increase in heart rate. According to Gottman's research, when the pulse rate of one member of a couple goes up 10 percent, that person is "flooded" with fight or flight hormones, which makes it almost impossible to have a productive conversation. Typically, men are more sensitive to flooding, and research shows that a husband's blood pressure and heart rate will rise much higher and stay elevated longer than a wife's. It also takes less intense negativity for men to become physiologically overwhelmed or flooded.

These physiological effects of fighting only highlight the importance of learning to fight fair. The ability to negotiate, listen to your partner during conflict, maintain your cool, and work through difficult moments is vital. This behavior is not instinctive for most couples, but it is a crucial relationship skill that must be mastered. Without it, the pain endured by relationship conflicts will be prolonged and long lasting. If you choose to practice these skills, however, you will increase intimacy and understanding in your relationship.

Twelve Rules to Fight Fair

Most couples get into bad communication habits, and when we are angry, frustrated or hurt, we tend to slip into them. Learning to fight fair is an advanced relationship skill, but probably one of the most important ones you can learn. Here are some rules to live by:

1. **Allow your partner to talk and really listen to what she says.**
   Interrupting will make the speaker frustrated and give her the impression that you are more interested in what you are saying than in listening to her perspective. In the heat of an argument, most people are not great listeners. Truly listening can give you great insight into your partner's perspective and help her feel heard, which can go a long way toward resolving a disagreement.

2. **Don't use absolutes.** Words like "always" and "never" are inflammatory generalizations that will put the other person on the defensive.

3. **Don't imitate, mock, taunt, use sarcasm, or make fun of the other person.**
   This type of rude and degrading behavior is insulting and shuts down any possible productive conversation. It also derails the discussion because it creates a new conflict in and of itself.

4. **Keep it between the two of you.** Don't speak for other people in your argument ("My sister couldn't believe how rude you were to me!"). Stick to your own experiences of one another. In addition, don't involve other people in your conflict by asking them to take sides ("I'm getting your mother on the phone right now! She knows how mean you can be!"). Don't bring up exes ("Brian used to always take me out to dinner; I don't know why you don't!") or other people from your past against your partner. This attempt

to triangulate others into your conflict distracts from the issues at hand. The only opinions that are relevant are those of the two people attempting to communicate at the time.

5. **Keep your hands to yourself.** Couples should *never* shove, push, hit, slap, restrain, or punch each other. Other types of aggressive behavior, such as slamming doors, throwing things, and hitting walls can be so threatening that they have the same result as actual violence. Physical force is abusive and makes it so that there is no safety in the relationship, which completely prevents the free expression of thoughts and feelings. We all have a right to be free of abuse and danger in our relationships. If your arguments escalate to the point of violence, it is crucial that you leave the house safely and get proper protection. You should have zero tolerance for violence in your relationship. Violence is a total deal breaker.

6. **No threats.** Threatening to break up, divorce, withhold love, deny sex, or anything else along those lines sends a message to your partner that you are not committed to the relationship. That kind of manipulation ("If you go to that nightclub, I am going to file for divorce!") pushes the other person out the proverbial relationship door. This includes veiled threats ("The last woman who did this with me is gone!"). Furthermore, making a threat can back you into a corner and make you feel that you have to follow through, even if you don't want to.

7. **Don't assume that you know what your partner is thinking.** Mind reading doesn't benefit relationships. Typically, when we assume that we know what our mate is thinking, our assumptions are filled with our own projections, expectations, and biases. It is especially important that you don't correct your partner's statements about his feelings or tell him what you think he should know or feel.

8. **Never fight if you are *too* anything.** If you are too hungry, tired, angry, or drunk, you can't have a constructive argument. Poor sleep will make your arguments worse. Studies show that couples are more likely to fight after a bad night's sleep. I know that I can be a cranky bitch if I get too hungry, and when Eric's blood sugar drops, things can get intense. We try to avoid high-conflict discussions during these times. A study of 107 married couples only confirmed our strategy when it reported that low blood sugar makes spouses touchy. Researchers found that the lower the blood sugar level, the more likely the subject was to act out with a voodoo doll of their partner. What they concluded was that we need glucose for self-control, and that anger is the emotion most people have difficulty controlling. Don't set yourself up to fail by having a discussion when you are too anything. It is best to table an argument until you are better equipped to handle it. You have to be in a clearheaded state for a discussion to be beneficial.

9. **Don't argue about details.** Arguments that focus on minutiae miss the bigger picture, which prevents it from getting resolved. It doesn't matter if your partner was eleven minutes late or seventeen minutes late, and if you spend all your time debating the specifics, the true issue at hand will get lost and won't be resolved.

10. **Watch your language.** This means no name calling, degrading language, or cursing at the other person. There is a big difference between using a curse word ("I feel so shitty about this fight we are having") and cursing at a person ("You asshole!"), which is hitting below the belt. Any type of disparaging language aimed at your partner is unacceptable.

11. **Don't participate in character assassination.** This type of low blow occurs when you overgeneralize in a negative way about your

partner's whole identity. You turn her shortcomings into major character flaws. Instead of addressing the issue at hand, you attack your partner personally. This alienates your partner and puts her on the defensive, preventing any productive conversation.

12. **Think before you speak.** Take a moment to stop and think before you speak. Ask yourself, "How is what I am about to say helpful to my partner?" and "How is it helpful to my relationship?" It can take years to develop a sense of safety and trust in a relationship, but only a few words to destroy it.

FIGHTING AND IMPULSE CONTROL

Work on developing and refining two basic impulse control skills in order to deescalate your fights:

1. **Editing.** Take a moment to calm down and think through what you are going to say. Ask yourself how your words will affect your partner.

2. **Leveling.** Reduce the intensity of what you are saying. Watch your volume, tone, and level of aggression.

Twelve Tips for Communicating Better and Deescalating Conflict

The way you communicate is often the difference between a positive result and an escalation into an unpleasant fight with your partner. Improving your communication skills makes a huge difference.

1. **Change the way you begin a discussion.** Gottman found that, 96 percent of the time, the way a discussion begins will predict the

way it will end. If you can start from a loving stance, rather than an accusatory or attacking one, the odds are better that you will resolve the conflict in a positive way.

2. **Know when it is time to abandon all hope of a productive conversation.** When you or your partner is in "Part X," that primitive state will keep any effective rational conversation from taking place. "Part X" is too invested in winning, being right, and destroying the opponent. When you feel yourself going there or sense that your partner is, tabling the discussion until you are both in a more adult state of mind is the best idea.

3. **Try reflective listening.** Reflective listening is repeating back to your partner what he just said, using your own words. For example, "Let me see if I understand you correctly. When I yell at you, you find it threatening and it scares you." Oftentimes, when couples fight they are so busy constructing their next argument, while their partner is talking, that they don't really listen to what the other person is saying. Feeling heard in a relationship is vital to good communication.

4. **Use "I" statements.** Instead of blaming your partner, use what therapists call "I" statements, like this: "When you _____[fill in the blank with a behavior], it makes me feel _____ [fill in the blank with a feeling or two]." For example, "When you raise your voice with me, it makes me feel scared." The point of these statements is for one person in the relationship to be able to express to the other how she feels without putting her partner on the defensive. "I" statements are not debatable because they don't blame and they take responsibility for the speaker's experience.

5. **Come up with a temporary solution.** When each of you is deeply entrenched in getting your own way, finding a temporary solution can help break through resistance. When Ethan and

Zac, a couple who came to me in my private practice, moved in together, they were excited about sharing a home, but their enthusiasm was dampened when they began to hang their art in the living room. Ethan wanted to hang a black-and-white photo on the wall and Zac was adamant about hanging his collection of framed movie posters. They each felt equally committed to their perspective and, in that moment, each of them felt as if they were making a life and death decision. It wasn't until they agreed to try putting the posters up for two weeks and then the photo for two weeks, before making a decision, that either was willing to budge.

6. **Take a time-out**. When an argument gets too heated, it ceases to be productive. Most couples can benefit from a cool-down period during an argument. It is important for you to establish this before taking a break, so your partner doesn't think you are simply walking away. It is helpful to say, "I think I need a time-out right now. I am too upset to think straight and need some time to calm down. Let's check back in an hour." Learning to take a loving time-out is a valuable skill.

7. **Let your partner influence you.** Let your partner influence your decisions. Gottman found that, even in the first few months of marriage, men who allow their wives to influence them have happier marriages, and are less likely to want a divorce, than men who resist their wives' influence. Statistically speaking, when a man is not willing to share power with his partner, there is an 81 percent chance that his marriage will self-destruct.

8. **Pretend you are an alien from another planet observing human relationships**. Try to observe not only your partner's behavior, but your own. This perspective can give you the distance you need to become aware of your own patterns and contributions

to a problem. It can also take some of the emotion out of your interpretations of your partner's behaviors and allow you to view them with greater objectivity. It is easy to focus on what your partner isn't doing. Instead, take a look in the mirror. If your behaviors are kind and loving, you are setting a good example and reducing conflict in your relationship. Keeping your side of the street clean also means doing your own insight work. Adults who lack insight about their own attitudes tend to perpetuate destructive behaviors that harm their relationships.

9. **Drop the rope.** Frequently in a relationship, fights become like that old camp game tug-of-war. Each person holds one side of the metaphoric rope and pulls and pulls, creating tension and struggle. This typically happens when partners are being stubborn and unyielding with each other. Sometimes, in order to resolve the conflict, one person just has to put down the rope to end the struggle. Putting down the rope doesn't mean giving up on something that is important to you in the relationship, but it does mean you are willing to be open to the other person's point of view, and willing to compromise and negotiate.

10. **Use the sandwich technique.** Start with the positive and end with the positive, even when you are not feeling especially positive. It makes a huge difference in the way your words are received. For example, "Honey, I love what an amazing provider you are for our family and I admire your work ethic so much. Sometimes all that hard work takes the man I love away from me, and I really miss our time together. I would really love it if we could plan some time together so that I can connect with you a bit. I feel really lucky that, unlike some of my friends, I have a husband I just love to spend time with, even after all these years!"

11. **Watch your Gottman ratio.** Researcher John Gottman has found that the biggest determinant of a stable relationship is the ratio of positive to negative interactions. According to him, you must have at least five times as many positive to negative interactions for the relationship to work. Once you are aware of this, you can use it in your relationship, both by making sure your ratio is on target and by identifying when your partner's ratio is off. Sometimes Eric or I will say, "Honey, your Gottman ratio is off," and we will adjust it accordingly. You would be surprised what a difference it makes.

12. **Keep your side of the street clean.** It is easy to focus on what your partner isn't doing. Instead, take a look in the mirror. If your behaviors are kind and loving, you are setting a good example and reducing conflict in your relationship. Doing your part means doing your own insight work. Adults who lack insight about their attitudes tend to perpetuate destructive behaviors that harm their relationships.

Anger Management 101

In and of itself, there is nothing wrong with anger. But anger management problems can be toxic to any relationship. Rage, personalization, and the inability to let go—all hallmarks of anger issues—make it impossible to create the feeling of safety needed for an intimate relationship to thrive. Volatile anger makes it impossible to work through problems, use new tools (like the fighting fair recommendations mentioned earlier in this chapter), and communicate well, all of which are crucial to a good relationship.

One of the most effective anger management tools is the anger management scale. Conceptualize your anger on a scale of zero to ten, with ten being the angriest most out of control you have ever been. Now think about what that experience of mounting anger is like for you. What is your "point of no return," that turning point when you know you are going to blow your cool and there is no going back? Maybe for you it is a seven. Throughout your day you want to constantly be taking your anger "temperature" and checking in with yourself. If you get into a heated discussion or feel something brewing, you should check your mood and rate your anger levels. As things start to escalate, you want to be prepared to step away from the situation before things get to that point of no return. So if you know that you are unable to control yourself when you hit a seven, you must practice stepping away from the situation when you reach a five. Please note that in this situation, six is too close to your loss-of-control point. You have to learn to step away long enough to calm yourself down and regain your rational brain so you can continue the discussion.

A few other things to keep in mind when you're seeing red:

1. **Don't be so quick to personalize.** People who have anger problems take everything personally, and are prone to what therapists call "narcissistic injury," or a perceived threat to their self-esteem or self-worth. Try to give your partner the benefit of the doubt, when it comes to making assumptions about her intentions to harm you. Don't take it personally when your partner does not meet your expectations ("If you loved me, you would be neater"). Instead, try viewing her shortcomings as her own personal struggle. It is important to see the other person for who she is, limitations and all.

2. **Put things in perspective.** Rageaholics often treat a minor incident, like being cut off in traffic, as if it were the same as someone taking a sledgehammer to their car. This tends to escalate emotions.

3. **Stop blaming others.** Taking responsibility for your own actions and contributions to the conflicts in your relationship is crucial. Blaming only prevents you from understanding and changing the problem.

4. **Start problem-solving.** Being proactive and productive is a great way to move away from the heat of the moment. Brainstorming solutions with your partner is one of the best ways to change the energy in the room and move toward a positive resolution.

5. **Speak up before your anger gets out of control.** Oftentimes, people with rage issues fail to speak up for themselves when someone upsets them. When you don't say anything at the time, you end up spending a lot of time thinking about things you wish you had said, ruminating about what happened, and getting worked up. It is always best to address issues as they come up, before the feelings spin out of control.

6. **Think before you speak.** Blurting out things you will later regret saying is the fast road to relationship destruction. Practice pausing and thinking before speaking, and if you're in doubt, don't say anything at all. It is better to sleep on what you want to say and then decide in the morning if you want to say it. Once something has been said, it can never be taken back.

7. **Work on letting go.** Lying awake at night thinking about things that upset you during the day puts obsessional thinking in overdrive. This kind of rumination fuels the anger fire. Instead, focus on changing your self-talk, having compassion for other people's struggles, learning from your experiences, and planning new ways to handle similar problems differently in the future.

8. **Stop thinking of yourself as the victim.** As long as you view yourself as the wounded one, you will feel powerless; this will merely fuel your

rage. Blaming others also leaves you feeling justified in intimidating and hurting others, which only exacerbates your own problems.

Because of temperament, family history, and personality type, certain people are more prone to anger issues than others. Due to the level of harm and destruction that anger issues have on a relationship, they must be addressed for a couple to thrive. If you or your partner has anger management problems, it is imperative that you enroll in anger management classes and spend at least one year working with a licensed therapist.

Domestic Violence

There is no "fighting fair" in a relationship where physical abuse is present. Being abused destroys the sense of safety and security in a relationship more dramatically and effectively than any other behavior. Once this has occurred, there is always an unspoken threat that it can happen again. This makes it impossible for the person who was abused to freely speak her mind and have productive conversations. Violence in an intimate relationship is a deal breaker and cannot be tolerated.

I Can Stop Any Time I Want: Addiction

Where addiction or compulsivity exists, intimacy cannot thrive. When one person in the relationship is acting under the influence of a substance like alcohol, for example, it becomes impossible to connect and to communicate. The bottle becomes the new lover. The substance is the priority. Getting it, sneaking it, thinking about it, ingesting it— these are the focus. Once that has been accomplished, the addicted person is no longer emotionally present because he is in an altered state. This leaves no room to care about his partner or the relationship.

Typically, addictions snowball. As they say in Alcoholics Anonymous, "Alcoholism is a progressive disease." Over the years, slowly and insidiously, alcohol begins to take more and more control. It starts out subtly, but eventually it comes to dominate all aspects of the drinker's life, preventing her from having meaningful relationships, even with those she cares about the most. Inevitably, this causes fighting and heartache. It is the same for any addiction.

In season 2 of VH1 *Couples Therapy with Dr. Jenn*, the core issue between Jodeci and K-Ci lead singer Joel "Jojo" Hailey and his wife Tashaunda "Tiny" Hailey was his alcoholism. He had literally drunk himself into the hospital, prior to the show, and arrived at the *Couples Therapy* facility straight from his hospital stay. In group therapy, Tiny captured the pain of living with an alcoholic partner when she said, "I just despise what alcohol does to us. This is not something that can be done casually any more. [It's] your life; [it] depends on it. I sit at the hospital bed with you, nobody else. I sleep in chairs at the hospital for days with you, nobody else . . . just me. I live that. And I don't want that any more. I don't want to be afraid . . . to lose you. I don't want to feel like that [any] more. I just don't."

If you are in a relationship with someone who is caught in the throes of an addiction or compulsive behavior, you cannot stand by and watch your partner self-destruct. To do that only enables him. The most loving thing you can do is to refuse to stand by and watch the addiction escalate. As painful as it is, it is an act of love and kindness to let your partner know that you are not available for a relationship until he gets help.

All's Fair in Love and War

Couples must be committed to learning to fight fair, because without this ability to work through conflict, the relationship is doomed. No matter how good your intentions are, without the ability to communicate them in a respectful way, the message is lost and the conversation is shut down.

While few couples can avoid fighting completely, all couples can learn to fight fair. Even in the most compatible of relationships, people have different views and ideas that often create tension. When couples are able to respectfully work through discord, it deepens their relationship and fosters a better understanding of each other, which, ultimately, creates true emotional intimacy.

STEP **3**

Negotiate

Sheila and Mark were both life coaches. Well educated and well read on relationship psychology, Sheila called my *Dr. Jenn* radio show after returning from what was supposed to be a romantic vacation with Mark. "We fought about everything! What to order from room service, how much to tip, whether or not to make the bed . . . we bickered nonstop about the silliest of things. We should know better than this; after all, we are *both* life coaches!" Eighteen months into the relationship, their conflicts were not limited to vacation squabbles. The couple, who genuinely loved each other, found that they were constantly arguing.

Let the Negotiating Begin

The strongest bonds are forged when you are able to love what is so,
not just what you hoped is so.

—JUDITH SILLS, PhD, AUTHOR OF *A FINE ROMANCE*

Once we get past the honeymoon stage of a relationship—which is all about projection—we move into the negotiation stage. This usually occurs sometime between six and eighteen months into the relationship. We start to let go of the fantasy of the person with whom we've fallen in love and begin to see who our partner really is. While this awakening may be jolting, it is not at all unhealthy—in fact, it is necessary for a couple, in order to forge a mature, emotionally intimate, connected relationship.

All relationships start out with a lot of projection. We fill in the blanks with our fantasies and hopes: A guy who is committed to the relationship isn't going to want to have boys' night out anymore, a woman may think to herself, while a man may assume that a woman who loves him will make sure he has a home-cooked meal every night. We base our projections on a cocktail of life experiences, family history, beliefs, hopes, and dreams. When the reality of our partner—his behavior and preferences—emerges, it typically generates disappointment and anger, because there is not going to be perfect alignment in all areas, as we had hoped.

As a relationship develops, so do expectations. No matter how much love there is between two people, they will *not* meet all of each other's expectations. Negotiating differences and accepting that you will not always get what you want is a sign of maturity, and will ultimately strengthen your relationship.

The discrepancy between our fantasy relationship and the reality of what it really is, forces couples to better define what it means to be "a couple." Each person in the relationship comes to it with preconceptions about how relationships are "supposed" to work and what the "right" way is to live, act, and love. There are two primary tasks that must be accomplished during this phase:

1. **Couples must come up with a commonly held set of operating principles.** What kind of couple are we? How do we handle the decision-making process? How do we express ourselves to each other?

How do we work through conflict? Some of this process is conscious, but much of it is unconscious.

2. **Couples must come to an agreement on how to handle anger in the relationship.** You can't bury it and you can't let it take over the relationship. You must find a healthy way to express anger and work through it together.

Conflict in Long-Term Relationships

For couples who are in long-term relationships and have moved past the negotiation stage, there are many reasons that conflicts arise. Typically, it comes down to two main problems that prevent couples from getting resolution:

1. **Unresolved issues.** Couples who allow too much water to go under the bridge allow anger and resentment to build up in their relationship and contaminate it, like a poison.
2. **Poor communication patterns.** Most couples have bad habits when it comes to conflict resolution. Some avoid talking altogether; many get too aggressive or confrontational; still others just don't know how to speak to each other, so conflicts only escalate, even as the partners attempt to resolve those conflicts.

Nothing to Fear But Fear Itself: Why You Can't Fear Conflict

Conflict is growth trying to happen.

—HARVILLE HENDRIX, PhD, AUTHOR OF *GETTING THE LOVE YOU WANT*

When handled effectively, conflict can be a great catalyst for change, on multiple levels. Conflict can help us to change each other and the dynamic of our relationships, as well as teach us about our differences.

According to Harriet Lerner, author of *The Dance of Anger*, "Human nature is such that when we are angry, we tend to become so emotionally reactive to what the other person is doing to us that we lose our ability to observe our own part in the interaction." Being aware of this loss of clarity is the key to getting it back and using conflict to grow personally. If you can turn the microscope on yourself and examine how you have contributed to a problem and, in turn, own it, you will have taken huge steps toward personal growth. When you can own that your behavior influences how your partner reacts to you, it's possible to change that behavior and ultimately diminish the conflict. You may not be able to change your partner, but when you change your own behavior, that changes the dynamics and, sometimes, your partner's reactions.

Typically, we think that to be close, as a couple, each of us has to think the same way. This is a very common relationship myth. In real, authentic relationships, couples disagree, but they love and believe in each other, and have so much faith in their bond that they can talk through their differences. To have a partner who calls you out on "your shit" is so much more valuable than being with someone who parrots what you say, thinks what you think, and just tows the party line. Healthy couples challenge each other while still being supportive.

It may be difficult to feel intimate and connected when there are disagreements—conflict creates a sense of distance between two people, making it harder for them to connect. We tend to be drawn to people who have strengths, where we have weaknesses, and when we can harness those strengths and learn to tolerate our differences, there is a tremendous opportunity for growth.

QUESTIONS TO ASK YOURSELF BEFORE YOU BEGIN NEGOTIATING

No matter what decision you make, whether it's choosing a restaurant to go to for dinner, where to go on vacation, appropriate punishment for your children, or bringing a new toy into the bedroom, negotiating is an important part of the decision-making process. In order to avoid letting your emotions get the better of you, ask yourself these questions:

1. What is my bottom line?

2. What does this conversation say about me?

3. How am I making it hard for my partner to give me what I want?

4. What past experiences might influence how my partner sees this issue?

5. What is the fear underlying this conflict for each of us?

6. What are my partner's intentions?

7. What is at stake for each of us here?

8. How am I contributing to the problem?

Beginning a Difficult Negotiation

The most stressful and critical moment of a difficult conversation is the beginning. The way you begin sets the tone for the rest of the discussion. As mentioned earlier (on page 71), a study by clinical psychologist John Gottman, executive director of the Relationship Research Institute, shows that 96 percent of the time the way a discussion begins will determine how it will end. It is important to utilize that leverage to influence the direction and tone of the entire conversation. Before beginning, do your best to calm down, if you are worked up, and choose your words carefully. If you come from a place of love and kindness, rather than being critical or aggressive, you will have changed the odds in favor of having a productive conversation.

Alex McCord of the *Housewives of New York* and her husband Simon Van Kemp have a long history of bickering and conflict. Even though they adore each other, the two of them fought constantly when they appeared on season 2 of VH1 *Couples Therapy with Dr. Jenn.* As my day counselor Tom Caruouso observed, "I immediately noticed that they argue and they fight about anything and everything. They're constantly contradicting and correcting each other. It's hard to even know what they are arguing about. They argue about the way they argue." Harsh start-ups were a regular part of Alex and Simon's communication repertoire. Here are a few examples of how some of their arguments began on *Couples Therapy*:

- "F*****g stop it."
- "That is something you do all the f*****g time and I'm pissed right now."
- "If you feel that way, it is your problem, not mine."
- "Can I tell you how f*****g sick and tired I am of hearing that?"

When you start a conversation with inflammatory statements like those, hostility and aggression are bound to escalate. No matter how angry or frustrated you are, you must begin to communicate with each other from a different place.

Even if your partner has used inflammatory language, you need to come from a place of openness and curiosity. Instead of trying to get your partner to see your perspective or change his mind, start the conversation by seeking to understand his point of view. Explore his perspective. Try to get into his head and understand what upset him and why. Seek to understand his intentions and reasoning, instead of assuming the worst. Attempt to understand how your choices, words, and behavior have contributed to the conflict. This can be extremely challenging when you are upset, but mastering negotiating skills can make all the difference between having a successful relationship or a volatile one. It is also important to look at how you may be contributing to the problem, what you may be doing that is preventing healthy negotiations in your relationship.

FIVE THINGS THAT SHOULD NEVER BE NEGOTIATED

1. **Monogamy.** If both partners do not want the same thing, it is not a good match. In order for a monogamous or an open relationship to work, both people need to be on the same page. Compromising on this issue will only lead to enormous pain and conflict.

2. **Marriage.** If marriage is important to you, you should not give up on this, no matter how much you love your partner. Staying in a relationship where you have to give up this level of commitment will lead to anger and resentment.

3. **Baby.** If having a child is important to you, you should not give this up. You also should not try to pressure, guilt, or force someone else into having a baby with you. Having a second or third (or more) babies is, however, negotiable. Those are decisions that both people should make together.

> 4. **Core Values.** Core values are defining values that guide your life and behaviors. You should not be with someone who wants you to compromise your morals and values.
>
> 5. **Character.** People can improve their communication, become more insightful, and learn new behaviors, but they cannot learn character. You cannot change someone's nature.

Stop! In the Name of Love: Ten Things That Prevent Healthy Negotiations

The ability to negotiate through conflict is a crucial skill for couples who want to have a healthy long-term relationship. The problem is that we all have triggers, blind spots, and bad communication habits that prevent us from healthy negotiations. Being aware of what they are is the first step toward changing them.

1. Blame

Blame is a barrier to resolution and insight. It prevents negotiation from taking place. Problems are never one-sided. Both people in a couple contribute to a conflict, even when it does not appear to be so, and blaming the other person only makes her defensive and prevents you from acknowledging your part in the conflict. Blame keeps you in a circle of negative, angry thoughts and feelings. It prevents both parties from examining what *really* caused the problem and makes it impossible to address the underlying issue, so that meaningful action can be taken to address it. Blame is also a distraction from talking about hurt feelings—a conversation that is necessary for conflict resolution.

You are probably in blaming mode if you are:

- **Saying "You," instead of I.** Saying, for example, "You broke your word" instead of "I felt hurt when you didn't come home early for dinner as you promised" invites resistance and excuses from your partner. Stick to describing your own experience.

- **Making blanket statements about personality.** "You are so controlling" is character assassination, as opposed to "When you told me not to go out with my friends, I felt controlled." Focus on the behavior that upset you without making sweeping statements about the other person's character.

- **Viewing yourself as the victim, and not acknowledging your role in the conflict.** Own up to your contribution, no matter how minor it may have seemed to you. Admitting to playing a role in the conflict reduces blame and lowers your partner's defenses, making him more willing to own up to his part.

2. Defensiveness

When you are on the defensive, you are so busy protecting yourself from a real or perceived attack—from exposing your own shortcomings or from a threat to your ego—that you go into a protective stance that prevents you from being open to your partner's feedback. Some people attack back, like rapper Treach Criss on season 5 of VH1 *Couples Therapy with Dr. Jenn*, who said, ". . . once I get attacked, the mentality is 'Back down from nobody!' We say everything in the book to each other," describing the conflict between him and his girlfriend Cicely Evans.

Blame is the number one trigger for defensiveness, another relationship killer. But just because your partner is in blaming mode does not mean that you are off the hook when it comes to your own defensive behavior. Don't let your partner drag you down into defensiveness.

If you find yourself denying any responsibility, making excuses, meeting your partner's complaint with one of your own, blaming your partner, or repeating yourself over and over again, you are probably in defensive mode. Here are some linguistic red flags that indicate when you are being defensive:

- "Yes, but . . ."
- "At least I didn't . . ."
- "You're the one who . . ."
- "You always . . ."
- "But you . . ."
- "I don't agree . . ."
- "You are blowing this out of proportion/being dramatic/ overreacting . . ."

Instead, try saying:

- "I get why you feel that way . . ."
- "I am listening. Please tell me more . . ."
- "I see your point . . ."
- "That isn't what I meant, but I can see how you might take it that way . . ."
- "I think my part in it was . . ."
- "I didn't think of it that way, but I can understand why that upset you . . ."
- "I see your point . . ."
- "What you are saying makes a lot of sense . . ."
- "Let's work together to find a compromise . . ."

The greatest antidote to defensiveness is taking responsibility. Owning your part in a conflict changes the dynamics, and melts the other person's resistance by allowing both of you to come to a mutually satisfying resolution.

3. Reactivity

Emotionally charged reactions and increasing intensity can cause our differences to become even more pronounced. When you meet intensity with intensity, it only escalates the argument and tension. Former porn star Jenna Jameson captured this dynamic in season 5 of VH1 *Couples Therapy with Dr. Jenn*, when she spoke about how she responded to conflict with her boyfriend John Wood: "You bust my balls? I'll bust yours right back." This kind of reactivity escalates conflict.

When we experience heightened reactive emotions, it prevents us from relating to our partner in a healthy way. The intensity and emotion can make everything blurry and prevent us from seeing what really matters. As Whitney Mixter of *The Real L Word* described her communication with her wife Sada Bettencourt, also of *The Real L Word*, on season 4 of VH1 *Couples Therapy with Dr. Jenn*, "The smallest thing can send us into a whirlwind of frustration, anger, confusion, misunderstanding." So many viewers related to that observation.

In order to become emotionally available to work through a conflict in a way that recognizes the point of view of both partners, and is productive, you need to deescalate the emotional intensity of the conversation. A few ways to do that include:

- **Take time to calm down.** Let your partner know that you need some cooling-off time. Make sure to be specific about how much time you think you will need so he doesn't feel abandoned.

- **Help yourself to develop an "observing ego,"** a term coined by psychologist Louis Ormont. In other words, be objective about what you see, by pulling yourself out of the emotions of the conflict to gain a clearer perspective.
- **Distract yourself with another activity.** Sometimes taking a break from the emotions that surround a conflict can give you the fresh perspective you need to reduce your reactivity to the problem.
- **Don't bottle things up.** Talk about issues that upset you as they arise.

TEN SIGNS THAT YOU'VE BEEN TRIGGERED

1. Your reaction is out of proportion to the event.
2. You are using absolutes ("You always. . . ," "You never . . . ," etc.).
3. You are making blanket statements ("You are controlling," "You're a terrible husband!").
4. You don't remember what you or the other person said. This also shows that emotions were running high.
5. You find yourself taking a stoic stance and being stubborn.
6. You are more invested in being right than in understanding what happened for the other person.
7. You are name-calling.
8. You are yelling.
9. You feel helpless.
10. You can't articulate the other person's point of view.

4. Being Overly Focused on the Other Person

When you are totally focused on your partner, you lose the ability to see your own shortcomings and how you contributed to the problem. As Harriet Lerner says in *The Dance of Anger,* "We become overfocused on the incompetence of the other and underfocused on the incompetence of the self." This prevents us from growing and keeps us stuck in whatever the problem happens to be in our relationship.

While you have a responsibility to your partner to lovingly call him out on his "stuff" and encourage him to grow, at the end of the day, you can't change him. The only thing you can change is yourself. Changing your own behaviors, thinking patterns, and the way you communicate can change the dynamics with your partner.

Be the leader in your relationship. Don't wait for him to change in order for the relationship to get better. Instead, take the high road and change yourself, regardless of what your partner does or doesn't do. It is a win-win proposition for you: You grow as a person, better yourself, develop new relationship skills—and all of this just might create a domino effect of positive change in your relationship.

Here are a few other things you can do to keep from overfocusing on your partner's contribution to the problem:

- Let go of trying to figure out who started it. Instead, focus on figuring out how to break out of it.
- Ask yourself how you may have provoked the other person, what you may be doing to perpetuate the conflict, and what you could do differently.
- Ask yourself what may have gotten triggered in you and what work you need to do on yourself to reduce those triggers.

5. *Arguing over Pseudo Issues*

One night at the *Couples Therapy* house, Taylor Armstrong of the *Housewives of Beverly Hills* returned to her room, only to find the heater blasting and a stopped-up toilet. She was already frustrated about some production issues and the food choices at the house, and when she saw the now infamous and, admittedly, unattractive "pea green towels" in her bathroom, she lost it and threw a massive fit—the biggest I have ever seen at the house. Taylor was totally justified in her frustration about things not working properly. The *Couples Therapy* house, in which we do treatment, was built in the 1940s, and the heating, air-conditioning, and plumbing are extremely erratic. As valid as Taylor's concerns were, the magnitude of her meltdown was out of proportion to the problems in the house. Taylor screamed at the house counselors, ranted to her housemates, flipped off the cameramen, yelled to stop filming, and then called me at 3:00 a.m., threatening to terminate therapy.

The next day in group therapy, I was determined to get to the real issue. I knew we had hit on something that was a lot more significant than the offensive "pea green towels." Therapy is a microcosm of how we function in the outside world, and I knew that the real issue was also playing out in her relationship with John at home. Taylor is an extremely strong woman who survived terrible domestic violence as a child, a physically abusive marriage, public scrutiny of her marriage as it was ending, and the suicide of her husband. Taylor is a survivor.

Once Taylor got past her frustrations and accusations, she got down to the real issue. "When I do have an outburst, it's about things that don't make any sense . . . it's because I don't know how to say it's about the things I can't control. So my home is perfect all the time, because everything about my life feels like chaos and it always has," she told me. It became clear that Taylor's anxiety was the underlying issue. She was spending her days and nights trying to contain her anxiety by controlling her environment, but what she really needed was to get help to control her anxiety, anxiety that was hurting her relationship.

Sometimes we have big explosions, as Taylor did; other times we have ongoing conflicts. These conflicts are not about what they seem to be about. The fight is the beard for the bigger issue that hides beneath it. Usually that "bigger issue" lies within us.

Kim and John, who came to see me in my private practice, had been dating for a year before they moved in together. They were barely out of the honeymoon stage when the movers arrived. It was only a week after unpacking their first box that the conflicts began, and the couple came in for therapy. John had a habit of leaving his clothes on the floor and dishes in the sink. Kim, who is a neat freak, found herself cleaning up after him and feeling resentful. John found Kim to be hypercritical. For her part, Kim felt disrespected, because John knew that his messes bothered her, but he chose not to clean up after himself. The couple found themselves having the same argument over and over again, with no resolution.

The truth is that John had a very controlling mother and was hypersensitive to feeling controlled. Moving in with Kim triggered his anxieties in this area. John was unconsciously creating a situation that guaranteed that Kim would want him to change his behaviors, and then he could point a finger and say, "See! All women are controlling." Kim, on the other hand, was a parentified child in her family, and had been put in a position where she felt obligated to take care of her parents. Her alcoholic mother was rarely present, so Kim had to take care of her siblings as well as clean up her mother's messes, literally and figuratively. So John's messes confirmed her worst fears that she would be cast in the caregiver role yet again.

Both sides of the argument are valid but nothing could be accomplished—that is, their conflict would never be resolved—if they stuck to the chores conversation again and again. If their issue really had been about chores, it could have been resolved with one conversation. The underlying fears and concerns that fueled their arguments were what needed to be addressed. Until John acknowledged his real fear—that he would lose his freedom, in this new stage of the relationship, and that Kim would behave the way his mother did—and Kim could admit that she is terrified of ending up as a resentful caregiver again—nothing will change.

If you find yourself repeatedly having the same fight over and over again with your partner, it is a sign that there is a deeper issue that needs to be discussed in order to resolve it. Until you identify the real issue, you will be wasting time fighting over pseudo issues.

To help you get to the real issue behind conflicts, ask yourself and your partner the following questions:

- What is this fight really about? Look for the real issue.
- What am I afraid of? Typically fear is at the root of most conflicts.
- What is it from my history that may be getting triggered in this conflict? We all get triggered from past issues, and until we own what those triggers are, conflicts will persist.
- What issues from my past may be affecting the way I see this problem? Past experiences with family and previous partners often color how we see things and determine which buttons our lover pushes.

6. Unwillingness to Compromise

As the song says, you can't always get what you want, but, sometimes, you can "get what you need." Jane, a prominent hedge fund manager, and Aaron, a plastic surgeon, came to see me in private practice. They are both very successful and used to their staff tending to them and meeting their needs. Both have been in relationships where they were in charge and got their own way the vast majority of the time—and they've each had a history of partnering with people who did not challenge them. Neither Jane nor Aaron was used to compromise. As a result, a simple task like planning a vacation could cause serious conflict between them. Neither wanted to give in on any issue, ever.

Having a mature relationship requires compromise and sacrifice. It doesn't sound sexy, but it's the truth. The ability to be flexible and accommodating is crucial to the well-being of a relationship. There has to be give-and-take for both people to feel respected, cared about, and loved.

The desire for freedom and the wish not to be controlled are valid needs in a relationship. We always have the freedom of choice. But the paradox of choice is that when we choose one option, we give up another one. When we choose to be in a monogamous relationship, we choose to give up sleeping with other exciting people. We are free to choose, but we are not free from the consequences of our choices. We may miss out on something that we could enjoy, but, hopefully we get something in return that is more meaningful.

The key to compromise is to make sure that you are not giving up something that is essential to the well-being of your soul or your authentic self. Giving up going clubbing and getting drunk with your girlfriends does not sacrifice your authentic self. It's a choice that shows maturity and a willingness to take steps to protect your relationship as well as your own health. There is a difference between a controlling or abusive partner who wants to isolate your from your support system, is critical of you, or wants to prevent you from succeeding in your career, and a partner who encourages you to make healthy choices for yourself and the relationship. Sometimes healthy choices can be hard, especially if, like Jane and Aaron, you are not used to making them.

The best thing you can do is to challenge yourself to make compromises that force you to grow and mature in your relationship. As difficult as that may be, the benefits are significant. Research shows that the willingness to sacrifice is associated with strong commitment, high relationship satisfaction, and superior functioning as a couple.

A few things you can do to help you become better at compromise are:

- Have an open mind.
- Be willing to sacrifice for your partner.
- Search for common ground.
- Be willing to adjust your perspective as you take in information.
- Ask questions.
- Put yourself in your partner's shoes.
- Recognize what is driving you.
- Choose your battles.

7. Avoidance

Nobody enjoys experiencing—and talking through—an upsetting conflict with a loved one. According to experts, men are at a disadvantage in this arena, in two ways. According to relationship authors Patricia Love and Steven Stosny, boy babies are born far more sensitive to stimulation than girls are, and have a propensity for emotional hyperarousal. Studies show that male babies startle five times more often than female babies. As a result, baby boys learn to guard against overstimulation from an early age. They do not handle eye contact and other intimate contact as well as baby girls.

In adulthood, men typically try to avoid the overwhelming feeling that goes along with a surge of cortisol, when they are hyperaroused during conflict with their partners. In other words, it is easier for them to avoid dealing with things than to face the music.

Women bond by helping each other through difficult times and talking about the troubles they experience. Typically, women seek comfort through connection and emotional bonds. Researchers refer to this tendency as "tend and befriend." As a result, women typically respond to stressful situations by protecting themselves and their young through nurturing, connected behaviors.

Men are far more likely to pull away from conflict and participate in a calming activity, like watching television, working on a hobby, playing a sport, or turning on the computer. Their natural instinct is to avoid uncomfortable feelings and go into what psychologists call "fight or flight" mode, where they are poised to either attack or retreat to their caves. Women, whose instinct is to "talk it out," typically perceive this behavior as a form of abandonment.

Women feel closer to others by exposing their vulnerability. To become closer to another woman, women trade personal disclosure with personal disclosure. But when a woman exposes her vulnerability to a man, he often feels inadequate as a partner and protector, which can trigger feelings of shame, causing him to get defensive and angry (fight) or to pull back (flight). This can feel very threatening to a woman and the emotional bond she is seeking to forge, particularly if her disclosure of vulnerability prompts her partner to pull back, which, again, may be perceived as abandonment.

Knowing that men are more physiologically reactive to emotional stimulation, it makes sense that men are more likely to get overwhelmed. Research shows that during a conflict, a man's pulse rate and blood pressure are far more likely to rise than a woman's. This physiological disadvantage leaves men more prone to stonewalling, which is considered to be one of the greatest predictors of divorce.

When a person stonewalls, he puts up a verbal and emotional wall, and refuses to engage. The usual "a-has" and "hmms" of normal conversation are abandoned. A great example of stonewalling occurred on season 4 of VH1 *Couples Therapy with Dr. Jenn* during a heated argument between Whitney Mixter and Sada Bettencourt. When Whitney was expressing her concerns, Sada cut her off by saying, "Let's just not talk about it. Bye. See you later," and walked out of the room, ending the conversation.

When one half of a couple stonewalls, it is impossible to have a dialogue and work through problems. Stonewalling is often accomplished through silence, monosyllabic mutterings, changing the subject, refusing to speak, saying the same thing over and over again, or disappearing for long periods of time. Research shows that 85 percent of stonewallers are men.

This is not to say that there aren't women who experience shame, avoid conflict, or stonewall in a relationship. But, statistically speaking, it is more likely to be a man. So what can you do to keep stonewalling at bay and the lines of communication open?

- Recognize when you are feeling overwhelmed during a discussion.
- Periodically check your heart rate during an emotional argument.
- Take twenty to thirty minutes to calm down, if things are getting too heated.
- Be sensitive to your partner's issues of shame and abandonment.
- Approach discussions about conflicts with sensitivity and gentleness.
- Make a pact to talk through conflict and not abandon each other, even if you need to take multiple time-outs during a heated discussion.

8. Judging Harshly

Intentions and judgment go hand in hand in our minds. If we believe our partner intended to hurt us, we are much more likely to judge him harshly. Typically, when we have been hurt by someone's behavior, we assume the worst. When talking about incorrect assumptions people make, Douglas Stone, Bruce Patton, and Sheila Heen, authors of *Difficult Conversations*, say, "The first mistake can be traced to one basic error: we make an attribution about another person's intentions based on the impact of their actions on us. We feel hurt; therefore they intended to hurt us. We feel slighted; therefore they intended to slight us. Our thinking is so automatic that we aren't even aware that our conclusion is only an assumption."

When we judge our partner harshly and make assumptions, we push her away and prevent closeness. We are tougher on her than we are on ourselves.

Most of us tend to assume the worst about others. When your partner is late for dinner, you don't give him the benefit of the doubt; instead, you judge him for being passive-aggressive, inconsiderate, irresponsible, and, on top of everything else, he doesn't appreciate your good cooking. But if the tables are turned, and you are late, you give yourself more leeway: The traffic was bad, you had to finish a big project, you're stressed out, and so on.

Judgments and assumptions are dangerous to relationships. Here are a few things you can do to avoid them:

- Give your partner the benefit of the doubt.
- Don't assume you know his intentions.
- Take the time to learn what your partner is really upset about, not what you think she's upset about.

- Don't play the victim.
- If you think he meant to hurt you, ask him if that is what he intended to do.
- Be aware that even when your partner understands that your intentions were not meant to be hurtful, she may still be upset.

9. Arguing Over Details

One of the most common communication problems occurs when couples fixate so intently on the details of a dispute that they miss more important issues. Everyone has his own subjective experience of an event that he sees through the lens of his own history and perception. Couples often have contradictory interpretations of the same event.

In the Japanese film *Rashomon*, various characters provide alternative, self-serving, and contradictory versions of the same event, based on their unique perspectives. The "Rashomon effect" is a term that refers to contradictory views of the same event, experienced by different people. For example, when two people are asked to recollect an experience or conversation, they typically offer substantially different, but equally plausible accounts of it. The Rashomon effect is always alive and well with couples.

The ability to experience the world through your partner's eyes while holding on to your own perspective is an incredibly important skill. Most people, however, get so focused on getting the details "right" and correcting their partner or arguing, that they keep from seeing any other perspective but their own. This prevents conflict resolution.

People don't change without first feeling that they have been understood. Telling your partner to change does not inspire change. If anything, it inspires rebellion. On the other hand, if you are able to get into your partner's head, understand her perspective, and verbalize it, you are on the way to change.

You can get so focused on the unimportant details of an argument that you literally can't hear your partner's pain. An almost comical example of this occurred with my client Roseanna and her boyfriend Pete. Pete received a care package from someone he worked with, which included an inappropriate note, setting off Roseanna, who already had trust issues with men.

I sat down with the couple in a session to figure out if the person who had written the note was indeed romantically involved with him. Pete admitted that before meeting Roseanna, he had had sex with her. Pete and Roseanna then proceeded to argue about whether she had given him one blowjob or two. Really? Does it really matter if it was one or two? The bottom line is this: It's understandable why Pete's sexual history with another woman, who clearly still had feelings for him, made Roseanna feel uncomfortable. Pete never got past arguing about the details of how many times they'd "hooked up" in order to address Roseanna's feelings. If he had said, "Roseanna, I can really understand why that would make you uncomfortable. Let's talk about what kind of boundaries I can make with other women to make you more comfortable," the session (and the relationship) would have played out much differently.

A relationship is not a court of law. Accuracy is less important than understanding the other person's experience. When you are so busy arguing over how often something happened, you are too busy being defensive to hear what your partner is saying, and your relationship will suffer.

Here's what you can do to avoid fixating on the details during a negotiation with your partner:

- Don't correct your partner and insist on specifics.
- Focus on feelings and emotional experiences.

- Learn what the experience was like for your mate.
- Don't tell your partner how she should express herself.
- Demonstrate empathy.
- Ask questions to understand your partner's experience.
- Look for opportunities to problem-solve together.

10. Assuming the Worst

Don't assume the worst about your partner. You have chosen to be with this person because you trust that she loves and cares for you. Work from the assumption that your partner has your best interests at heart. If you approach difficult conversations with this in mind, you are more likely to give your partner the benefit of the doubt, instead of assuming the worst.

If you don't think the person you are with loves and cares about you, you may want to get out of the relationship, because it is not healthy for you to stay. You should *not* give the benefit of the doubt to a partner who is abusive, a serial cheater, a drug addict or alcoholic, or who has a long-standing, pervasive history of lying. If that is the situation you are in, you should get therapy to better understand why you are with this person, and you should get out of the relationship. You should also seek out the help of a professional therapist or crisis hotline counselor to figure out how to get out safely.

The reality, however, is that most people tend to assume the worst about their partners, whether or not those assumptions are justified. Usually it boils down two grievances that are not always connected:

- **You are trying to hurt me.** Most people operate from the mistaken belief that if their partners have hurt them, they must have intended to hurt them.

- **You are lying.** The reality is that everyone lies to some degree ("No, Honey, those pants don't make your butt look big"). All of this occurs on a continuum, with some offenses being more hurtful than others. There is a big difference between a partner who lies and says he picked up toothpaste at the market, when he didn't, and a partner who lies and says he didn't sleep with that woman at the bar, when he did.

The way you communicate with your partner in those doubting moments is the key to negotiating difficult conflicts. If you go on the attack and become accusatory and belligerent, you don't leave any room to get answers.

Here are a few things you can do to prevent yourself from assuming the worst about your partner:

- Give your partner the benefit of the doubt.
- Watch your own reactivity.
- Ask open-ended questions.
- Be respectful in your responses and tone.
- Cut your partner some slack.

WHAT WE MUST ACCEPT ABOUT OURSELVES GOING INTO A CONFLICT

In the book *Difficult Conversations*, the authors talk about three crucial characteristics that are important to accept about yourself in difficult conversations:

1. You will make mistakes.

> **2.** Your intentions are complex.
>
> **3.** You have contributed to the problem.
>
> We like to think that we are above these, but none of us are. Accepting these things about ourselves will help us judge our partner less harshly and be clearer in our own communication.

Spheres of Influence

Lorenzo came from what he described as a hotheaded Italian family. Dinnertime was filled with loud debates, passionate arguments, and even family downtime was intense and often heated. Lorenzo was used to a high level of conflict and talking about every problem that came up. His husband Preston, on the other hand, came from a more subdued family. "We are WASPs. We don't talk about anything unpleasant or upsetting," he half-joked in therapy with me. Preston's experience and skills at talking through conflict and dealing with high levels of emotion was low. Of course, it was Lorenzo's intensity and passion that drew him to Preston, but he found their debates and arguments exhausting and overwhelming. Lorenzo was frustrated by his inability to talk through things and angered by what he perceived as his habit of shutting down when things got heated.

No matter whether we love or hate our family of origin, we are influenced by their negotiating style, and it is vitally important to be aware of how this affects our tolerance for conflict, and our ability to work through it, in our relationships with other people. We typically choose partners who have strengths where we have weaknesses, and from whom we can learn. Lorenzo, for example, needs to learn to reduce his emotional reactivity during conflicts, and Preston, for his part, needs to learn to tolerate conversations about difficult things. Learning from each other makes us stronger, more whole, and more capable of a healthy relationship.

Given the high level of influence that our family of origin has over our relationship skills, it is important to be aware of how that affects us. Ask yourself the following questions:

- How did my family handle conflict? What was their style?
- How does this influence my own negotiation abilities?
- What baggage am I bringing to this relationship from my own family and how they handled disagreements?
- What were my mother's strengths and weaknesses in this area? My father's? My siblings'? My own?
- How did my partner's family handle conflict? How does this affect his negotiating style? Which of my buttons might this push?
- What do I need to work on to be a better communicator in my relationship?

More Than a Feeling

We like to believe that feelings are unimportant and that logic always prevails, but that is not the nature of relationships or conflict. Feelings are far too significant to go unexpressed without serious consequences in a relationship. As Stone, Patton, and Heen say so astutely in *Difficult Conversations*, "Feelings are too powerful to remain peacefully bottled. They will be heard one way or another, whether in leaks or bursts. And if handled indirectly or without honesty, they contaminate communication." In other words, talk it out or it will come back to bite your relationship in the ass.

Talking about feelings doesn't come easily for most people. It is scary to make yourself vulnerable and risk the possibility of getting hurt or being let down. And, of course, we fear upsetting the other person. This leaves us feeling vulnerable and exposed, which often creates tension. Not to mention that most people do not grow up in homes where the expression of negative feelings—anger, hurt, sadness, jealousy—is encouraged, much less accepted and embraced. When you come from a family like that, it hurts your ability to tolerate your own feelings as well as your partner's, a dynamic that also hurts the relationship.

Shayne Lamas, daughter of Lorenzo Lamas, and winner of the twelfth season of *The Bachelor*, is a great example of this. On season 2 *of* VH1 *Couples Therapy with Dr. Jenn*, I did a session with Shayne and her husband Nik Richie of TheDirty.com, where he poured his heart out to her about how alone and lonely he felt in their marriage. Shayne's cold response surprised even me.

> **Shayne**: OK, we get it! He feels f***ing lonely. At some point it's like, okay, now we know your feelings, let's move past it. I get it. I got it. I got it. I got it.
> **Me**: Cut that s***t out. Cut it out. It's killing your f***ing marriage. Do you get that? Your dismissiveness, your inability to let him feel his feelings. Did nobody ever let you feel your feelings? Is that what it is?
> **Shayne**: I mean, I know what feelings feel like. I love . . . I just . . .
> **Me**: So you are telling me that . . . you had loving consistent . . .
> **Shayne**: So, I have no feelings 'cause my father never showed me feelings. We all love each other, but we all don't know each other. There is no emotional bond. And then, whatever. It is what it is. But . . .
> **Me**: But what "it" is, is the template from which you spring off to this relationship. You didn't get that connection, and now you are struggling to make it with your husband. Are you afraid that if you let him in he won't stick around?

Shayne: I've just never let anybody in. I don't know what it's like. [She bursts into tears.]

When we are able to safely express our feelings and allow our partners to do the same, we take our relationship to a new level of connection, closeness, and safety. Ultimately, Shayne learned how to do that and it saved her marriage.

When your partner is expressing his feelings, try to connect, in the following ways:

- Treat him tenderly. This is a moment of vulnerability.
- Listen carefully to what is important or upsetting to your partner and reflect it back to him.
- Do not tell him that he is wrong for feeling the way he feels.
- Do not judge, evaluate, or criticize. This will shut him down.
- Don't try to fix it. Emotions need to be understood, not fixed.
- Let him know that his feelings matter to you, and that you are working to understand them.
- Connection and compassion are the antidote to negative emotions. Provide these two things for your partner in those difficult moments and it will be transformative.

YOU SHOULDN'T FEEL THAT WAY

Dealing with your partner's upset feelings and strong emotions can be challenging. Even worse, it can push our own buttons. It can make us—consciously or unconsciously—want to shut them down. This is often done with comments like "You shouldn't feel that way," "Stop being so dramatic," and "Just calm down." Comments like that inflame and make your partner feel even worse. Here are six reasons never to make those statements to your partner:

1. Your partner now feels "bad" for having those feelings.

2. She opened up to you in a search for understanding and compassion. Telling her she shouldn't feel that way shuts her down and doesn't make her feel understood.

3. Feelings that are free to be expressed and explored don't get acted out in the relationship in destructive ways.

4. Being told to stop feeling a certain way doesn't change the fact that the feeling is present. But now, in addition to feeling bad, your partner feels guilty and frustrated for experiencing her natural emotions.

5. This is likely to create more hurt, resentment, and distance between the two of you.

6. Energy that is wasted trying to repress feelings is not available for more constructive behaviors.

Six Skills You Need to Reduce Conflict in Your Relationship

Having a healthy, mature, emotionally connected relationship requires skills that don't just fall into your lap—they are acquired through the use of self-restraint and relationship tools, and by becoming a compassionate partner. While many important skills and abilities are needed to build a great relationship, these are six of the most crucial things you need to do:

1. *Listen*

I will never forget the words of my clinical supervisor right before I went into my very first session as a therapist. He said, "Just listen. Listen really well. Most people are never truly heard and when you give that, it's magical. You don't have to solve her problems, just listen well and you will help her heal." He was so right. Most people don't really listen. They are distracted by their own wandering thoughts, busy preparing what they are going to say in response, or distracted by their electronic gadgets. Listening, really listening well, is a gift you should give your partner.

Attentive listening shows that we care. It is loving and respectful. It also allows us to understand our partner on a deeper level because, when we are focused, we hear the nuances and get to know our partner in a more profound way. The well-known family therapist Virginia Satir once said, "I believe the greatest gift I can conceive of having from anyone is to be seen by them, heard by them, to be understood and touched by them."

But what if your partner is not giving you that respect? Give it to him anyway. You will benefit on multiple levels. Your partner is more likely to pay attention when you speak, if you pay attention to him first. It is an effective strategy. It is also a great way to change the dynamic of your relationship.

2. *Develop Empathy*

Empathy is the ability to understand another person's condition from her perspective, being able to imagine what an experience is like for her, and to feel what she is feeling. Empathy creates a bridge between two people with different backgrounds, life experiences, and perspectives. Empathy engenders sensitivity and connection, which creates a safe place for vulnerability in a relationship. Empathy opens the door for a deep level of intimacy and closeness.

Empathy also leads to compassion, which makes a person want to alleviate the pain and suffering of the other. When you are connected with that desire, in the context of a relationship, you are less likely to lash out and say things you'll regret. Empathy gives you greater capacity to work through conflict in a loving manner.

Just showing an effort to be more empathetic makes a big difference in relationship satisfaction. According to a study published in the *Journal of Family Psychology*, the "perceived empathetic effort," meaning the degree to which one appears to be attempting to understand why another person is feeling a certain way, makes a huge difference in the level of fulfillment that partners feel with each other. This skill is particularly powerful for a man who is in a relationship with a woman. For women, satisfaction in a relationship is most strongly associated with feeling that their partners are making an effort to understand them, regardless of whether or not they actually do understand them. This attempt to understand goes a long way for a woman because it indicates that her partner is investing in the relationship and expressing the desire to be emotionally attuned to her needs. For a man, this effort goes a long way, too, but an even stronger indicator of relationship satisfaction, according to the study, is whether or not he is able to identify when his partner is happy.

3. Become Emotionally Attuned

When I talk about emotional attunement I am referring to the ability to read your partner's cues and pick up on micro-expressions. The capacity to tune in to your partner and accurately take his emotional temperature is key to creating a strong connection and bond. It is the vaccination against disconnection, which, in my clinical experience, is the single greatest cause of breakups.

You don't even have to know exactly what your partner is thinking. Simply acknowledging a shift in energy and asking what he's thinking is enough to show that you are invested and tuned into him. On the third date with my boyfriend, Eric, we were at a charity event. I was wearing a really special outfit and it was getting cold. Eric offered me his jacket, but at that moment I wasn't cold enough to need it. About an hour later, though, when we were sitting at the table, watching the show, the air-conditioning began to kick in, and I thought to myself, "I am getting really cold, but I don't want to cover up my cute outfit with his jacket." I had not said a word to him. I wasn't even making eye contact, when this thought flashed through my mind. We were both watching a musical performance. All of a sudden he looked at me and said, "What just happened? Your whole energy just changed. Is everything okay?" Before I could finish my first sentence, his jacket was around my shoulders. To have someone so attuned to my needs made me feel connected, adored, and taken care of. It was incredibly sexy to have him so tuned into me.

The ability to read another person's state of mind and emotions is one of the most seductive things you can do, especially for a woman. We all want to feel seen and appreciated. If you don't already do this, it requires a conscious effort to tune into your partner's emotional state. It means you have to step outside your own thoughts, feelings, and needs in the moment. Tuning into your partner in this way is most challenging during tense moments in your relationship because you have to manage your own fears, insecurities, anger, and judgment.

The good news is that, just like any relationship skill, emotional attunement can be learned. When you believe you have observed an important mood shift in your partner, share your observations, even if you are not 100 percent sure of the specifics. This opens the door for conversation and connection. "Hey, I noticed when your aunt Sally was talking about your mom, you got a look on your face. What was going through your mind?" A good formula for this is to pair an observation with a question. "You seem upset. Does it have to do with the call you got from your boss?"

A study in the *Journal of Family Psychology* found that couples are better at recognizing "hard" emotions (anger, annoyance, irritation, aggravation) than they are at recognizing "soft" ones (sadness, hurt, concern, disappointment). Softer emotions express vulnerability and are more focused on relationship and connection. Therefore, recognizing them is important to draw couples back together. Being too focused on being angry during a conflict prevents you from addressing the hurt your partner is feeling and deprives you of an opportunity to tune in and resolve the conflict.

4. Practice Good Timing

Steve's company was laying off people left and right. His boss sat him down and let him know that if he didn't get his numbers up, he could be the next to go. On his way home from work, Steve got a call from his mother's nursing home saying that she was refusing her medication, and, as he turned into the driveway, his son's school called to say that the boy had ditched class again. All Steve wanted to do was to decompress and have a peaceful dinner with his wife Stephanie. Instead, he was greeted by his wife, who was pointing at her iPad (open to Facebook) and saying, "Who is this Sophia and why did you 'like' her picture?" Actually, Steve had done nothing wrong. His boss had asked him to "like" the post to help support the boss's adult daughter's singing career.

Steve's fuse was short and his temper quick to flare. Even though Stephanie could see that he was tense when he came home from work, she went in for the kill. Stephanie had contained her anxiety all day long and could take it no longer. Instead of asking for time to calm down from his day, Steve reacted by yelling at Stephanie for being insecure and threatened to block her from his Facebook account. Things escalated from there.

In life, timing is everything. Had the same conversation occurred after Steve had unwound from his day and shared his stresses with Stephanie (including his boss's inappropriate request that Steve "like" his daughter's Facebook page), it would have been a benign conversation, instead of World War III.

It takes tremendous restraint to postpone a conversation that you need to have with your partner. The ability to delay gratification is crucial for successful conflict resolution. Starting a difficult conversation when you or your partner is caught off guard, angry, hurt, anxious, or upset is a recipe for disaster. Try some of these methods to help you time a difficult conversation:

- Be aware of your emotions.
- Take your partner's emotional temperature before starting a difficult conversation.
- Schedule a time to talk.
- Go to a public spot where you can't yell or scream.
- Ask, "Is this a good time to talk?"

Here are a few things you can say to buy yourself time to calm down:

- "I'm sorry. This isn't a good time to talk about this."
- "Let's take a break and talk more about this later."
- "Let me think about this and get back to you tomorrow morning."
- "I am feeling really triggered. Please give me twenty minutes to get my head on straight."

- "Let me take a minute and get some fresh air."
- "I would love some time to digest what you have just said."
- "Let's take a time-out and talk again in an hour."

5. Develop Emotional Intelligence

Developing a high EQ (Emotional Intelligence) is far more important than having a high IQ when it comes to relationship success. Psychologists Peter Salovey and John Mayer, who are credited as the first to coin the term "emotional intelligence," define it as "a subset of social intelligence that involves the ability to monitor one's own and others' feelings and emotions, to discriminate among them and to use this information to guide one's thinking and actions." People who have a high EQ exhibit impulse control, problem-solving skills, empathy, the ability to delay gratification, the capacity to read other people's emotional cues, self-soothing skills, high self-esteem, adaptability, and resilience, and are able to identify, express, and understand feelings.

Mastering these skills is a guarantee for reducing volatility and conflict, and increasing your ability to meet your partner's needs and have your own needs met, as well. Very few people can push our emotional buttons like our partners. The ability to manage our own negative emotions, so that they don't overwhelm us and affect our judgment, is a very advanced EQ skill. Like a bad flu, emotions can be contagious. Therapists call the experience of catching your partner's anger, anxiety, or frustration "emotional contagion."

The ability to regulate emotional contagion is the best defense for not "catching" your partner's negative feelings. The first step is being aware that your emotions are heightened. The second step is to verbalize this to your partner. Next, you need to take steps to calm yourself down—with deep breathing, a time-out, or asking your partner to change the subject temporarily. If both of you are able to do this, it will improve the state of your union.

6. *Learn from Your Struggles*

Relationship struggles are inevitable and should be used as vehicles for growth. To experience pain, and not grow and learn from it, is to waste an opportunity to learn how to do better in your relationship. If you can see conflict as opportunity, it will make you react differently when it arises again, and provide you with a more positive attitude as you face the challenges ahead.

I have a strong personality and opinions. My boyfriend Eric is the same way. Despite these traits, we are always very respectful of each other and our opinions, but sometimes things can get intense. Fortunately, one of the strengths of our relationship is that we have a great ability to talk through things. He has the most emotional stamina of anyone I have ever met, when it comes to talking through conflict.

We came up with some questions that we like to ask each other at the end of a conflict. You may want to try using them the next time you and your partner have had a contentious conversation:

- What did we learn from this?
- What could we do differently next time?
- What do I need to work on?
- What was my part in this?
- What is it from my past that got triggered?
- What is the underlying fear behind this conflict?

There is nothing to fear when it comes to conflict in your relationship. That said, you have a responsibility to your partner and yourself to hone your relationship negotiation skills and work on your reactions and communications. Using the right skills, conflicts can be transformed into opportunities for growth for both you and your partner. Make sure you seize that opportunity.

STEP **4**

Work Through Your Childhood

We all pay for each other's childhood. We all pay for each other's
   past. We all pay.
But this is where we change that. This is where we have the
   opportunity to heal.
—Dr. Jenn Mann, during a childhood trauma group therapy session,
Season 1, VH1 *Couples Therapy with Dr. Jenn*

The single most important, poignant, and dramatic group session I
do every year with my Couples Therapy clients is what we call the
"childhood trauma group." This four- to five-hour session is often the
turning point for couples. The experience of sharing their childhood
pain, trauma, and struggles opens the door for connection, compassion,
and understanding in their relationships. Of all the group sessions that
I lead, this is the most difficult and painful one—where couples are
the most vulnerable.

When my clients share their childhood struggles, it always becomes
clear what issues they are reenacting in their relationships, why they
are acting out the way they are, what familial patterns need to be
broken, and how they are sabotaging their romantic relationships.

Sharing their pain and struggles always brings them closer to their partners and helps their partners have compassion for them.

No matter how many times I see it, it always amazes me how we act out our family dynamic in our romantic relationships and re-create our historical traumas. We don't even know we are doing it most of the time. Even when we are unaware of our family traumas, they still have an effect on our ability to be close to our romantic partners.

In this chapter, I am going to share with you the many ways that your own family history, just like that of the clients I work with on VH1 *Couples Therapy with Dr. Jenn*, affects the way you interact with your partner and what you can do about it so you can have a healthier relationship.

Parents Are Our First Mirrors

Parents are the psychological mirrors that reflect back to us who we are, how we define ourselves, and how we fit into the world. An infant is born without a sense of self and parents help create the first images of who she is and what her value is in the world. As children get older and their world becomes bigger, they discover more mirrors—friends, relatives, teachers, coaches, child-care workers—people they come across every day. For better or for worse, our primary caregivers—typically our parents—create the foundation for our sense of self through all of our interactions. Their words and actions are particularly powerful in this regard.

The way we are parented helps us form core beliefs about ourselves. Children are egocentric, meaning they think that anything that happens is all about them. This is a normal part of child development, not narcissism. The child whose father screams at her doesn't think to herself, "Wow, he must have some serious mental health issues. His parents must have yelled at him and he never worked through his rage. This guy really needs therapy!" Instead, she thinks, "There must be something terribly wrong with me. I must be a bad kid. If I were better, Daddy wouldn't yell at me so much. I really must not be very lovable." These internalized messages are played out in our relationships, and do the most harm, when we pick unhealthy or hurtful partners or when we sabotage good relationships.

Because children are dependent on their parents, no child wants to accept that his parents are imperfect, inadequate, or pathological. They must idealize their parents to keep themselves safe, even if—and many would say especially if—they are being abused. It is easier to think of themselves as "bad," given that most abusive parents convey that message ("If you weren't such a bad girl, I wouldn't have to hit you. Next time behave!"). As author John Bradshaw points out in his book *Bradshaw On: The Family: A New Way of Creating Solid Self-Esteem*, "The great paradox in child-parent relationships is that children's beliefs about their parents come from the parents." Typically, a child makes himself the "bad" one in order to maintain a relationship with his parents and have care and protection from them, however flawed it may be.

We all form what clinical psychologist Robert Firestone, author of *The Fantasy Bond*, refers to as the "fantasy bond." This is the illusion of connection with our caregiver when our emotional needs are not being met. This occurs in all parent-child relationships, but is at its most extreme when abuse is present. Paradoxically, the more a person's emotional needs have been neglected, the stronger the bond, due to the increased need to idealize the family.

It is difficult and painful to recognize the wounds inflicted by those we love, especially when we were helpless children. I can't tell you how many times someone has walked into my office telling me about her "perfect childhood" and "perfect parents," only to find out after years of work together that she had, in fact, been abused, molested, or neglected by them. People underestimate the impact that a home with substance abuse, yelling, or volatility has on them. There is no such thing as a perfect childhood or perfect parents; there are only degrees of dysfunction.

Until we recognize where our childhoods and parents fell short, we cannot heal our wounds. This is especially important for survivors of abuse who tend not to have empathy for the wounded child they once were. Psychologist and psychoanalyst Alice Miller describes this best in her book *The Drama of the Gifted Child: The Search for the True Self*: ". . . if they are aware of having been misunderstood as children, they feel that the fault lay with them and with their ability to express themselves appropriately. They recount their earliest memories without any sympathy for the child they once were, and this is more striking as these patients not only have a pronounced introspective ability but also seem, to some degree, to be able to empathize with other people. Their access to the emotional world of their childhood, however, is impaired—characterized by lack of respect, a compulsion to control, and manipulate, and a demand for achievement." To recognize where your needs were not met and where you were hurt is crucial to the healing required to be a great partner.

It has been said that family life is our first school for emotional learning: The interactions, experiences, and messages that we absorb over the course of childhood teach us the most fundamental lessons about ourselves; and have a profound effect on our daily interactions, relationships, emotions, communication, love, and marriage. This is where we learn whether or not it is okay to express our feelings; which topics are acceptable to talk about; whether or not it is safe to be vulnerable; how to communicate with our loved ones; if the world is a safe place; if people are trustworthy; and, of course, if we are lovable.

Parents who do not feel lovable themselves and did not get the message from their own parents that they were loved, are not equipped to parent their children in a way that helps the youngsters develop good self-esteem. For some people, whose parents are unable to convey their love for them, there is at least one other person—a coach, a grandparent, a scout leader, or a teacher—who does. This experience of positive regard from an adult figure is crucial for healthy development. It takes only one loving person to engender self-esteem in a child, and while it is ideal for the parent to be that person, sometimes it cannot be. Because our sense of self is formed in the social context of our lives, it is crucial that we have at least one lovingly attuned adult who validates our worth. Without that, we constantly search for love, validation, and attention . . . usually in the wrong places.

Why We Marry Our Parents and Why It Hurts So Much

Despite the thousands of books and research studies I have read on relationships, the many degrees I have, and over two and a half decades of clinical experience, I am still stunned by how people consistently choose mates who are just like their parents, with both their good and bad characteristics, even when they are not consciously aware of these qualities. I see it in my private practice, the calls I get on my radio show, and the celebrities on my television shows. It is such an unconscious process that most people aren't even remotely aware of it.

On season 1 of *Family Therapy with Dr. Jenn*, Britney DeJesus from MTV *Teen Mom* talked to me in session about an abusive boy she had dated. He was controlling, verbally abusive, emotionally unavailable, and, eventually, physically abusive. Because she was so young when her father left, she did not even remember what he was like or know why his relationship with her mom had ended. I brought in her mother, for a session with Britney and her sister Briana, to answer their questions about their childhood and their father. When her mother described the man who had raised them, he was identical to Britney's boyfriend—and she didn't have any conscious memory of her father. She was stunned. History always repeats itself when it doesn't get processed.

Your Imago

The unconscious mind doesn't know the difference between past, present, and future. It is always trying to heal old wounds in current time. As a result, we pick mates who have many of the same qualities—positive and negative—as our parents. According to Dr. Harville Hendrix, author of *Getting the Love You Want: A Guide for Couples* and creator of Imago Therapy, our unconscious mind creates a composite picture of the traits of the people who influenced us the most in childhood. Of these impressions, the ones that are most vivid and powerful are the ones of being wounded. This data is recorded in our unconscious, along with experiences and interactions with these people, and form what Hendrix calls our "imago"—the template we unconsciously use to pick our partners. Without being conscious of it, we compare every potential partner we encounter to our imago. Whether or not you are attracted to someone is largely dependent on how well that person matches your imago.

According to Hendrix, the primitive part of our brain seeks to re-create the conditions of our childhood, so that we can correct them. This requires our romantic partners to have our caregiver's negative traits, which means they are bound to reopen our most sensitive wounds. In order for this unconscious process to play out, the person we pick has to be someone who stirs a deep sense of recognition within us, someone who makes our unconscious believe that this person can make up for the wounds of the past. This imago match is necessary for us to fall in love.

You don't have to be an abused child to have unmet needs or wounds from childhood. The wound may be the result of parents who never really understood or accepted you; a home where you were unable to express your authentic feelings; or narcissistic parents who expected you to meet their emotional needs. No parent is perfect and it is impossible to meet the needs of a child all the time. Infants constantly need attention. Their needs for food, comfort, diaper changing, and soothing are 24/7. During the first three years of life, we learn whether the world is a safe place—or not—based on our parents' abilities to meet our needs. Whether it is postpartum depression, work stress, demands of other children, and/or other stressors, no parent is able to meet every single need a child has. It just isn't possible, even under the best of circumstances.

Our unmet needs are filed away in our unconscious, and we carry them around into adulthood and into our romantic relationships. We unconsciously look for partners who will meet those needs. According to Hendrix, "You fell in love because your old brain had your partner confused with your parents! Your old brain believed that it had finally found the ideal candidate to make up for the psychological and emotional damage you experienced in childhood."

In the honeymoon period of a relationship, the unconscious rings a bell: "Ding! Ding! It's a match! This person will make you whole again and heal all your pain! You will never be lonely again!" When this imago match occurs, we fall into a relationship. The more "perfect" the match, the more intense the fall.

During this honeymoon phase, we unconsciously believe that we have found the person who is going to make it all good for us. The intimacy increases and we share our history, struggles, passions, and fears with each other. Couples in this phase seem to naturally intuit each other's needs and thoughts and are typically kind, understanding, and supportive of each other. We instinctively work hard to present ourselves so that we appear to be healthier than we really are and attempt to be everything we think our new partner is looking for in a mate. We put our best foot forward. We take pains to meet the other person's needs and to seem as if our own needs are minimal.

We unconsciously identify ourselves with our partner's ideal. So much of falling in love is projection. We connect the dots and fill in the gaps about things we don't know about the other person with what we hope, believe, or desire to be true. You don't really know whom you are with, however, until you have been together for about a year and a half, the time frame it takes to move past our projections.

The combination of being on our best behavior, the unconscious hope that we have found the one to end our past suffering, the magic of early romance, the way we minimize our own needs and focus on meeting the other person's needs—the projection that occurs during a typical courtship—all this makes us look like ideal partners. Without consciously meaning to, we appear to have minimal emotional needs. This gives our partner the mistaken idea that our goal is to nurture, not be nurtured, which makes us desirable.

But we have needs of our own . . . and we have our own triggers. As Hendrix points out, we don't get into relationships to give and help others heal; we fall in love because unconsciously we believe the other person is going to meet all our unmet needs and love us in a way that will heal our past. But once we get past the honeymoon phase, when each of us starts to have our own needs that conflict with the other's, we have less of a desire to meet their needs. We want our needs to be met. Top that off with the fact that we tend to pick people who embody our disowned parts. In other words, if we grew up in a house where we weren't able to be loud, passionate, and expressive, we pick someone who is, and when we see that disowned part of ourselves in our partner, it triggers us, making us uncomfortable and pissing us off. We don't even know why.

It has been said that we can get an accurate picture of what we didn't get in our childhoods by looking at our chronic complaints about our relationship. Our romantic relationship is typically our greatest trigger, but it is also our greatest opportunity to heal. It holds a mirror in front of us and asks us to look at the things we need to work on, individually and as a couple. While we want to believe that we can heal just by merging with another person, the truth is that we can only heal by working on ourselves. A romantic relationship is the greatest catalyst for personal growth that exists.

Family Systems 101

The best illustration of how family systems work was shown in a video I saw while I was in grad school, a few decades ago. The footage was of a session that was done with the well-known family systems therapist Salvador Minuchin. He was working with a mother and a father and their two kids. At some point in the session, he walks over to the father, who is sitting on a couch with his family, and hands him a rope. "Hold this," Minuchin says. The dad, looking bewildered, takes the rope. Minuchin walks in circles, loosely tying the whole family together on the couch. Then he tells the mother to grab the pencil sitting on a table to her right. She reaches for the pencil and the whole family, still tied together, is shifted to the right. "Would you please get that glass of water over there?" he asks the son. As the son reaches for it, everyone shifts in that direction. He then explains that everyone in a family is connected, and every member is affected by the moves, emotions, and experiences of the other members of the family, just as they are in the rope exercise.

Every family is a mini society. There are rules (spoken and unspoken), expectations, leadership, and power hierarchies that bind everyone together. There are rituals, habits, belief systems, structures, expressions, and subtle nuances in language that are only understood by family members. Every family is unique. Outsiders don't know the family language or cues, but the insiders do. Jenna, for example, knows that when her mom walks into the kitchen, opens the refrigerator, and sighs she is having another bout with depression, and Jenna's role is to try to cheer mom up. When Hank walks into the house with a certain expression on his face, Susan knows that she'd better get dinner on the table fast or there will be hell to pay. All of their history together—good and bad—is alive in the family system. Every family has its own behaviors, culture, beliefs, and dynamics.

Your own family of origin had, and continues to have, its own unique dynamics. Those dynamics affect you individually and impact your romantic relationship, not to mention how you run your own family. What was your family like and how did it impact you? What did it teach you?

YOUR FAMILY OF ORIGIN AND HOW IT HAS AFFECTED YOU

- What did you learn from your family about relationships?
- What did your family teach you about yourself? What message did you get about yourself from your parents? Your siblings? Your grandparents?
- What was your role in your family?
- Was your family insular or inclusive? What did that teach you about people outside your family? Can they be trusted?

- Were your family members trustworthy? Did they keep you safe? Did they have your back?
- Were you free to express your feelings and emotions in an honest and authentic manner?
- Was your family chaotic or well-organized? What did your family of origin teach you about discipline and structure?
- Did you feel loved?
- Was there fear, coercion, threats, or violence?
- How were things handled when mistakes were made?
- Were your boundaries respected?
- How did your parents handle their own conflicts?

Children bear the brunt of their parents' unresolved issues. They inherit whatever issues their parents didn't address, keeping them emotionally tied to the family system and passing down the same problems to future generations. Kevin's father, Rick, had a temper. His inability to handle any problem, big or small, led him to lose control. It could be something as small as Kevin spilling his milk at the dinner table or as catastrophic as Rick's struggle with unemployment. Any difficulty that came up led Rick to scream, yell, and become violent. He beat the crap out of Kevin on a regular basis. The whole family walked on eggshells around him. Kevin, now an adult, came into my office to seek help after hitting his son for the first time. Full of shame and remorse, he couldn't understand how he could have done the exact thing to his son that had caused him so much pain in his own childhood. He had always vowed never to be like his father. But he was. His wife walked on eggshells around him, fearful of the next blowup, just as his mother had done. Had Kevin not come to me for therapy, so that he could work through this issue, his son would have continued the cycle of family violence with his own family, and passed it down to the next generation, and so on. In my business, we call this the multigenerational transmission process. What we don't deal with, we continue to act out and pass down. This is why we have a responsibility to ourselves and our partners to work through the issues of our own family of origin.

Families are like sensitive ecosystems. When one thing is altered, there is a ripple effect within the system. Every single member of a family affects the others, even when the issues are behind closed doors. Scott and Marsha had been married for eighteen years when they walked into my office. Scott was the breadwinner and worked long hours to support his family. Marsha, a stay-at-home mom, felt resentful of her absentee husband and kept telling him that she didn't care about the money. She wanted more time with him, and wanted him to spend more time with the kids. Scott felt unappreciated and threw himself deeper into work, where he felt competent and capable, unlike at home, where he felt he could never do enough to please his wife. Feeling unheard and resentful, Marsha started to withhold sex. She felt unloved and disconnected in the marriage, which never leads to sex. She focused her attention on her kids to distract herself from her empty marriage. What ultimately brought Scott and Marsha into therapy were parenting issues. Their teenage son Ian had gotten a girl pregnant and their daughter Ava appeared to be developing an eating disorder.

When adults' marriage needs—emotional intimacy, sex, connection, conversation—are not met, they seek to have those needs met elsewhere in the family system. No normal adult seeks to have sex with his or her child. This is incest and is deeply pathological and damaging. Yet all too many parents discuss their sex lives with their children, as Marsha did with her son, complaining about her unmet needs. This kind of stimulating talk breaks appropriate parent-child boundaries; it puts children in an adultified position, which exposes them to provocative adult information that is inappropriate and typically gets acted out. The sexual tension in the house led Ian to act out. Meanwhile, Ava, a sensitive child, absorbed much of her mother's pain, and unmet needs from her father as well. This led Ava to act out with food and exercise in order to gain control of the uncontrollable in her life and ultimately to get attention and bring the family together.

Children are the greatest bearers of family dysfunction. It was no coincidence that Marsha and Scott had an anorexic sex life . . . and now, an anorexic daughter and a son who was acting out sexually. When kids act out, it tends to force parents to come together and pay attention to the crisis. This acting out serves many unconscious purposes. You would be amazed at how often fixing a marriage makes the children's symptoms go away. So, if you were the child who acted out, I hope this helps you to have compassion for yourself and address the deeper issues. And if you are the parent with a child who is acting out, I hope this information inspires you to tend to your marital relationship.

A healthy family system allows members to become autonomous and independent. Differences are honored, conflicts are worked through, competencies are encouraged, and feelings are expressed. If you came from a family that did not provide that, you will be challenged to provide it in your relationships. And if you came from a home where you were abused or neglected, the challenges are even greater.

But That's How You Discipline a Kid!

Because abuse is so commonplace in this country and because victims always seek to protect their abusers, child abuse has been greatly downplayed in the United States. Even as adults, survivors of abuse are constantly rationalizing what their parents did ("I was a bad kid," "She was a single mom," "It could have been worse," "That's how you discipline kids"). Violence against children is a serious problem that has a massive ripple effect. The problems created by abuse are some of the biggest barriers I see to healthy self-esteem and intimacy.

The American Academy of Pediatrics "strongly opposes striking a child" and cautions parents that spanking is "the least effective way to discipline a child." Nevertheless, it has been estimated that 90 percent of American parents spank their children. In certain communities, beatings are commonplace. In season 6 of VH1 *Couples Therapy with Dr. Jenn*, after returning from court to face a domestic violence charge, *Love and Hip Hop* star Joe Budden was questioned by former supermodel Janice Dickinson about his childhood.

Janice: Were you abused as a child?

Joe: No.

Janice: Did your dad ever hit you?

Joe: No.

Janice: Your mom never hit you?

Joe: My mom used to beat my ass.

Janice: There you go. Bam! There it is.

Joe: That's good parenting

Janice: It's not good parenting!

Joe: In a black household that is good parenting. Your kid does something crazy and you're going to beat their ass.

Janice: What did you do to warrant a beating? Did you break her favorite vase? Did you fart at the dinner table? It's really bad for people's souls.

Joe: Wait. You think kids shouldn't get beaten? Is that what you're saying?

Janice: Hell, no!

Joe: Oh, you're buggin'.

Janice: Hell no! You can't beat your kid!

Joe: F**k, you can! Yes, you f@#*in' can!

Janice: Listen, now you're crossing a serious f@#$%&*g line. I got beat as a child and I know how it's affected me. It took me fifty-five years to get over it.

Joe: OK, but that's you. If my kid does something stupid, he's going to get his ass beaten.

Janice: I'm still not getting the truth from you. Now that I know you hit children, it makes me just have more bones to pick with you.

Joe: I am definitely "with" beating children.

Janice: You're with it? I'm against it, motherf@#$er.

Janice is right. Violence against children hurts their souls. Just because something is the norm, or is culturally acceptable, doesn't make it right. There are areas of Africa where women undergo clitoral circumcision. It is considered part of the community and a rite of passage, even good parenting, but that doesn't make it right. It, too, is brutal, violating, and harmful on multiple levels. Sharon Evans, a VH1 *Couples Therapy with Dr. Jenn* viewer, said it best in a post: "I will never understand why people think that because you are born black it is okay to be beat on by your parents. His excuse was 'That's what happens in a black household.' That is sad. And, yes, I am sure that the circle of abuse stems from that. I got my ass beat. It was abuse. But I got help, and ended the circle so my children did not have to endure beatings and I have raised two wonderful black men."

That spanking and beating children is acceptable or the norm in some cultures does not make abuse right. One in four Americans was beaten by a parent to the point of leaving a mark on his body. One in five has been sexually molested. One in three couples engages in physical violence, and of those couples who have children, 90 percent of their children witness this violence. Twenty-five percent of people in this country grew up with alcoholic relatives. Every year there are over three million reports of child abuse involving more than six million children. That it is common doesn't mean that there aren't enormous consequences.

How Trauma Changes Us

The past is never dead. It's not even past.
—WILLIAM FAULKNER, *REQUIEM FOR A NUN*

Growing up in an atmosphere of violence has both emotional and physical repercussions. According to the US Centers for Disease Control and Prevention, individuals who reported six or more adverse childhood experiences had an average life expectancy two decades shorter than those who reported none. Ischemic heart disease (IHD), chronic obstructive pulmonary disease (COPD), liver disease, and other medical problems have all been linked to child abuse. If you suffered childhood abuse, you are at a higher risk for intimate partner violence, alcoholism/drug addiction, illicit drug use, depression, and suicide attempts, and you are more likely to have tried smoking and drinking at an early age. Survivors of abuse are more likely to have had multiple sexual partners, contracted sexually transmitted diseases, become sexually active at an early age, and, for female survivors of abuse, experienced unintended pregnancies and had a teen pregnancy.

Trauma is not just about the actual event that occurred; it actually rewires the brain. Psychiatrist and expert in post-traumatic stress, Bessel Van Der Kolk described it best, in his book *The Body Keeps the*

Score: Brain, Mind, and Body in the Healing of Trauma, when he said, "Research . . . has revealed that trauma produces actual physiological changes, including a recalibration of the brain's alarm system, an increase in stress hormone activity, and alterations in the system that filters relevant information from irrelevant. These changes explain why traumatized individuals become hypervigilant to threats at the expense of spontaneously engaging in their day-to-day lives."

The combination of numbness, hypervigilance, and hair-trigger reactions can be difficult to be around. Because of this fundamental reorganization of the way the brain manages perceptions, survivors often have big reactions to small things. Their brains are unable to differentiate past threats from current situations. The man whose violent father shot his mother will have the same physiological reaction when he hears a car backfire as he would hearing a gunshot. The woman whose uncle wore a particular cologne when he molested her will feel as if she were a little girl being raped again when her unknowing husband wears that cologne to bed. The woman whose dad screamed at her and criticized her will have a primitive reaction if her boyfriend raises his voice or questions how she handled something.

Trauma survivors tend to be quick to overreact and are hypersensitive to rejection and criticism. This hyperreactivity compromises social abilities and can be particularly challenging to intimate partners. To complicate matters further, survivors are slower to recover. According to Van Der Kolk, "The stress hormones of traumatized people take much longer to return to baseline and spike quickly and disproportionately in response to mildly stressful stimuli." This is the result of changes in the brain, and is not a reflection of the person's character. In other words, heightened responses and poor ability to recover emotionally are not about the trauma survivor's personality, temperament, or nature. They are the result of the brain's being rewired by trauma. This does not excuse the behavior or make it okay, but it is helpful for spouses in this position to understand that it is not personal. In order to change this reactive pattern, therapy is crucial.

Oftentimes, the emotional repercussions of trauma are subtle. Surviving abuse requires children to develop defenses. They must repress their pain, hurt, fear, anger, and other negative emotions. They learn to go into denial and numb their emotions. They often turn the anger they feel toward their parents inward, directing that anger toward themselves; years later, this may surface in the form of depression, anxiety, cutting, eating disorders, aggression, poor grades, sexual acting out, and the like. Kids in homes where there is abuse create illusions of love and connectedness where they don't exist; this harms their ability to choose good partners later. They idealize their parents (sometimes just the nonabusing parent, but often both of them) and minimize the hurt they suffer. They learn to read the room quickly because it may be a matter of life and death, so they must become attuned to micro expressions, body language, and the subtlest of cues from adults. But this often puts them in a position to misread cues and expect the worst from partners later in life.

These defenses allow a child to survive very difficult and painful experiences, but at a cost. They force the growing child to have a diminished awareness of the reality around her. In addition, the defense mechanisms that are necessary skills in childhood can become barriers to emotionally intimate relationships once the child becomes an adult.

Trauma prevents people from realizing they are reacting to their past. As Van Der Kolk points out, "When something reminds traumatized people of the past, their right brain reacts as if the traumatic event were happening in the present. But because their left brain is not working very well, they may not be aware that they are reexperiencing and reenacting the past—they are just furious, terrified, enraged, ashamed, or frozen.

After the emotional storm passes, they may look for something or somebody to blame for it. They behave the way they did because you were ten minutes late, or because you burned the potatoes, or because you 'never listen to me.' Of course most of us have done this from time to time, but when we cool down, we hopefully can admit our mistake. Trauma interferes with this kind of awareness."

On a more subtle level, survivors of childhood abuse tend to treat their partners with the same anticipation of betrayal as they viewed their abusers. Their defense mechanisms and unconscious mind get the better of them and they are quicker to lash out and anticipate duplicity or harm. On season 6 of VH1 *Couples Therapy with Dr. Jenn*, former supermodel Janice Dickinson shared the heartbreaking story of the sexual abuse she and her sister suffered at the hands of her father. Janice even went to the police to report it and they did nothing. Her mother acted oblivious to what was happening. "Why didn't she know what was going on in that house?" she cried, tears falling down her cheeks. Nobody protected Janice, even those who were supposed to keep her safe. Janice was betrayed by them all, which explained the verbally abusive way that she treated her fiancé, Rocky. Janice reacted to him as if he were one of the people who had betrayed her. When I pointed this out in group therapy, Rocky's only words were "It's true." For Janice, that became a lightbulb moment. She just looked at him and said, "I'm so sorry." That began a crucial healing process.

But we don't have to be victims of trauma or of our childhood. Once you understand what happened to you, you can do something about it. You can address the abuse, heal the pain, and move past it. You must make a conscious effort to be aware of your triggers, monitor your reactions, and work hard to be open and vulnerable in your relationship. You must be mindful about not projecting onto your partner the hurtful experiences you have had with other people.

You must choose not to let the sins of your abuser run your current relationship. That is how you move from victim to survivor.

Trauma and Intimacy

Christina called my radio show unsure as to whether or not she should let her boyfriend know that she had been sexually abused seven years earlier. She reported that, as a result of being raped, she had experienced sexual issues with previous partners, but not with her current boyfriend of two years. I suspected that this trauma was probably affecting her more than she realized. She revealed that if her boyfriend touches her in the middle of the night she has a heightened startle response (a classic posttraumatic stress disorder symptom). She told me that she envisioned herself marrying this sweet, kind, accepting man and wanted to know if she should tell him. My response? "Only if you want to have a deep and meaningful relationship with him." We have to share this kind of information, no matter how difficult and painful, with the person we love the most. Withholding it prevents Christina's boyfriend from better understanding her and being the best partner he can be.

Most survivors come up with a "cover story" that explains their symptoms. "I'm crying because I just found out an old friend died"; "I have always startled easy. Don't worry. It's not a big deal"; "I just have a lot on my mind, that's why I was up all night"; "No, the sex was great! I didn't have an orgasm because I was distracted." These stories hide a history of abuse and shame and make it more palatable for others.

Trust is a huge issue for survivors of abuse. When trust in the adults who were supposed to protect and take care of you, and keep you safe, has been violated, it becomes very difficult to trust anyone. The rate of retraumatization for victims of abuse is very high and, as a result, the world becomes an increasingly dangerous place for many. Given that most survivors don't have great people-picking skills because of what they have been through, it can be even more challenging.

I would argue that you cannot have an emotionally intimate relationship without sharing your childhood pain with your partner. In Christina's case, not sharing that information with her partner was not only a barrier for her, sexually, but an emotional barrier between them. When we are willing to tell our lover what we have been through, we create closeness by being open and making ourselves vulnerable. While it is not appropriate to tell everyone you know about this part of your history—being discriminating and having good boundaries are essential for self-care—it is crucial for your significant other to understand your history and how it impacts your relationship.

If you are unable to tell your significant other on your own, you may need the help of a therapist. Sometimes feelings of shame or anxiety get in the way. If, on the other hand, you don't feel it is safe to share your history with your partner, then you have a more significant problem. You may need the help of a professional to determine if it is your fear or paranoia that is holding you back or if you have truly picked someone with whom you cannot share this sensitive information.

The Five Abuses

All abuse has lasting effects and, if left untreated, it creates a massive ripple effect for the relationships and loved ones of survivors. The only way to move past abuse is to understand what happened to you and address it. All too often people deny the painful experiences they have had, don't give them the proper weight, or don't recognize the injustice that they experienced. You have to know you are good enough not to have deserved the treatment you got in order to move past it. You also have to be able to recognize maltreatment for the abuse it is in order to recover.

Here are some of the most significant types of child abuse, along with descriptions, so you can better recognize if this has happened to you. Also listed are typical effects of that abuse, so you can understand the symptoms in yourself or your partner. Believe it or not, because of the defenses that people are forced to develop to survive abuse, it is somewhat common not to recognize that you have been abused at all.

1. Emotional/Verbal Child Abuse

Among the signs of emotional/verbal abuse are calling a child insulting names, making degrading comments, offering belittling criticism, shouting, intimidation, emotional blackmail, verbal attacks on the child (about her appearance, intelligence, competence, or value), threats, repeated jokes at the child's expense, teasing, sarcasm, and cruel comments.

Typically, there are two types of verbal abusers. Direct abusers are openly vicious in degrading their children ("You're stupid," "I wish you had never been born," "Get out of my face, you fat slob"). Indirect abusers use teasing, sarcasm, insulting nicknames, and subtle put-downs. Typically they hide their abuse under a veneer of humor, and when the abused or any other witnesses complain, the abuser tells them they are "too sensitive" or lack a sense of humor. Sometimes parents rationalize their verbal abuse under the guise of helping their children learn to face life's harsh realities or become stronger people. One father I worked with justified his cruel verbal behavior toward his son by saying, "I don't want him to become a pussy. The world is cruel. I have to be cruel to him so he is prepared." Because the world is cruel, children need to receive unconditional positive regard and support at home and have a safe place to weather life's storms. That is what creates resilience.

One US study found that 25 percent of undergraduate students reported suffering some kind of emotional abuse at the hands of their parents, but children can be abused by teachers, coaches, and other grown-ups in positions of power as well. Some parents are emotionally abusive without being physically or sexually abusive. However, parents who are physically or emotionally abusive are almost always verbally abusive as well.

Emotional abuse gives children a negative message about themselves, reduces self-efficacy, and creates poor self-esteem and a sense of inadequacy. This internalized hurt and rage often develop into depression or anxiety in adults. Adults who experience this are often sensitive to criticism, verbally aggressive, and quick to lash out with similar put-downs. They are more likely to experience weight problems, addictions, and compulsive acting out.

2. Physical Abuse

Any physical aggression that is directed at a child is abuse. While many of the child protective organizations define physical abuse as any "nonaccidental trauma or physical injury" to a child, there is no agreed-upon definition by experts. Slapping, bruising, hitting, kicking, shaking, burning, pushing, shoving, cutting, hair pulling, beating, hitting with an object, and whipping all constitute physical abuse. Injuries inflicted by parents, such as bruises, broken bones, red marks, welts, burns, broken bones, lacerations, and internal injuries, are all clear signs of abuse. As therapists and mandated child abuse reporters, we are taught to look for signs of physical abuse, but oftentimes the marks are not visible or on a part of the body where they can't be seen. Savvy child abusers know this.

The most common abusers I see in my office are parents whose "discipline" of their children gets out of control. Parents may not think that what they are doing constitutes abuse because either they believe other parents are doing it, too, or their own parents treated them the same way. Injuring a child is never okay: In fact, it is against the law in the United States and may result in parents being reported to child protective services or the police, and could result in a child being taken out of the home. I have seen too many clients in my office who should have been removed from their homes for their own safety and well-being, but never were.

The effects of child abuse have a long shelf life and leave victims vulnerable to a host of physical and emotional problems. According to the US surgeon general, ". . . severe and repeated trauma during youth may have enduring effects upon both neurobiological and psychological development altering stress responsively and altering adult behavior patterns . . . these individuals experience a greatly increased risk of mood, anxiety and personality disorders throughout adult life."

As we have discussed, parents are a child's first mirror, reflecting back to them whether or not they are lovable. Children's lives revolve around their parents, who are supposed to be their source of safety, security, love, comfort, and connection. According to Adults Surviving Child Abuse, "Child abuse violates the trust at the core of a child's relationship with the world. When the primary relationship is one of betrayal, a negative schema or set of beliefs develops. This negative core schema often affects an individual's capacity to establish and sustain significant attachments throughout life. Survivors often experience conflictual relationships and chaotic lifestyles, frequently report difficulties forming adult intimate attachments and display behaviors that threaten and disrupt close relationships."

Typically, survivors of abuse have a more difficult time assimilating experiences, develop a negative self-perception, experience feelings of isolation, and suffer from amnesia. Studies have shown that survivors have higher rates of depression, anxiety disorders, addictions, eating disorders, sexual disorders, and personality disorders, especially borderline and antisocial personality disorders. They are more likely to exhibit aggressive behaviors, signs of posttraumatic stress disorder (PTSD), disassociation, and self-harming behavior; some even attempt to commit suicide. They are also more likely to be in poor health generally, and to suffer from chronic pain syndromes, headaches, fibromyalgia, chronic fatigue, and irritable bowel syndrome.

3. Sexual Abuse

Any time an adult or another child (four or more years older than the victim) uses a child for sexual stimulation, sexual abuse has occurred. Pressuring a child to engage in sexual activities (regardless of the outcome), indecent exposure of the genitals, showing pornography, any sexual contact with a minor, physical contact with the child's genitals, viewing the child's genitalia without physical contact, using a child to produce pornography, and selling the sexual services of a child are all forms of sexual abuse and are crimes in this country.

Sometimes a predator will use overt threats or physical force, but more often sexual abuse involves coercion and manipulation. Abusers take advantage of innocent children and often try to convince their victims that the activity is an expression of love, that the victims are "special," or that the child brought the abuse on herself.

Childhood sexual abuse is an epidemic in this country. It has been estimated that as many as one in three girls and one in six boys is a victim of child sexual abuse before the age of eighteen. According to the *FBI Law Enforcement Bulletin*, child molestation is one of the most underreported crimes in the country; only 1–10 percent is ever disclosed. In most cases of abuse, the abuser is a member of the family or someone who is considered to be part of the victim's "circle of trust."

This betrayal by a trusted adult is devastating, just as it is when a child reports abuse and a parent does not believe or protect her.

Many years ago I was a guest on a segment of the *Oprah Winfrey Show* dealing with betrayals. On the show, I worked with Luis, a man who had been sexually abused by his father. Initially, his mother acted as if she understood the violation Luis had experienced, and kicked her husband out of the house. But ultimately she cared more about her own desperate need for companionship, and took her husband back. Luis was still living at home at the time, and was then forced to live with his abuser. A parent or adult who does nothing when a child reports sexual abuse is a participant in that abuse. To passively stand by, knowing that your child is being abused, is to be an abuser, too. If you had a parent who did that, you have been doubly victimized.

Sexual contact between a child and a caregiver is never acceptable. It is the ultimate violation of trust and power. To take advantage of a child you are supposed to protect and care for is a heinous act. Sexual contact in this type of relationship is a vile breach of trust, because, for the child, there is always a loss of choice. There is nothing a child can say or do, even if she is perceived as being seductive, that ever warrants crossing this line. If you were molested, it was not your fault. The responsibility always rests with the perpetrator.

Male survivors of child sexual abuse face unique challenges. Those who were raped by same-gender adults may question their sexual orientation and be quick to blame themselves for not stopping the assault. Men who were violated by opposite-gender, nonfamily members are typically reluctant to recognize what happened as sexual abuse.

In his book *Silently Seduced: When Parents Make Their Children Partners*, Dr. Kenneth Adams, a leading expert on covert incest, sex addiction, and childhood trauma, clarifies this point: "Children are not property. They feel terrified and degraded when a parent, or any adult, is sexual with them. Cooperation does not equal enjoyment. They are too scared, too emotionally needy, or too starved for affection to say no. Even if children report that at some level they enjoyed the sexual contact, it is still emotionally damaging. Children are generally too needy and confused to understand inappropriate sexual touch. Their enjoyment is, at some level, a source of guilt and shame later in life: 'It was my fault because I enjoyed it and didn't say no. All my life I carried guilt because I thought I seduced my father. It wasn't until I went over the wreckage of my life that I realized I was a victim of incest.'"

When I started out my career, working for the Los Angeles Commission on Assaults Against Women (now known as Peace Over Violence) as a rape and domestic violence counselor, I frequently got calls from women and men who had been sexually abused. To me, this is one of the most difficult forms of abuse to process because of the emotional confusion it creates. Sometimes the body betrays the victim with feelings of sexual excitement, despite feeling uncomfortable, fearful, or scared. Children do what they have to do to survive and maintain a connection with the person who abused them—typically a caregiving adult. The shame that goes along with this is agonizing and life-altering for most victims.

The effects of childhood sexual abuse extend far and wide. It is hard for survivors to know what to do with the anger, fear, rage, and powerlessness that they once felt. Without therapy these feelings often get turned inward. Survivors have higher rates of depression and anxiety, and are at higher risk for suicidal thoughts or acting out. Most struggle with poor self-esteem, feelings of self-loathing, and self-destructive behavior. Many feel stigmatized and isolated because of their experiences. Survivors have higher rates of addiction; compulsive acting out with food, sex, or other behaviors; body dysmorphia, which causes sufferers to obsess about perceived flaws (imagined physical defects); and eating disorders. Many suffer from PTSD; as a result, sleep disturbances, nightmares, and flashbacks are common.

Surviving childhood sexual abuse brings a host of challenges to relationships and to partners. Most survivors experience trouble with intimacy, including hypersensitivity to being controlled and trust issues. Poor boundaries and sexually inappropriate behavior can cause problems in a relationship.

Trust issues are consistent across the board. On season 2 of VH1 *Couples Therapy with Dr. Jenn*, Tashaunda "Tiny" Hailey made the courageous choice to share that she had been molested as a young child. After she told her family, she never saw the abuser again, but she is still pained by the abuse. "Why would he violate that trust? That made me not trust men, period," she said. This sentiment is a normal and understandable reaction to sexual abuse.

Abuse also affects sexual development. Traumatic sexualization, the process whereby a child's sexuality is shaped in an inappropriate and dysfunctional way, is a result of sexual abuse. When a child is forced to be sexual in order to receive affection, attention, status, privileges, or gifts, she learns to use sexual behavior to manipulate others, which continues through adulthood. A person who is used to getting inappropriate attention for her sexuality can often become hypersexual as an adult. In an attempt to regain power or to re-create trauma, many survivors find themselves acting out promiscuously with multiple partners, sometimes of both genders. Typically, those experiences leave survivors confused, feeling bad about themselves, and questioning their worth.

Victims of sexual abuse have higher rates of revictimization. One study found that 63 percent of women who had suffered sexual abuse by a family member also reported a rape or attempted rape after the age of fourteen. Children who have been sexually assaulted during adolescence are 13.7 times more likely to experience rape or attempted rape in their first year of college. Some research claims that those with a prior history of sexual victimization are over 1,000 percent more likely to be revictimized. Revictimization creates more trauma and a whole new slew of issues.

Revictimization often results in a number of different types of sexual maladjustments and intimacy issues. Women typically show greater evidence of sexual disturbance or dysfunction than men and are more likely to have had lesbian or bisexual experiences; have an aversion to sex; experience flashbacks during sexual contact; have difficulty with arousal and orgasm; suffer from vaginismus (painful sexual intercourse); and have negative attitudes toward sexuality and their bodies. Male victims often experience disturbed sexual functioning, struggles with feeling "unmasculine," sexual acting out, such as compulsive masturbating, watching pornography, and sexual compulsivity. They are also more likely to victimize others. Many men struggle to process emotional and sexual intimacy after abuse. When sexual contact is associated in a child's memory with revulsion, fear, anger, a sense of powerlessness, or other negative emotions, it can contaminate later sexual experiences and may grow into a generalized aversion to all sex and intimacy with either gender.

4. Neglect

Neglect is failure of the parent or caregiver to provide needed, age-appropriate care. It is one of the most common forms of abuse. While neglect is an act of omission, it can be as damaging, if not more so, than physical abuse. As one patient said to me, "If my parents had abused me physically, at least I would have known they cared enough to hit me." To be neglected is not to be cared about or loved by the most important people in your life, or at least that is the way the psyche interprets it.

Neglect typically falls into one of six categories:

- **Supervisory neglect:** The absence of a parent or guardian, which can lead to physical harm, sexual abuse, or criminal behavior.
- **Physical neglect:** Parental failure to provide the basic physical necessities, such as a safe and clean home.
- **Medical neglect:** Guardians fail to provide needed medical care.
- **Emotional neglect:** The child does not get the needed attention, love, nurturing, encouragement, and/or support.
- **Educational neglect:** Caregivers don't provide the child with an education and the resources to actively participate in the school system.
- **Abandonment:** A parent or guardian leaves a child alone for long periods without a babysitter.

There are many homes where children are neglected due to socioeconomic challenges. This is still abuse and has repercussions. But it is not only poor families where children are neglected. This happens across all socioeconomic strata. This is especially common in the context of substance abuse, unemployment, and/or domestic violence.

Neglect has a wide range of consequences. The physical consequences of neglect range from minor injuries to hospitalization or even death. Typical psychological consequences vary from low self-esteem to a dissociative state, which makes the person feel detached from people or even from reality. Cognitively, the effects may be anything from attention problems and learning disorders to more serious organic brain syndromes. Behaviorally, neglect may spawn poor peer relations and even violent behavior. Studies show that developmental delays, attention deficit, poor social skills, and emotional instability are particularly common in instances of neglect. While the majority of neglected children do not show severe disturbances, it always has long-term effects without therapy.

Maternal detachment, which may occur as a result of postpartum depression, substance abuse, or other mental health issues, is harmful to bonding and attachment between child and parent. Studies show that this form of detachment hurts a child's expectations of adult emotional availability, affect (the way a person expresses emotions), problem-solving abilities, social relationships, and the ability to cope with stress. A study by psychologists J. Lawrence Aber and Joseph P. Allen, published in *Developmental Psychology*, found that the cross-cultural effects of parental neglect and rejection are poor self-esteem and emotional instability. Study after study shows that children of emotionally unavailable mothers are anxiously attached and have more issues in their romantic relationships.

5. *Spiritual Abuse*

A spiritual abuser uses religion or God's name to physically, emotionally, or sexually abuse another person, and claims that the intentions and character of God are behind the abuse. Spiritual abusers use religion and God's name to control, coerce, and manipulate the life, behavior, thoughts, and future of another person. One website on spiritual abuse clarifies it this way: "When a parent uses force to punish their child in an abusive way, that is physical abuse. When a parent claims God wants it that way, or recites Bible verses while doing it, that is spiritual abuse."

I first encountered the concept of spiritual abuse when I was working with Scott Stapp, Grammy Award-winning artist and founding member of the band Creed, during the childhood trauma group session on season 6 of VH1 *Couples Therapy with Dr. Jenn*. Scott talked about being beaten by his stepfather Steve "in the name of God." His stepfather would beat him for listening to rock music (even though he was not), having impure thoughts, or doing bad things that Scott never did. Steve forced Scott and his sisters to strip naked and watch as he abused each of them, while he cited biblical references to justify the abuse. Scott describes many of these "scripture-based punishments" in his memoir *Sinner's Creed*. Steve kept his stepchildren socially isolated, sent them to a school that promoted his distorted values, and regularly abused the children. Much of what Scott experienced is typical in spiritually abusive homes.

To commit spiritual abuse is to abuse another's soul and undermine a child's relationship with God and religion. It robs a child of a loving image of God. According to David Henke of the Watchman Fellowship, an independent Christian research and apologetics ministry focusing on new religious movements, cults, the occult, and the New Age, there are five typical traits of a spiritually abusive home:

- **Authoritarian leadership.** Parents exert complete control over others and demand complete obedience. Expectations are unreasonable and authority may never be questioned. Love is totally conditional on obedience and performance.
- **Image consciousness.** Extreme emphasis is placed on how things look, often with a focus on looking like "good Christians." There is a lot of secrecy in these households, which is needed for the abuse to continue.
- **Suppression of criticism.** Questioning authority in these homes is perceived as a threat to family values. To question the leader/abuser is to potentially undermine his power and influence over children and spouse—the whole family system. The challenger typically gets labeled as a "troublemaker" to disempower him and keep others from listening to him.

- **Perfectionistic standards.** Spiritually abusive parents are invested in having "perfect" children as evidence of the success of their controlling, abusive measures. They use performance-based love to manipulate and coerce their children.
- **Imbalance.** There is a severe lack of balance in the homes of this type of abuser. Oftentimes, these kinds of abusers claim to possess a special grasp on the truth, have a closer relationship with God, believe they are more holy or enlightened than others, and are extremely self-righteous.

According to the literature on spiritual abuse, some of the common repercussions among victims of spiritual abuse are anger due to feelings of powerlessness in childhood, anxiety, depression, unhealthy or distorted views of God, loss of ability to trust God and others, low self-esteem, poor self-worth, codependency, poor boundaries, and controlling or abusive behavior with romantic partners or people in other relationships.

It is possible to heal this type of abuse, but treatment and support from healthy religious leaders are crucial. As one spiritual abuse writer put it, "For those of you haunted and wounded through a spiritually abusive family, one thing essential to understand is that God does not condone what has been done in His name. It is also important to acknowledge that true abuse has occurred: until then, denial will prevent lasting healing—for denial perpetuates falsehood and suppresses truth."

Everyone Is Here But No One Is Home

Many of us did not grow up in a home where actual abuse occurred, but where there were other dynamics that altered our ability as adults to have a close and intimate relationship with others. These more subtle family dynamics affect most people. Take a look and see if you or your partner experienced any of them. It should give you insight into your relationship dynamics.

1. Addiction

To grow up in a home with alcoholism, addiction, or compulsive behavior is to grow up with unpredictability and chaos. Children love their imperfect parents, but need stability and consistency to feel safe. When you live with an addict, you never know who will show up to dinner—Dr. Jekyll or Mr. Hyde. In the groundbreaking book *Adult Children of Alcoholics*, psychologist and researcher Janet Woititz talks about the characteristics of adult children of alcoholics. These traits have been modified and are part of the literature for the adult children of alcoholics (ACA) 12-step program.

The ACA website lists the following as traits of an adult child of an alcoholic:

- We became isolated and afraid of people and authority figures.
- We became approval seekers and lost our identity in the process.
- We are frightened by angry people and any personal criticism.
- We either become alcoholics, marry them, or both, or find another compulsive personality, such as a workaholic, to fulfill our sick abandonment needs.
- We live life from the viewpoint of victims and we are attracted by that weakness in our love and friendship relationships.
- We have an overdeveloped sense of responsibility and it is easier for us to be concerned with others rather than ourselves; this enables us not to look too closely at our own faults.

- We get guilt feelings when we stand up for ourselves instead of giving in to others.
- We became addicted to excitement.
- We confuse love and pity and tend to "love" people we can "pity" and "rescue."
- We have "stuffed" our feelings from our traumatic childhoods and have lost the ability to feel or express our feelings because it hurts so much (denial).
- We judge ourselves harshly and have a very low sense of self-esteem.
- We are dependent personalities who are terrified of abandonment and will do anything to hold on to a relationship so as not to experience painful abandonment feelings, which we received from living with sick people who were never there emotionally for us.
- Alcoholism is a family disease; and we became para-alcoholics and took on the characteristics of that disease, even though we did not pick up the drink.
- Para-alcoholics are reactors rather than actors.

2. Affairs

Children suffer when parents have affairs, even when the parents succeed in keeping the affairs secret. The adulterer's attention and energy are focused elsewhere. The excitement of a new relationship and feelings of love or lust take center stage. The parent who is having an affair typically becomes so swept up in his personal needs and the affair that he doesn't realize the impact it is having on the children.

According to a *New York Times* article, titled "Psychology Experts Find Extramarital Affairs Have a Profound Impact on Children," "The common assumption has been that unless a marriage is in jeopardy, a discreet affair has little if any impact on a child. Increasing clinical evidence and a recent study suggest that the subtle changes in an adulterous parent's behavior can unsettle children, regardless of whether the truth leaks out and even if the children are too young to understand what is happening." Children sense that a parent is expending emotional energy outside the family and they notice that the parent is less attentive to them. This shift is anxiety-provoking and feels like rejection to the child. When parents have an affair, they are not only betraying their spouse, they are betraying their children and their whole family. As one client of mine said in therapy, "My mom didn't just cheat on my dad, she cheated on all of us."

When a parent engages in an affair, that prompts children to question the viability of marriage, to develop trust issues, and to worry about their own ability to be faithful when they are older. Children are robbed of a role model who could show them what a constructive, loving, and committed relationship looks like. Granted, relationships where affairs are occurring are missing those qualities to begin with, but the affair further prevents a couple from making healthy changes in their marriage. An affair is a symptom of the relationship's weaknesses and problems. The devastating effects are even more far-reaching when a child is asked to divide his loyalty and pick sides or when he is asked to keep a secret from one of his parents.

If you had a parent who cheated, you're more likely to have poor boundaries, insecurities, lower self-esteem, and sensitivity to abandonment and betrayal. The experience you had in childhood is likely to make it harder for you to trust your partner and allow someone to be close to you, out of fear of being hurt.

It has been said that parental affairs can also become the training ground for a child's adult behaviors. If one or both of your parents had an affair, you are more likely to have one, too. According to Annette

Lawson, a Stanford University sociologist and researcher, in instances where fathers bragged to their teenage sons about their affairs, as many in her research sample did, philandering is more likely to be viewed as a sanctioned family tradition and be acted out by the sons later in life. Girls whose fathers cheated were more likely to grow up angry at men and unsure of their relationships. When mothers have affairs, children of both genders tend to lose confidence in marriage and family. History is not destiny and it is up to you to work through the pain of infidelity from your early years or reenact it and hurt your partner.

3. Controlling Parents

When I was about ten years old, I had a neighborhood friend named Lisa. We used to hang out together, play David Cassidy albums, and talk about boys. We ate pizza, had sleepovers, and did all the normal stuff girls do at that age. But Lisa came from a home that would make today's "tiger moms" and "helicopter dads" look low-key. The rules at Lisa's house were extremely strict—there was an arranged marriage in the works, she had no privacy, and her mother regularly eavesdropped on our phone conversations. This was in the day before cell phones and mute buttons. I would hear her mother breathing on the phone and used to repeatedly ask the woman to get off the phone and give us privacy, until I would hear the phone click, indicating that she had finally hung up. Lisa was a good kid growing up in bad circumstances, which ultimately took its toll. Eventually, we lost touch. A couple of decades later, I turned on the television to see my childhood gal pal in a police chase, on heroin, with her toddler son in the car. The first thing that ran through my mind was the hell she went through growing up.

Growing up with controlling parents is a suffocating experience, where your wants, needs, and desires are not taken into account, and where rules can't be questioned and feelings are not to be felt.

Controlling homes are not democratic, and disagreement is not allowed. If you grew up in this environment, you were probably intimidated, manipulated, and overpowered on a regular basis.

A study published in the *Journal of Positive Psychology* found that controlling parents—those who did not let their children make their own decisions, intruded on their privacy, and encouraged dependence—had a lifelong impact on their children that was similar to the impact of bereavement. Adults from homes like this are more likely to experience depression, substance abuse problems, and eating disorders. They are perfectionists, frequently feel scrutinized, and are sensitive to criticism or perceived control. Growing up in a controlling household makes it difficult to be in touch with your feelings and know how to express them. It can also give way to strong reservations about having children.

4. Death and Suicide

Those who lose a parent during childhood are never the same. It is a life-altering experience that changes the way a person views the world. It is a child's worst nightmare come true. American culture is not prepared to help grieving children and, typically, neither is the surviving parent, who is struggling with his or her own grief and fear.

For those who lose a parent to suicide, the impact is even greater. The guilt and pain that go along with this type of loss are especially acute. In these situations, the family has usually been dealing with extreme depression or mental illness prior to the suicide, which has its own painful associations. Studies show that children who experience a parent's suicide are three times as likely to commit suicide themselves in their later years.

The research shows that the younger a person is at the time of the loss, the more likely it is that she will develop mental health issues, especially anxiety or mood disorders or substance abuse later in life. Good parenting practices, positive relationships, and strong support act as protective factors against psychopathology. People who lose a parent during childhood are more vulnerable to depression, anxiety, and troubled relationships later in life.

The early death of a parent can make people more resilient, responsible, and independent. It can also make them more compassionate toward the suffering of others. On the negative side, the early death of a parent causes many children to forfeit their childhood and grow up with a fear of being close because they live in anticipatory fear of future loss. This may make intimacy and closeness especially difficult.

5. *Divorce*

While being the child of divorce is not an unusual experience—it has been estimated that one million marriages in the United States end in divorce every year—it is a unique experience for every child who experiences it.

Family and home life are the foundations for children. To experience a divorce is to have a bomb go off in your world, emotionally speaking. The experience of going through your parents' divorce is not a single isolated event but a series of losses, difficulties, and changes that threaten life as you know it. Divorces don't come out of nowhere. Typically, children are exposed to tension, conflict, fighting, and other signs of trouble for years leading up to the actual event. And when children don't witness the run-up to divorce, they are often blindsided by its announcement. Once the divorce actually happens, children have a lot of fears and anxieties about what their new world will be like, and if they will be cared for and safe.

How parents handle divorce has a huge impact on how much their children are affected. Children who lose a parent to divorce—a mother who abandons her children for her new boyfriend, or a father who abandons his first kids for his new family—suffer more. Due to remarriages, many adults have to suffer through more than one divorce during their childhood. Statistically speaking, adult children of divorce have higher rates of depression and relationship issues. They are 26 percent less likely to marry than their counterparts from intact families, and 50 percent more likely to divorce when they do marry.

According to the authors of *The Unexpected Legacy of Divorce: The 25 Year Landmark Study*, "Contrary to what we have long thought, the major impact of divorce does not occur during childhood or adolescence. Rather, it rises in adulthood as serious romantic relationships move center stage. When it comes time to choose a life mate and build a new family, the effects of divorce crescendo. A central finding . . . is that children identify not only with their mother and father as separate individuals but with the relationship between them. They carry the template of this relationship into adulthood and use it to seek the image of their new family. The absence of a good image negatively influences their search for love, intimacy, and commitment. Anxiety leads many into making bad choices in relationships, giving up hastily when problems arise, or avoiding relationships altogether."

In my private practice I've seen a few different themes in adult children of divorce. For one, they frequently have a sense of waiting for "the other shoe to drop," that anxious sense that something could go wrong at any minute. The life experience of divorce makes it harder for them to trust, especially in intimate relationships. Children of divorce also usually have a lot of fear that their own marriage won't work out, or seek to avoid marriage altogether in order to avoid a potential abandonment.

That said, much of the new research shows that these trends are changing. The way divorce is handled by parents, and the amount of support the children receive, are big determinants in outcome. Divorce has lost much of its stigma. More couples, recognizing that children need both parents, are sharing custody 50/50. They are also becoming savvy about therapy, and getting help for their children early on, to help reduce the negative effects of divorce. According to *For Better or For Worse: Divorce Reconsidered*, by author John Kelly, new research shows that only 15 percent of adult children of divorce experience problems, compared to children whose parents did not divorce.

6. Spousification and Emotional Incest

As we know from Family Systems Therapy, when marital needs are not being satisfied they seek to get met elsewhere in the system. When a marriage is troubled, a divorce occurs, or when couples are not meeting each other's needs, it is all too common to see an adult lean on her child. This occurs in the form of confiding in the child with complaints about the marriage, needy behavior, inappropriate requests, adultifying the child, and extreme focus on the child.

Emotional incest or covert incest occurs when a child inappropriately becomes the object of a parent's affection, love, and preoccupation. Kenneth M. Adams explains it best in his book *Silently Seduced: When Parents Make Their Children Partners*: "The parent, motivated by the loneliness and emptiness created by a chronically troubled marriage or relationship, makes the child a surrogate partner. The boundary between caring love and incestuous love is crossed when the relationship with the child exists to meet the needs of the parent rather than those of the child. As the deterioration in the marriage progresses, the dependency on the child grows, and the opposite-sex parent's response to the child becomes increasingly characterized by desperation, jealousy, and disregard for personal boundaries. The child becomes an object to be manipulated and used so the parent can avoid the pain and reality of a troubled marriage."

I see adults who were cheated out of their childhoods all the time. It is emotionally confusing and creates tremendous guilt. And it always damages the child's ability to have a healthy romantic relationship in adulthood. Bob's wife always gave him foot rubs when the marriage was good. After the divorce, she moved on and remarried, but he was not having as much romantic luck. His feet ached and he missed the affection and physical touch he had once received from his wife. So he decided to start having his seven-year-old daughter rub his feet instead. This kind of behavior is totally inappropriate (children are not there to meet the needs of adults) and creates a dynamic where a child believes it is her job to service adult men, leaving her more vulnerable to molestation down the road. Breaking this kind of boundary teaches a child not to have appropriate boundaries with men. When Bob got a girlfriend, and she started giving him foot rubs, his daughter, who had been put in the position of a surrogate wife, became very jealous and angry at the new girlfriend and with her father. She felt she had been replaced.

I see a lot of this with men, in the form of neglecting their wives' needs in favor of taking care of their mothers. This is particularly common with single moms and their oldest sons or only children. Many times the son becomes "the little man of the house," emotionally taking care of the mom. When he grows up and marries, it becomes very hard to give up that role. The guilt is overwhelming. I frequently get calls from the girlfriends and mothers of these men on my radio show. Just last night I got one. Courtney had been dating "a great guy" named Andy for three years. He has two daughters with whom she gets along famously. She called me because Andy's mom had come into town to stay with them, and was lying to and telling Andy's daughters that Courtney hated them, as well as inventing other fabrications to sabotage her relationship with the girls. Andy did nothing. He did not stop his mother, establish a boundary, or tell her that her behavior was unacceptable. When I probed Courtney further, she revealed that Andy's mother had successfully sabotaged his previous relationships, using the same strategy, and Andy had done nothing about it. He didn't want to "upset" his mother.

It isn't always the opposite-sex parent who creates an emotionally incestuous relationship that prevents the adult child from having successful relationships. Just the other night I got a call from Bridget, who couldn't stop thinking about a man she dated thirty-seven years ago for two months in high school. Her alcoholic, widowed mother guilted her into breaking up with the guy because she wanted all of Bridget's attention and focus for herself. Her neediness and dependency on Bridget kept her from dating and developing normal, healthy relationships for her whole life.

Sometimes parents are overly seductive without actually crossing the line into sexual contact. Parents who walk around naked, talk about sex, ask inappropriate questions about their child's sexuality and preferences, or are seductive with their children are committing emotional incest. Creating a sexually charged atmosphere at home is extremely destructive and harmful to children.

If you had a parent who made you take care of his emotional needs, made inappropriate sexual remarks, confided in you about his personal business, idealized you, wouldn't let you date, sabotaged your relationships, or was inappropriate with you, you are probably a victim of emotional incest. It is crucial that you enforce good boundaries with that parent, if he is still living, and do some work in therapy so that you can learn what appropriate boundaries look like to protect your relationship with your partner.

7. The Emotionally Troubled Parent

Having a mentally ill or disturbed parent can mean many things. Sometimes a schizophrenic parent is barely coping. Other times, a mother or father may have a personality disorder, may be narcissistic, or may have a borderline personality disorder, which, though covert, may be just as difficult to handle. Or a parent may struggle with depression or anxiety. No matter what the condition, the child is always affected.

I will never forget season 2 of VH1 *Couples Therapy with Dr. Jenn*, hearing Doug Hutchison talk about his depressed mother in a session with me that was never shown on air. It explained so much about his relationship with his child bride Courtney Stodden. He recalled a significant moment, when he realized what his mother's mental state required of him. He described it like this: "I was playing kickball with my friends and I came into the house because I had to pee really badly. I walked into the living room, and as I was heading to the bathroom, I saw my mother sitting on the couch with her head in her hands. I knew she needed me to take care of her. In that moment I knew that it didn't matter how badly I had to pee. It didn't matter that I wanted to play with my friends. My needs no longer mattered. What mattered was that I had to take care of my mother. I walked over to the couch and sat down with her to comfort her. I didn't go out to play again."

If you have a mentally ill or depressed parent, you end up setting your own needs aside. You're catapulted into adulthood and forced to be a caregiver at an early age. Children in these unhealthy situations grow up without having their own physical and emotional needs met. They learn to ignore their own needs and prioritize the needs of the ill parent. They are deprived of their own childhoods in order to take care of a broken parent. They often feel inadequate, not only because they have to deal with the stigma of a mentally ill parent, but also because they are unable to make things better. Typically, families like these are dysfunctional and impose inappropriate boundaries, expectations, and responsibilities on kids.

If you have a narcissistic parent, you are an extension of that parent's ego. You receive conditional love, solely based on your achievements and how well you please your parent. You are the child of someone whose own needs were unmet and, therefore, is incapable of meeting yours. Being the child of a narcissistic mother or father makes it difficult to separate from that parent in a healthy way and develop your own priorities, values, and goals. It forces you to create what therapists call a "false self" to please the parent. The real self is split off or hidden, and becomes a lost inner child. According to Alice Miller, author of *The Drama of the Gifted Child*, the child who did not experience acceptance will eventually want to live out her "true self" and not want to be forced to earn love.

The child of a mentally ill person tends to be keenly sensitive to other people's pain and has a tendency to rescue and take care of people. She finds it hard to allow others to nurture or care for her. Emotional intimacy and authenticity tend to be very scary for her. These parentified children like to be in control at all times and have a hard time letting go. They find their own dependency needs to be unacceptable and frightening, since they did not have the necessary experience of having them met in childhood. They grew up in a chaotic, emotionally disconnected environment, where safety, predictability, and structure were absent most of the time. No one was there to guide, comfort, or set appropriate limits for them. They took on their parents' problems as their own, and when they were unable to solve them, felt guilty, sad, and bad about themselves. Poor self-esteem is common among them.

A University of Michigan study found high rates of psychiatric and behavioral problems in adults with mentally ill parents. These adults were less likely to complete high school and more likely to have relationship problems. Other literature suggests these adults are more likely to have psychological, addiction, and legal problems. They are particularly vulnerable to depression, anxiety, ADD/ADHD, and bipolar disorder.

WHY GETTING SPANKED PROBABLY AFFECTED YOU, EVEN IF YOU THINK IT DIDN'T

According to sociologist Murray Straus, author of *The Primordial Violence: Spanking Children, Psychological Development, Violence, and Crime,* spanking is a poor choice of discipline for children, and it has significant deleterious long-term effects. In his research, it was found that spanking does not work better than other nonviolent forms of discipline, and has long-term effects on aggressiveness and mental health. According to him, "More than 100 studies have detailed these side effects of spanking, with more than 90 percent agreement among them. There is probably no other aspect of parenting and child behavior where the results are so consistent."

If you came from a home where you were spanked, it probably has affected you in certain ways in your relationship, however slight. Here are some of the most common ways:

- **Aggression and antisocial behavior.** In her analysis of spanking studies, Elizabeth Gershoff, one of the foremost researchers on the effects of spanking, found convincing evidence that spanking can lead to problems such as delinquent and antisocial behavior, along with aggression, criminal and antisocial behavior, and spousal or child abuse as an adult. The studies also link spanking with increased rates of fighting. According to the study, titled "Physical Punishment of Children: Lessons from 20 Years of Research," ". . . virtually without exception, these studies found that physical punishment was associated with higher levels of aggression against parents, siblings, peers, and spouses."

- **Domestic violence.** Spanking has the potential to harm children's future intimate relationships by leaving them vulnerable to becoming a victim or a perpetrator of domestic violence. Studies of spanking and corporal punishment have found that children who were spanked are more likely to assault their parents, and boys who were spanked to assault their girlfriends, years later.

- **Rape, and unprotected and risky sex.** In an analysis of spanking studies, it was found that spanking and other forms of corporal punishment are associated with an increased probability of verbally and physically coercing a dating partner to have sex; engaging in risky sex, such as premarital sex without using a condom; and participating in masochistic sex, such as spanking during sex.

- **Poor cognitive development.** A two-year study by Shari Barkin, a pediatrician at the Children's Hospital at Vanderbilt University in Nashville, found that two- to nine-year-olds who were spanked developed less rapidly than other children, based on cognitive testing. According to Elizabeth Gershoff's study cited above, examining twenty years of spanking research, imaging studies have shown changes in the brains of children who were physically punished. These changes include decreases in gray matter in regions connected to IQ and alterations in the dopamine system, which leaves those who were hit more vulnerable to addiction problems.

- **Stress and fear.** A 2003 study on how the brain chemistry of children under the age of one is changed as a result of corporal punishment found that those who were spanked frequently showed huge spikes in the stress hormone cortisol when they were subjected to new situations. The researchers concluded that people who were spanked are also more easily frightened and experience more anxiety.

- **Mental health and addiction.** Harsh corporal punishment (HCP), which is defined as one spanking a month for more than three years, frequently done with objects such as a belt or a paddle, has been linked to reduced gray matter in the prefrontal cortex, which has been linked to depression, addiction, and other mental health disorders. A study called *"Physical Punishment and Mental Disorders: Results from a Nationally Representative US Sample,"* published in the journal *Pediatrics,* looked at this type of violence against children and concluded, "Harsh physical punishment was associated with increased odds of mood disorders, anxiety disorders, alcohol and drug abuse/dependence, and severe personality disorders."

- **Impulsivity.** The loss of gray matter in the prefrontal cortex is strongly correlated to poor impulse control. According to a study in the *Journal of Cognitive Neuroscience,* "The more gray matter you have in the decision-making, thought-processing part of your brain (the prefrontal cortex), the better your ability to evaluate rewards and consequences." The irony is that kids are typically spanked because of their inability to control their impulses and the research shows that the more you were spanked as a child, the more you likely you are to struggle with issues of self-control and impulsivity.

- **Expecting the worst.** Spanking is associated with what researchers call the "hostile attribution bias," which basically means that when you have a history of being spanked you have a greater expectation that people will be mean to you. This bias may make the world feel like a hostile place. And this tends to make those who anticipate this type of behavior more likely to be on edge and have hostile responses themselves. It can actually create a self-fulfilling prophecy.

Victim No More: Moving Past Your Childhood and Having a Healthy Relationship

Seldom or never does a marriage develop into an individual relationship smoothly and without crisis. There is no birth of consciousness without pain.

PSYCHOANALYST CARL JUNG,

FROM THE ESSAY *"MARRIAGE AS A PSYCHOLOGICAL RELATIONSHIP"*

I don't trust a relationship where people never have disagreements, conflicts, or fights. I believe, as Harville Hendrix does, that "Conflict is growth trying to happen." In my clinical experience, couples who don't ever fight usually have at least one, if not several, dynamics going on in their relationship. Sometimes one person has lost her voice. She is too apprehensive or scared to express herself, or perhaps she is conflict-avoidant and with a person who is aggressive or conflict-seeking. Other times, a couple may not know how to communicate, so both people shut down and don't talk about things. It is easier not to talk than to talk through things because they don't have the skills. Oftentimes, the lack of conflict is just a sign of two people who don't have a deep relationship. If you are engaged in an emotionally intimate, connected relationship, you are going to trigger each other's wounds in some way.

A relationship that is superficial, not committed, or purely sexual will not trigger conflict. In these types of relationships, people move on at the first sign of difficulty.

Given that you *will* have conflict in your relationship and knowing, from having read this chapter, that your childhood has a huge impact on the dynamics between you and your partner, it is important to work on yourself as well as with your partner, as a couple, so that you can use conflict and childhood wounds to grow, not destroy your relationship.

Here are some suggestions that will help you to manage your historical triggers and enhance your emotional connection with your partner:

1. **Recognize that you are getting triggered in the moment.** Being self-aware, when you are feeling flooded with emotions, is really challenging but important. Take a moment to look at the "Ten Signs You Have Been Triggered" on page 92 so that you can recognize when this is happening.

2. **Know your historical triggers.** Know what pushes your buttons. Make a list on your own and again with your partner so you can both identify what is likely to trigger you and you can work together to notice when it happens. If you felt disrespected in your childhood, respect is likely to be a trigger. If you were abandoned, fear of abandonment might be your trigger. If you had an emotionally unavailable parent, not being heard might be your hot button. Making sure you are aware and that your partner knows this about you helps you both.

3. **Stop blaming yourself for abuse.** A child is never responsible for being abused. You can't heal from the issues in your past until you admit them to yourself and to another person. When you

don't recognize abuse, you think you deserved it or it was somehow acceptable. When you blame yourself, you absolve the perpetrator of responsibility. When you act as if you deserved to be harmed, you prevent yourself from seeing the injustice that was committed. When you allow a partner or a family member to be verbally abusive, you rob yourself of dignity and self-esteem. We must recognize the traumas we experienced and see them for what they are in order to heal. Denial does not make things disappear; it makes problems grow and fester. As Alice Miller said, "We only have one enduring weapon in our struggle against mental illness: the emotional discovery of the truth about the unique history of our childhood." The toughest, bravest, strongest thing you can do is recognize where you have been harmed and get help so you can heal, which also increases exponentially the odds of having a healthy, loving relationship.

4. **Individuate from your parents.** There are key times in a person's life cycle when individuation is supposed to occur. Becoming separate and independent from your parents is an important part of becoming an adult. You can be close to your family and still be individuated. This means that while you respect and may be interested in your parents' opinions, at the end of the day, you do what you believe is right and in your own best interest, regardless of their reactions. This is especially challenging if you came from a home where you were enmeshed, experienced emotional incest, sustained any type of abuse, addiction was present, or where your parents were invested in keeping you dependent on them in any way. You cannot have a healthy relationship with your partner without

becoming separate from your parents. Your spouse must always come first, above your family of origin.

5. **Let go of relationships with abusive people, even if they are your parents.** When it comes to parents, we get dealt a particular hand. We don't always get the cards we hoped for. If you have a parent or family member who is cruel and hurtful, you cannot continue to have a relationship with him.

You have to mourn the loss of the parent you hoped to have. Holding on to the image of the mother or father you wished for prevents you from moving forward. If you have a parent who can't meet your needs, you may want to take the advice I gave Farrah Abraham in a session with her mother Deborah on season 4 of VH1 *Couples Therapy with Dr. Jenn.* You have to mourn the loss of the mother you hoped to have.

If you have a parent who abused you, and continues to disrespect and hurt you, you should not have a relationship. To maintain that relationship invites more abuse. As a child you did not have a choice, but as an adult you get to pick who is in your life. Too often callers to my radio show tell me that other family members or friends have told them they "should" have a relationship with an abusive parent. "But she is your mother!" they say. I say, DNA does not give a person the right to abuse you, and you always have the option to step away if that person does not own her hurtful behavior, make amends, work to develop new insight and change her behavior.

6. **Be willing to do the work.** In order for a relationship to work, both people have to be willing to work on both themselves and the relationship. I recently interviewed Drs. Harville Hendrix and Helen Hunt, creators of Imago Therapy, on my radio show. They both shared very openly that they had each been divorced prior to meeting each other. They talked about a time in their own

relationship when they thought they weren't going to make it. They went to the Imago Therapy community and shared their crisis. They prepared to get a divorce, but at the last minute decided to try their own techniques on themselves. They saved their marriage, further developed their techniques, and came to the realization that any relationship between two people can work if they are both deeply committed to working on it. Interestingly, when I asked them if they could have made their relationships work with their previous partners, they both said they could have, if the other person had also been committed to doing the work.

As I mentioned earlier, doing the work means going to therapy. I recommend one year of weekly individual therapy and at least six months of weekly couples therapy with a licensed therapist, not a "life coach." If finances are an issue, please know that there are mental health clinics all over this country that see people based on their ability to pay. Other ways you can work on yourself and your relationship include reading books about issues that have come up for you, attending workshops, journaling, working with a spiritual or religious leader, meditation, prayer, visualization, writing exercises, 12-step work, self-help workbooks, and attending lectures (or watching videos of them).

7. **Take responsibility for your stuff.** Always be willing to examine how your own issues and childhood experiences affect the way you approach your relationships, and be willing to own your issues when they come up. Always work to make the unconscious conscious and take responsibility for your actions While you can't change your past, you are responsible for how you react to it, and it is your choice to take steps to heal from it or not.

8. **Share your history with your partner.** In order to have a deep, meaningful, connected relationship, you have to be willing to be vulnerable and share your pain. This brings you and your partner

closer, and helps you understand each other better. You cannot fully appreciate or understand how your partner works without this valuable information.

There is no intimacy without personal disclosure, authenticity, and vulnerability. Furthermore, not sharing what has happened to you prevents you from being seen. It also allows shame to flourish. According to Brené Brown, author of *Daring Greatly: How the Courage to Be Vulnerable Transforms the Way We Live, Love, Parent, and Lead*, shame needs three things to grow exponentially: secrecy, silence, and judgment. Talking about your shameful experiences with a partner who has proven to be trustworthy is part of the healing process.

9. **Recognize that you and your partner are together in order to heal each other.** We are drawn to our imago match in order to resolve our old childhood issues. When I interviewed Drs. Harville Hendrix and Helen Hunt, I asked them if it is possible for a person to heal without being in a relationship. They said definitively that they thought it was *not* possible to heal without being in a safe and intimate relationship with another person. According to them, love relationships are the best possible vehicle for change and self-growth.

Typically, it is the thing that one partner needs that is hardest for the other one to give. That is also the arena where they most need to grow. Sarah had a dependent, alcoholic mother who never acknowledged her needs or feelings, made Sarah take care of her, and allowed Sarah's stepfather to beat her. Sarah's withholding mother made her into a caregiver, which she resented. She looked forward to the day when she could leave her mother's home and not have to respond to anyone else's needs. But it is not possible to have a relationship where you do not tend to the other person's needs. Part of being a couple is caring for each other emotionally. It involves sacrifice. Every time Sarah's husband asked for something, even something as small as texting him when her plane landed from a business trip, he was met with resistance or else she would agree and then passive-aggressively "forget" to do it. This came from a very wounded, childlike place. In order for Sarah to recover from her past, and become an adult woman and a good partner, she needed to learn how to give and respond to her husband's extremely reasonable requests.

10. **Practice expressing feelings and listening to each other without getting defensive.** Most people came from homes where they were not encouraged to feel their authentic feelings, much less express them. Doing this is an important part of your healing as well as a healthy part of bonding in a relationship. Being able to hear each other and feel heard creates an atmosphere of acceptance and open communication. It also allows you to know your partner on an intimate level.

11. **Give, even when you don't feel like it.** This is a true act of love and it helps you to overcome your own limits. Give, not because you want something in return, but just because your partner deserves to be loved and cared for. Come home with flowers, not because you screwed up or want something from her, but because you know it is meaningful for her and will make her feel loved. Give him a blow job, not because he did you last night or because you want him to mow the lawn, just because he is a good man and you love him. These selfless gifts are healing for both people and create an atmosphere of generosity in the relationship.

12. **Give your partner the benefit of the doubt.** Unless you have picked a partner who has a history of being abusive, it is best to give your partner the benefit of the doubt. We all make mistakes at times. Some are big and some are small. Given that we may be getting triggered from our own childhood, it is important to look at our partner's intentions, behavioral history, and patterns with us. We also have to take into account our partner's level of remorse and ownership of behavior. (See page 184 for more on this.)

Forgive and Make Amends

A happy marriage is the union of two good forgivers.
—Ruth Bell Graham

I am not a therapist who blindly believes in forgiveness. I hear too many stories in my work from people who have been guilted into "forgiving" because someone told them it was the "right" thing to do, they were too afraid of losing an important relationship to process their true feelings, or they were instructed to just "let it go," without the emotional due process needed to heal and move past the offense that was committed against them.

Forgiveness in a marriage or a romantic partnership is unique because of the special, multilayered bond two partners have with each other. We are invested in our relationship, our future, and, in many cases, share our finances, work, or family. We share everything from our beds to our hearts. I witnessed my own parents, Barry Mann and Cynthia Weil, go through their own ups and downs over the course of over five decades of marriage. Because they wrote songs together, many of which have won gold records and Grammy Awards, their work kept them invested in their marriage, even during the most difficult of times. The early years of their marriage were chronicled in the Broadway show *Beautiful*, but I am one of the few who had a front-row seat to their personal stories of love and forgiveness. Their ability to forgive and make amends has kept them married all these years.

It doesn't matter what keeps you "in" your relationship—work, children, or religious beliefs—as long as you are "in." Some of you may be debating whether or not you want to stay "in." I believe this chapter will help you to open your heart to forgiveness, when appropriate, and teach you how to make amends, when necessary, a process that will ultimately help you make a healthy choice for your own future. This chapter offers the tools you need to help resolve conflict and heal the wounds that we inevitably experience in coupledom. It will also help you get a clearer picture of your own contribution to the problems in your relationship, so that you can apologize and help heal your partner, as well.

Get Off Your High Horse

No matter how amazing your relationship, spectacular your partner, or great your relationship skills, you will both make mistakes. You will hurt each other, intentionally and unintentionally. At some point, you will disappoint one another, slip up, say things and speak in tones you'll later regret, be insensitive, inconsiderate, disrespectful, judgmental, or harsh. You will irritate each other at times and alienate each other at others. It is the nature of the beast—relationship tenets we must accept. The more we resist and resent them, the less likely we are to put time and energy into healing and solving problems, and the more likely we are to stay stuck in our self-righteous anger and indignation. We've all done it. We've all been there. When you are up on that high horse, it is impossible to have the difficult conversations that you have to have, and to make or receive amends.

Give your partner the benefit of the doubt in regard to his intentions. Unless you are with an abusive, cruel, or sociopathic partner—in which case you should get out of that relationship—you have to assume that what he did was not intentionally malicious. You can feel two things at once. You can love someone and be angry with him at the same time. You have to look at the totality of the relationship.

As psychotherapist Nathanial Branden points out in his book *Taking Responsibility: Self-Reliance and the Accountable Life*, "One of the characteristics of a mature, responsible love is the ability to know that we can love our partner deeply and nonetheless know times of feeling angry, irritated, or alienated, and that the truth and value of our relationship is not to be judged by the moment-to-moment or day-to-day fluctuations in feelings. In healthy relationships there is an equanimity born of the knowledge that we have a history with our partner, we have a context, and we do not drop that context under the pressure of immediate hurts or disappointments. We remember. We retain the ability to see the whole picture. We do not reduce our partner to his or her last bit of behavior and define him or her solely by means of it."

In our hurt and anger it is easy to engage in what therapists call "splitting." Splitting is a failure in thinking to bring together the positive and negative qualities of the other person in order to form a cohesive, realistic whole. Generally speaking, people are not all good or all bad. You must see your partner clearly—both his strengths and his weaknesses—to forgive him and also to humble yourself to ask for his forgiveness. When you come to terms with your own flaws, it makes it easier to have compassion for your partner's flaws.

It's Not Personal

So much in life is not personal, even though it feels that way. We get triggered because of issues from our past and interpret words and behavior through our own biased lens. Sometimes, our pain is rooted in misunderstandings, assumptions, or our own sensitivities.

QUESTIONS TO ASK YOURSELF ABOUT YOUR PARTNER'S BEHAVIOR

- Was this really about you?
- What was going on in his life that made him feel so fragile that he behaved the way he did?
- Is there anything from her past that might have been triggered in this situation?
- How might lack of experience have contributed to his bad choice?
- How might negative experiences from her childhood or previous relationships affect her perception of what happened?
- What incorrect assumptions (you are trying to hurt him, control him, get back at him, etc.) did he make that caused him to behave this way?
- Was her behavior altered by drugs, alcohol, or medication?
- Did he hear you accurately?
- What are her limitations?

To understand the underlying cause of your partner's poor behavior is not to *excuse* it, but instead to help you not to take it so *personally*. Understanding what he did does not free him from responsibility or entitle him to hurt you. It does, however, leave more room for understanding and, ultimately, repair.

When you get past the honeymoon period, you must grieve the loss of the idealized partner you thought you had. You must see him for who he is, not who you built him up to be with your projections, assumptions, and fantasies. Typically, the traits that initially drew you to your partner are the first ones to upset you or cause problems. Marissa was drawn to Jason because he was so kind and generous. He was the kind of guy who would give you the shirt off his back. He literally took his shirt off once, and gave it to a homeless man. She loved his generous spirit and it felt so good when he shared that with her. Years later it felt very different when they were a struggling married couple and Jason gave his younger brother $3,000 to start a new business without asking Marissa. When it was time to pay the rent and they were short a few thousand, Jason was forced to reveal his secret loan. Marissa was livid.

What Jason did was wrong. He should have consulted his wife before giving his brother the money. He needed to make amends to Marissa. But things are never black and white. We contribute to the problems we have in our relationships. We teach our partners how to treat us. Even though Marissa knew that her husband had terrible money boundaries, she let him handle their finances. She handed him the checkbook and turned the other cheek. Because of her own issues and anxieties relating to money, she did not make bill paying a collaborative process, and never set up a protocol in the event that anyone would ask either of them for money, or if they wanted to make a big purchase. Marissa never checked on Jason or asked him how the money was being spent. She put her head in the sand. That was Marissa's contribution to the problem that was set into motion because of her own limitations.

You are not so perfect yourself. I know I'm not! (You'll hear more about that later in this chapter.) Just like your partner, you've come to your relationship with baggage, triggers, issues, imperfections, and limitations. Your deficits and weaknesses affect the relationship and do harm to it. Sometimes you screw up.

Like your partner, you hope that when you mess up in the relationship he handles it with sensitivity and kindness and gives you the benefit of the doubt. You need to do the same. Generally speaking, one person sets the standard. Be the role model in your relationship in this way.

Create an atmosphere of forgiveness and take responsibility by being quick to look at your part in conflicts. Have empathy for your partner, and be quick to make amends. Humility is an important quality in an enduring relationship. Just to clarify, I am not talking about forgiving abuse. There is *nothing* that warrants violence in an intimate relationship. I am talking about making amends for the more typical problems that couples have.

QUESTIONS TO ASK YOURSELF ABOUT YOUR PART IN THE CONFLICT

- What was my contribution to the problem?
- How might my issues (heightened sensitivity to abandonment, ridicule, disrespect, etc.) have led me to misinterpret events?
- How might my own negative experiences in childhood or previous relationships be coloring how I see this event?
- What got triggered in me?
- How good a job did I do listening and trying to understand my partner's perspective?
- Did I create a self-fulfilling prophecy?
- For my own growth, am I willing to ask my partner how I contributed to the problem?

Relationship Crimes and Misdemeanors

A dog distinguishes between being stumbled over and being kicked. There is a difference between intentional and unintentional wrongdoing, ongoing hurtful patterns versus one-time offenses, and big offenses versus small ones. There is a difference between a lie we tell to avoid hurting our partner's feelings ("Yes, I love your new haircut") and ones that are more destructive ("I set up a profile on that dating site as a joke. I wasn't really planning to use it!"). The more significant violations of human connection are the ones that tend to hit us the hardest—and they come in all forms.

COMMON CRIMES OF THE HEART

- Betrayals
- Breaking a confidence
- Breaking a promise
- Contempt
- Criticism
- Cruelty
- Deceit
- Dishonesty
- Disrespect
- Drinking or using drugs
- Embarrassing each other in public
- Failing to offer support
- Forgetting plans or important occasions
- Gossiping about each other

- Ignoring the other person
- Impatience
- Inappropriate-boundaries with other people
- Inconsiderate treatment
- Infidelity (emotional or sexual)
- Judgmental attitude
- Letting the other person down
- Lies
- Making unilateral decisions
- Meanness
- Misjudgment
- Negative attitude
- Not doing household chores
- Not participating in child care
- Not taking an interest in your partner
- Put-downs
- Rudeness
- Secrecy
- Sexual betrayals
- Spending money irresponsibly
- Spending time at bars or clubs
- Tardiness
- Unfairness
- Unreasonable expectations
- Yelling

How we respond to hurt runs the gamut, and is based on a number of factors, including how our own family of origin handled offenses, our culture, gender, temperament, level of rigidity, unresolved issues, and the ability to put ourselves in another person's shoes. These things also have an effect on our ability to recover quickly. Usually, the passage of time helps us to calm down and be open to making or receiving amends. We rebound from minor offenses much more quickly than big ones. We may think there are offenses, like infidelity, for which we have zero tolerance, but once it actually happens to us we feel differently than we thought we would. Forgiveness is not so black and white.

Most of us need to work on situational forgiveness (forgiving a specific act), as well as dispositional forgiveness (becoming a more forgiving person). It is impossible for you or your partner to forgive without making proper amends. And there's much more to it than just saying, "I'm sorry." Words are not enough. In order to repair the disconnection, you must know how to make a sincere, deeply felt apology.

Part A: The Four Rs of Apology

To make an effective apology, four things must be present. I have come to this conclusion based on decades of clinical experience in private practice and counseling people in the media, as well as through extensive research about the psychology of forgiveness. The four Rs that I recommend have changed and evolved over time. In my experience, if all four are not addressed properly it is difficult, if not impossible, to let go of the pain and heal the fracture in a relationship. Hurt people are always looking for inauthenticity in an apology. They are looking for the holes: "Are you saying this to placate, silence, or dismiss me?" Because of this, it is especially important for an apology to be genuine, authentic, and heartfelt. In order to do that, no matter which side of the apology you are on (giving it or receiving it), your apology must have these four elements:

1. Remorse

"It pains me to know I have hurt you so. I am so terribly sorry for the pain I have caused."

A heartfelt apology comes from the realization of the hurt you have caused, even if it was unintentional, and your feelings of remorse. This expression of regret serves as the first step toward reparation. You must verbalize that you are hurting because of the pain you have caused the other person, while keeping the focus on him.

Empathy is a key part of expressing remorse. Showing that you are moved by the pain you have caused is powerful. This gives the other person hope that he can trust you not to reinjure him. It is the first step toward reestablishing trust. It lets him know that his pain has penetrated your heart and made a difference. He has not suffered in vain.

While showing remorse often involves an apology, to say you are sorry is not enough. Too often people say those words to shut the other person up or make the conflict go away. If that is what you are doing, your partner will sense it and your apology will be meaningless, if not downright offensive.

While expressing remorse, you must avoid attacking, blaming, or making excuses, regardless of how justified you think your actions may have been. Conflicts are two-sided and cause both people pain. No matter how much you are hurt, this is not the time to seek empathy for yourself or try to get the other person to apologize. Sometimes you have to put your own pain aside to help your partner heal. As my cotherapist on VH1 *Couples Therapy with Dr. Jenn,* Dr. Mike Dow, always asks, "Do you want to be right or do you want to be happy?"

2. Responsibility

"You have every right to be angry with me. I shouldn't have said those things to you. There's no excuse for my behavior and I know I hurt you deeply. I'm so sorry for that."

To take responsibility is to take ownership of your actions as well as their impact, even if it was unintentional. It is a statement of regret for having caused inconvenience or damage. That damage may be concrete ("I wasn't careful and I knocked over your vase and broke it") or it may be about damage to the relationship ("I know you have trouble with trust, and my lying to you makes it harder for you to trust me now"), but it must be acknowledged. When you take responsibility, you let your partner know that you understand the gravity of the situation you have caused, and recognize that what you did was wrong.

About nine months into the relationship with my boyfriend Eric, I made a terrible and costly mistake that I had to own in a big way. To this day, I am still racked with guilt, even though Eric handled it beautifully. I am amazed at his ability to forgive me.

Eric and I were going on a family trip to Montana for winter break and were busy making last-minute arrangements before we left. His gorgeous black Ferrari California was parked on the busy street where I live. Because there have been so many accidents on my block, specifically people hitting parked cars, we decided to move his car into my garage. When I went to open the garage I discovered that the garage-door motor was broken. We were rushing to the airport and I told Eric that I would call someone to have the garage door fixed and make sure his car got moved into the garage. I then completely forgot about it. You can see where this is going.

A few days into the trip, I received a text message from my neighbor, telling me that someone had crashed into Eric's parked car, along with the photographic evidence of the wreck. There were pieces of that beautiful Ferrari everywhere! It looked like an automotive massacre had occurred in front of my house. I was devastated. I had broken my promise to get the garage door fixed and have the car moved! This was totally out of character for me. I pride myself on being someone who keeps her word, so this was particularly tough on my own sense of self. I was terrified to tell him.

I was already in love with Eric and I worried that he would be so angry and disappointed in me, and the devastation that my mistake had caused, that he would end the relationship. I wouldn't have blamed him if he had. All I could do was to take responsibility for my actions and let him know how remorseful I was for not following through. I owned my mistake.

There were many reasons why it slipped my mind at the time. I was under enormous stress. I was in the process of moving to a new network for my radio show. My ex-husband and I were going through a high conflict time. I was worried about my kids. My nanny was on the verge of leaving—and any single working mom knows that you can't do your job if you don't have support for your kids! But none of that mattered. I did the wrong thing. To make excuses would have diminished my apology by not fully acknowledging what I had done wrong. It would not have lessened his loss or disappointment in any way. I would have run the risk of appearing as if I were trying to excuse my behavior. It didn't matter what other stresses I was under, no matter how legitimate they were. I made a promise and I broke that promise and I had to own it.

We are responsible for our behavior and the consequences of it, regardless of outside circumstances. Facing the wrongs we have done is a humbling process. When we are rigorously honest, we feel vulnerable, anxious, and ashamed of ourselves. It is uncomfortable. But growth always is.

Taking responsibility is harder for some than for others. You may be particularly challenged in this area if you are a man, come from a home where you were shamed for making mistakes, or have very black-and-white thinking. Understand that taking responsibility is not only healing to your partner, but it also allows you to create a more positive self-concept. Being responsible for your actions is a sign of maturity and strength.

3. Recognition

"I know you are upset, and rightfully so. Tell me what this was like from your perspective and what upset you the most. I want to hear about your feelings."

To help your partner heal, you have to provide him with a forum to talk through what happened from *his* perspective, even if you see it differently. The French novelist Gustave Flaubert said, "There is no truth. There is only perception." This is especially true in romantic relationships.

Feelings and perceptions must be processed and recognized. Too many couples undermine their apologies by trying to prove to that their partner's perception is wrong; they argue over the details or invalidate their partner's feelings.

Seek to understand the other person's pain. He needs you to see it from his perspective and understand how you hurt him to feel close again. You don't have to agree with his perspective; you only have to provide support. This is what closes the emotional gap after a rift. In psychology, they say that separation leads to deeper understanding. But that can't occur unless you talk it through. This requires two things: (1) You must let the other person articulate his pain and (2) you must allow him to talk about what happened from his perspective.

We cannot carry our pain in silence in an intimate relationship. Pretending that we are not hurt, angry, sad, or upset does not make the pain go away. On the contrary, pushing those feelings underground makes them snowball. Not talking keeps people stuck in their pain and anger. The Nobel Peace Prize winner Bishop Desmond Tutu described this perfectly in *The Book of Forgiving: The Fourfold Path for Healing Ourselves and Our World*, when he said, "Marriages crumble under the weight of unspoken hurts. When we ignore the pain, it grows bigger and bigger, and like an abscess that is never drained, eventually it will rupture."

Elaine, who called my radio show, is the perfect example of that. She had been married for thirty years and had four children, three of whom were already in college. Seventeen years earlier, her husband had had an affair with someone he had worked with. After she found out, she and her husband went into therapy to try to work through what happened. They had a few sessions and then, according to Elaine, the therapist told her that if she was going to choose to stay in the marriage she could never mention the affair again. In an attempt to be a good wife (and therapy client), she agreed.

Sixteen years later, she was an hour late coming home from her ladies' book club and her husband got upset—nothing out of control; he was just annoyed—but Elaine lost it! All her anger about the affair that she had not talked about, her humiliation, her unexpressed rage bubbled to the surface and she used the affair against him. She made a spiteful, nasty remark about it that cut her husband to the core. Once the dam had broken they were both unable to recover. Her comment created a great divide between them. By the time she called me, they had spent a whole year at a cordial but uncomfortable distance, not discussing what happened.

If Elaine understood the therapist's direction correctly, I have to believe she was trying to keep her client from beating her husband up for years over the infidelity. She probably wanted the couple to be able to move on. But when your partner has betrayed you on that level, it must be processed over time.

Grief occurs when we lose something precious to us: trust, faithfulness, innocence, and the fantasy of how the relationship will be. Grieving is a *process*, and it's not a linear one. Different milestones, emotional realizations, triggers, and experiences are going to emerge and create the need to further process what happened. Grief is all about feelings. We need some time to soak in them, but not so much that we drown our relationship and ourselves. It is normal to obsess about a hurt or betrayal. But at a certain point you have to work on moving forward. I love how Dr. Fred Luskin, Director of the Stanford University Forgiveness Projects, puts it in his book *Forgive for Love: The Missing Ingredient for a Healthy and Lasting Relationship*, "Forgiveness can wrap up the grief, but it does not prevent the suffering. When there is a serious injury or loss, there is no way to avoid pain."

It is important not to torture your partner for his indiscretion forever, put his mistake at the center of every conversation for years, or constantly punish him. For couples who are unable to have productive conversations about what happened, or if one partner constantly torments the other for his mistake, boundaries need to be put in place. Some couples save the discussion for therapy or assign a limited time each day for the hurt party to vent. There should be a limit to these conversations, however, in order to keep them productive and result in healing.

4. Remedy

"I'm so sorry for what I have done. I am going to shut down my Facebook account and give you all my passwords. I'm going to go to therapy so that I can understand why I act the way I do."

I can't tell you how many calls I have gotten from people whose spouse has done something terrible—has an ongoing pattern of this behavior—and the caller has chosen to take him back. I ask, "What did he do to make you think it would be different this time? What plan of action did he have to correct this bad behavior?" The answer is always the same: nothing. "He said he was sorry and that he wouldn't do it again," she tells me. Without a plan of action, nothing changes. To take someone back who has repeatedly harmed you, but is not committed to doing anything differently, is to sign on for more of the same hurtful behavior. To apologize without implementing a plan is to set yourself up to reoffend and hurt your partner.

Remedy is twofold. For change to occur, two things must happen:

1. You must take steps to avoid repeating the behavior. You must set yourself up to succeed with a plan of action.
2. You must do the work to repair the damage you have caused.

These are crucial elements to the healing process, and they increase the success rate for the couple.

Without transformation, apologies are nothing but empty words. You have a responsibility to your partner and to yourself to implement change. Reparations are not enough if you continue the behavior. Changing is your "living amends" to your partner. A "living amends" is a 12-step concept that we can all use. It means amending the way you live, and making genuine changes in your behavior. It is your partner's insurance policy that you will not hurt her again. It is what will ultimately restore her trust, and allow her to feel close to you again.

Apologizing to your partner for forgetting your wedding anniversary two years in a row is insulting, unless you offer assurances that it won't happen again. What are you going to do differently this time? It might look like this: "I will set two alarms before the date to remind me. I will make reservations for a special weekend away together right now to make it up to you. I will also make reservations at your favorite restaurant right now, for next year's anniversary, so you know that this will not happen again. I don't believe I am ever going to mess this up again, but if I do, you have my commitment to take it to therapy and find out why I might be sabotaging our relationship when I know how important this is to you." Taking steps to ensure that you will not make the same hurtful mistake again is key.

For bigger offenses, the remedy usually involves more than one behavioral action or commitment. On the following page are some typical examples of conflicts and action plans I have used with clients. Make sure to put your plan someplace where you will be reminded of it several times a day, or set an alarm on your phone as a reminder of your commitment. You may not want to do everything listed for the offense; it may be overkill for your situation. On the other hand, you may choose to do everything listed and even add a few things. You and your partner have to come up with a plan that is proportional to what happened, and feels right for your personal relationship dynamics and situation.

RELATIONSHIP CRIME	POTENTIAL MULTIACTION PLANS
Drinking or drug problem	1. Inpatient treatment and detox.
	2. After inpatient treatment is over, commit to working a 12-step program starting with ninety meetings in ninety days, and after that a minimum of one meeting a week, actively working with a sponsor and working the steps.
	3. Attending weekly therapy with a professional who specializes in substance abuse issues.
	4. Both parties agree to keep a totally sober home—no drugs or alcohol in the house.
	5. Weekly or monthly drug testing.
	6. Cut ties with drinking or drug-taking friends.
Anger problem	1. Weekly anger management classes until the leader determines that he has "graduated."
	2. Weekly therapy with a therapist who specializes in anger management.
	3. Get evaluated by a psychiatrist to see if medication is advisable and comply with the doctor's suggestions.
	4. Implement an agreed-upon "time-out" strategy when discussions get heated.
Cheating	1. End affair and completely cut off all contact with the cheatee.
	2. Total transparency with phone, computer, and other devices. Willingly install spyware so partner can monitor your communications.
	3. Willingly share all passwords.
	4. Agree not to get any other phones without your partner's knowledge. If one is found, it is understood that the marriage is over.

	5. Postnuptial agreement that includes an affair penalty fee.
	6. Individual therapy to help offender understand why he acted out.
	7. Couples therapy to heal the marriage and understand why the offender was so vulnerable to the affair.
	8. Spouse accompanies you on business trips.
	9. No going out drinking with pals.
	10. Willingness to give a full accounting of how the offender's day-to-day time has been spent, along with permission to make phone calls to any people he reports he was with throughout the day to verify what has been shared.
Emotional affair	1. End contact with the other person.
	2. Change boundaries with outside friends or colleagues. For example, no text messaging after certain hours, no talking about personal life with outside friends of colleagues, etc.
	3. Transparency with phone, computer, and other devices.
	4. Individual therapy.
	5. Couples therapy.
	6. Plan to have daily face-to-face time with partner to repair your connection.
	7. Weekly date night to bring back connection and romance.
Financial secrets	1. Plan of financial transparency. Partner may look at finances any time; no secret accounts.
	2. 12-step program. Debtors Anonymous for the debtor, Alcoholics Anonymous for the partner who stole money due to addiction, etc.

RELATIONSHIP CRIME	POTENTIAL MULTIACTION PLANS
	3. Third-party monitoring. Have an accountant, business manager, or trusted friend monitor finances to avoid secrecy.
	4. Weekly business meetings to discuss finances.
	5. Commitment to learning more about financial management to become better educated in this area.
Inability to voice needs	1. Assertiveness training.
	2. Bibliotherapy (reading books on assertiveness).
	3. Individual therapy to address self-esteem issues.
	4. Commitment to being more open and honest about your needs.
Poor social media boundaries	1. Unfriending or unfollowing people who are not personal friends; are ex-boyfriends or girlfriends; are flirtatious, unsupportive of the relationship, or feel unsafe to your partner.
	2. Friend or link to your partner on all social media.
	3. Make "relationship status" on all accounts show "married" or "in a relationship" and with whom.
	4. Do not flirt, compliment the appearance of, or make sexually suggestive remarks to others.
	5. Do not private-message or direct-message anyone without sharing with your partner.
	6. Have an agreed-upon protocol for accepting or declining social media requests.
	7. Share password codes.

	8. Post pictures that show you are in a relationship and say nice things about your partner on social media.
	9. Do not share any information about fights or vent about your partner on social media.
	10. Do not post any racy pictures of yourself on social media.
	11. Do not post any pictures of each other without the other's approval.
	12. Set an agreed-upon time limit for using social media.
Not standing up for partner with your family	1. Pick your partner's preferences over your family's.
	2. Set limits with family members about the way they treat your partner.
	3. Commit to never participating in secret visits with your family that your partner does not know about.
	4. Make it a policy that if you are both not welcome at a family member's house, no one is coming (including your children).
	5. If you cannot resolve these conflicts, attend family therapy together.

After the Action Plan

Once you have created your action plan to avoid repeating the same bad behavior, you must start working on repairing the damage you have done to the relationship. Sometimes there is some overlap. For example, going to couples therapy may have been part of your action plan, but it is also an important step toward repairing your relationship. Typically, the behavior that nurtures your connection as a couple is most valuable in repairing the relationship. As Dr. Gary Chapman points out in his terrific book *The Five Languages of Apology: How to Experience Healing in All Your Relationships*, ". . . in the private sphere of family and other close relationships, our desire for restitution is almost always based upon our need for love. After being deeply hurt, we need reassurance that the person we hurt still loves us. After all, successful . . . relationships . . . are ultimately based on love."

When you commit to remedying the damage done, by taking steps to avoid repeating the behavior as well as repairing the damage you have caused, you bolster your relationship. Sometimes people say, "Why do I have to do so much to fix this? Shouldn't he just know that I love him and I'll do better next time?" No, he shouldn't. These steps show that you are apologetic and committed to doing better with actions that are far more powerful than words. When you do this, you are not only healing your partner, you are also restoring your goodwill and investing in your own personal growth.

Part B: Your Contribution

Typically, this is how the call goes. I welcome the caller to the show, and she then tells me how she has been wronged. The pain she has suffered is tremendous, the anger she feels is justified, and the hurt is immense. She wants to know if she should forgive the guilty party and stay in the relationship. I tell her what to look for in an apology—that it should include the four Rs—and make sure it is heartfelt and likely to lead to change. Then, inevitably, I ask her, "What was your part in this?" Not everyone is able to answer that question. "If I got him on the phone with me right now, what would his complaint about you be? What would he be most frustrated about?"

The answer is always revealing. The caller who has no idea what she might have done to contribute to the problem has told me, without realizing it, that she is not self-aware, in touch with her partner's needs or feelings, and is invested in being the victim. This is a problem. Without the willingness to look at your part of a problem, nothing will change. With the exception of abuse, we are always participants in our relationship problems. It takes two to tango.

We are accomplices in creating the character and dynamics of our relationship. We cannot be, as Nathaniel Branden calls it, "cognitively passive," lacking in internal responsibility. We must be aware of our issues, triggers, poor choices, and bad behavior, and how they affect the other person. We must take responsibility for our part.

Just today, Eleanor, a follower of mine, posted on social media telling me that she was upset about how I counseled Angela "Big Ang" Raiola and her husband Neil Murphy on season 6 of VH1 *Couples Therapy with Dr. Jenn*. She felt that I had come down too hard on Ang and let Neil off the hook.

The painful dynamic in their marriage was that Ang made the lion's share of the money. She knew when she married Neil that he was not a big money earner. She came from a well-known crime family, dated some heavy spenders, and made a great living, especially with her hit show *Mob Wives*. Neil works for the Sanitation Department. He struggled with alcoholism and depression and was not the proactive partner that she wanted him to be. In her frustration to effect change in their marriage, she called him names, yelled at him, and emasculated him. I completely empathized with her frustration and anger. His follow-through was poor. He was often passive-aggressive, and she felt she could not count on him to do what he said.

But here's the thing. Ang saw who he was before she married him. She picked a man she'd met in a bar and partied with, and who did not make a lot of money. Then she got angry with him for being who he was. Of course, Neil had a responsibility to himself and to Ang to improve himself, address his addiction, get treatment for his depression, keep his word to his wife, and find ways to add value to the relationship, even if it was not in terms of finances. But Ang had choices. She was not a victim. People are most likely to change in a relationship when they feel loved and inspired, not criticized and devalued. Once she saw that he was not changing, she had a choice to leave. When she chose not to leave, she had to accept the man she'd married.

As it turned out, my fan Eleanor had her own experiences in a passive-aggressive marriage, so this really pushed her buttons. It is not that Neil was right and Ang was wrong. It is easy to look at a situation like that and say, "She is right and he is wrong." Relationships are more complicated than that. Both people participate in the dysfunction. When Ang shifted the way she interacted with Neil, it changed the way he responded to her.

I am grateful that I got to help them before she passed away from cancer, eight months after we finished shooting. We stayed in touch after we wrapped, and our work made a big difference in their relationship.

At the end of the season she wrote Neil this beautiful heartfelt note of apology.

> *Dear Neil, my love:*
> *I just want to let you know how much I love you and appreciate you.*
> *I know that it's been a bumpy road and I know that I've hurt you so*
> *much. First, I want to apologize from the bottom of my heart. You*
> *have a great big heart and that's what made me love you.*
> *Love, your wife forever,*
> *Ang*

We play an unconscious role in creating our life circumstances. You picked your mate to fill a role in your life, even if you didn't realize it or consciously welcome it. We choose people because they represent the repressed parts of ourselves; we're reenacting painful childhood hurts, acting out our own poor self-esteem; and for a host of other reasons. But at the end of the day we are responsible for our choices: the partner we pick, how we relate to that partner, whether we escalate or deescalate a conflict, and whether we stay or go.

I AM RESPONSIBLE FOR THESE THINGS IN MY RELATIONSHIP

- How I respond
- My behavior
- The way I speak
- My attitude
- Expressing my needs
- Establishing boundaries
- Being consistent in my words and actions
- My contributions to the relationship
- The agreements I make
- Taking care of my own emotional life
- Seeking to understand my partner's perspective
- Working on my issues
- Choosing whether or not to accept my partner's behaviors
- Choosing to stay or to leave

As I have pointed out throughout this book, connection and attachment to your partner are the keys to your relationship. When you don't do your part in nurturing that, problems always develop. When you don't tend to your relationship and nurture that bond, you leave the relationship open to intruders.

Having an affair is one of the most painful betrayals in a relationship. There is *nothing* I can say that will excuse this kind of hurtful, destructive behavior. Only the person who has the affair is responsible for the affair. But after the 4 Rs of apology have been made and everyone has had time to digest what happened, you *have to* look at what left your relationship vulnerable to infidelity in the first place, in order for the relationship to recover. In my experience, nine times out of ten, the relationship has been neglected.

Mariah and Tyler came to see me three years into their marriage. Tyler had started his own business. He realized that getting it off the ground would require working long days, weekends, and traveling a lot, but he did not anticipate the toll it would take on his marriage. Typically, he would come home at 9 or 10 o'clock at night, grab a bite to eat, and get back on his computer. Mariah might have been able to tolerate this if it had only been five days a week, but it was seven. She felt like an entrepreneur widow. She never saw her husband and, when she did, he was too exhausted to talk about his day. He was so stressed out and obsessed with his work that he didn't ask much about hers. Sex became infrequent, because he was "too tired," and the date nights they used to have became a thing of the past. They were totally disconnected.

Mariah decided that this was a good time for her to start training for a marathon. It had been a lifelong goal of hers and she figured it wouldn't take time away from her marriage, since her husband was never home. She joined a training group that met for long runs on the weekend and recommended running three days a week during the week. She organized a weekday running group with two women and a man who lived near her house.

Howard was recently divorced and not at all her type. When the four of them ran together, the other two ladies were a bit faster than the two of them, which meant they often spent hours together running alone, talking, and watching the sun come up. She started confiding in him about her frustrations in her marriage. He talked about what had caused his divorce and shared his dating trials and tribulations. They started looking forward to their special runs together and found excuses to do other activities with each other. Eventually, the emotional affair turned into a physical one.

What Mariah did was *wrong*. It is inexcusable. She made a commitment to her husband and she betrayed him on the deepest level. She broke her vows. That said, their marriage didn't stand a chance. Tyler was a good man who was working hard to build a business to support his family. He was investing in their financial future, but, in doing so, he neglected their emotional present. He did not realize the damage he was doing, even though Mariah had voiced her feelings about it. She had pleaded for time with her husband, and she had told him how neglected she felt, emotionally and sexually. She talked to him reasonably, she tried yelling, she begged, but nothing got him to change.

It wasn't until he faced losing his wife to another man that Tyler woke up. After he got past his hurt and anger, he set about restructuring his business day. He came home for dinner every night, during which he put down his phone and shared with his wife what had happened in his day and asked her about hers. He made a commitment to have one weekday night and one weekend night where he did not go back to work after dinner, and on the nights he did go back to working, he did it at home. He made sex and connection with his wife priorities.

That his wife had an affair was wrong, but after some time in therapy, he realized that his checking out of the marriage in favor of his work was wrong, too. It did not justify her transgression, but it did put it in context.

We tend to feel entitled to be loved by our partners. Somehow we think we are owed great love without giving it. But love is a two-way street. It requires us to step up to the plate and look at our reactions and behaviors, especially when we have been hurt. To succeed in a relationship, we must exercise consciousness and self-responsibility. You chose your partner, but you don't have to stay. If you do stay, you are just as responsible as your partner is for the quality of the relationship.

To Forgive or Not to Forgive, That Is the Question

Until we have seen someone's darkness we don't really know who they are.
Until we have forgiven someone's darkness, we don't really know what love is.
—Marianne Williamson, spiritual teacher, bestselling
author, and lecturer

You can do everything I tell you to do in this book—create connection, fight fair, negotiate well, work through your childhood issues, have great sex—and you will still need to learn to forgive. Couples always have personality differences, disagreements, and conflicts. Problems and hurt feelings are inevitable, and in order for your relationship to thrive, you have to learn to forgive and move on.

There may be some things that happen in your relationship that are easy to forgive—a cranky attitude after a rough day or a forgotten birthday. There are other issues that are harder to move past; for example, when your partner publicly humiliates you or makes a large purchase that puts the two of you in financial jeopardy. Then there are problems like serial infidelity or addiction that are so massive that they may become deal breakers. You may choose never to forgive. Just as relationship crimes happen on a continuum, so does forgiveness.

Forgiveness is not as black and white as people would like to believe. As Dr. Gary Chapman points out, "When we commit actions or speak words that are detrimental to another, the consequences of those actions and words are never fully removed, even with genuine forgiveness." There are repercussions to actions, even when there is forgiveness. After a problem occurs, it takes time and good behavior to heal and create the sense of safety that is so important in a relationship.

Self-help books, religious leaders, and society itself place a premium on forgiveness. It has become a moral issue, which it should not be. We are told that forgiveness heals our hearts, bodies, and souls. It is the "right" thing to do. But those who spout the virtues of forgiveness usually overlook that it is a process and that it does not erase hurt feelings. Sometimes we think we have forgiven, but then something triggers the memory of the betrayal—a phrase, an anniversary, a location, or seeing a person who was involved. Forgiveness is not a simple process.

The concept that either we forgive or we don't forgive is wrong. In reference to this all-or-nothing concept, Rabbi Susan Schnur writes, "But this, in relation to deeply felt violations, is reductive, a misrepresentation of our experience, and a mockery of the complex continuum of resolutions that crystallize in the aftermath of betrayal. We may partially forgive, vengefully forgive, contingently forgive, not forgive yet reconcile. We may mourn but yet not forgive; achieve understanding yet only forgive a certain part of betrayal, become indifferent; become detached. Forgiveness is comprised of lots of things."

Cheap Forgiveness

This leads me to what experts in the forgiveness field refer to as "cheap forgiveness." In her book *How Can I Forgive You?: The Courage to Forgive, the Freedom Not To*, author and clinical psychologist Janis Abrahms Spring defines it as ". . . a quick and easy pardon with no processing of emotion and no coming to terms with injury. It's a compulsive, unconditional, unilateral attempt at peacemaking for which you ask nothing in return." You give up your safety and integrity in order to preserve the relationship at any cost. Typically, *you* pay the price.

Sometimes, not wanting to make waves, people forgive too quickly. They don't realize that forgiveness is a process. Anger may be an important and validating emotion, one that helps to avoid future mistreatment. It takes self-esteem to say, "This is not okay. I deserve to be treated better than this! I am not going to just move on!" That sense of injustice is important to effect change and establish boundaries. In his research article "Two Cheers for Vindictiveness," Jeffrie G. Murphy points out that when a person lets go of all his angry or vindictive feelings, he may also be letting go of self-respect, self-defense, or allegiance to moral order. Needless to say, you cannot have a loving, kind relationship if you are permanently stuck in this stage, but you can't deny those feelings exist and work through them at the same time.

To forgive too quickly is to forgo the transformative process that the relationship needs to truly heal and repair the fractured relationship. It is ineffective in the long run. That kind of cheap forgiveness gives the offender the green light to hurt you again. It also prevents him from doing the work to help release you from pain. Janis Abrahms Spring says, "You're free to reserve forgiveness for someone who has the fortitude to admit his culpability and the decency to help release you from pain he has made you suffer. I would go so far as to say that you don't restore *your* humanity when you forgive an unapologetic offender, he restores *his* humanity when he works for forgiveness."

Brushing what happened under the carpet prevents you from growing by analyzing your own contribution to the problem. This head-in-the-sand approach prevents you from forming a more intimate bond.

Unless you process what happened and work through it, which the four Rs can help you do, an invisible wall stands between you. Monkey see no evil, hear no evil, speak no evil does not make the hurt go away. As we discussed earlier in this book, pains that are not worked though don't disappear; they tend to grow when they are pushed underground and eventually get acted out. The stress of carrying repressed anger is likely to harm your physical and emotional well-being.

What Is Forgiveness Anyway?

The perspectives on forgiveness are so varied that the word is hard to define. According to forgiveness researchers, forgiveness is *not*:

- forgetting the harm done to you
- going into denial
- pretending the injury was not hurtful
- condoning unkind actions
- preventing you from seeking justice
- an attitude of superiority or self-righteousness
- a commitment to reconcile
- condoning bad behavior
- giving up the right to be angry
- a pardon

Nor does it mean you have to stay together. It does not mean that you will forget what happened. That would not be to your benefit and would invite further injuries. It is not a get-out-of-jail-free card. It doesn't make what happened right or remove the pain of the other person's failures. It does not mean that you will never discuss it or feel pain stemming from it again in the future. Forgiveness is not being a doormat, nor is it giving permission for you to be abused.

So then what is forgiveness? There are so many definitions that I disagree with or believe to have the potential to do more harm than good. Here is how I look at forgiveness in the context of a romantic relationship: Forgiveness is giving up hope of a better past. It means that, as much as you are hurt or angry about what happened, you have moved to a place of acceptance. You recognize that neither of you can go back in time and take back the things that were said or done. It means not continuing to punish or shame the other person for her mistake, even if you are still hurting. It is letting go of revenge. It is an attempt to see what happened through your partner's eyes and to have empathy, even if what she did was truly terrible. It is a pledge to practice compassion. It is merciful. It is a commitment to restore closeness, even if that is a process. It is a means of healing the sadness, anger, and pain because we recognize that not only do these feelings hurt you, but they also hurt your relationship, and you have a desire to move forward and heal.

In a relationship, both you and your partner are accountable to each other. Forgiveness does not absolve a person of responsibility. On the contrary. In his book *Forgive & Forget: Healing the Hurts We Don't Deserve*, renowned author, ethicist, and theologian Lewis B. Smedes writes, "You do not excuse people by forgiving them; you forgive them at all only because you hold them to account and refuse to excuse them."

Being a "Human Bean"

Nobody is perfect. We are all human beings. As I mentioned before, my parents are songwriters. My dad, Barry Mann, writes the music, and my mom, Cynthia Weil, writes the lyrics. They have always been collaborative, creating music together, and have been incredibly honest with each other in giving feedback, for better or for worse. Long before I was born, an incident happened that gave my father his nickname "Bean" or "Beany."

My parents always went to recording sessions together. But on one occasion, my dad went to the studio to create a demo (a demonstration record) without my mom (for reasons no one can remember). When he came home, he played the demo for her, and my mom, who can always be counted on to give extremely honest feedback, hated it. "This is not what I thought you were going to do! This isn't what we talked about!" she exclaimed. "This doesn't represent our work! The one time I don't come with you to the recording studio you record this? How could you have done this?" My dad, who had been up all night recording for hours on end, and who was pained by the idea of disappointing his wife and writing partner exclaimed, "I'm just a human being!" My mom, who misheard him, said, "What? You're a bean?" This bizarre misunderstanding broke the tension and made them laugh so hard that tears streamed out of their eyes. My mother recognized that my dad was just a "human bean" and everybody makes mistakes and they moved on.

Study after study shows that the ability to forgive transgressions is linked to overall relationship satisfaction. Forgiveness was listed as one of the top ten most important characteristics in the study "Characteristics of Long-Term First Marriages," which looked at 147 couples in long-term marriages (twenty years or more). Researchers who participated in the study "Interpersonal Forgiving in Close Relationships: II. Theoretical Elaboration and Measurement" found that forgiveness in romantic relationships is directly related to the levels of satisfaction and commitment that both partners feel. Findings in the study "Forgiveness and Conflict Resolution in Marriage" showed that couples who practice understanding and willingness to forgive were better at conflict resolution. This study also found that the capacity to seek and grant forgiveness was one of the most significant factors contributing to marital longevity and happiness.

As Dr. Gary Chapman points out, forgiveness is a choice, not a feeling. It is "a commitment to accept the person in spite of what he or she has done." But what if you are just unable to forgive, despite the desire to be forgiving and the knowledge that forgiving can help your relationship?

What to Do When You Want to Forgive But Can't

Forgiving is difficult. Anyone who tells you otherwise is a delusional Pollyanna. There are many reasons that people have a terrible time forgiving, but the number one reason I see is the fear of being hurt again. It is easier to obsess, stay stuck in your anger, and put up walls. All those activities keep your partner at a distance and keep you safe.

Sometimes the other person has done everything to make it right, but you still hold on to your anger. You cling to it the way a toddler holds on to his favorite teddy bear. Other times, you hold on to your anger because the amends you received did not address the four Rs and were not sufficient. You just don't feel it's safe to trust again.

Andrea called my radio show about her husband of ten years, who had had an affair with a woman he worked with. He broke the news to Andrea via text message a year and a half before her phone call to me. He had lied about ending the affair during the first two months they were in counseling, but the woman he had cheated with called to inform Andrea that they were still involved. He finally did end the affair and left the job, so he would no longer be working with the "other woman"—and he became totally transparent with his phone.

Andrea's husband didn't go back to therapy with her because he "couldn't bear to see her cry." Of course, he should have thought of this before he put his penis in another woman's vagina. I guess hindsight is 20/20. His inability to perform the fourth R—recognize and process feelings—left Andrea stuck, thinking obsessively about the affair. "Is that something you ever get over?" she asked. "I have never forgiven him for it. I think about it every day. I wake up and I think about it. I go to work and I think about it. I come home and I think about it. I can't get it out of my mind." Andrea and her husband need to go back to therapy so that, with the help of a professional, Andrea's husband can learn to hear his wife and soothe her pain. Without that, it is unlikely she will be able to forgive him and move forward.

Other times, the person has addressed the four Rs, but you just can't let it go. It is scary to be so vulnerable. I always say, "Love is being vulnerable to someone. It means handing him all the tools to break your heart, but trusting that he won't." When your partner does, it is devastating. It takes time and consistent behavior. We are all afraid of being hurt.

TENETS THAT WILL LEAD TO A FORGIVING MIND-SET

- We all make mistakes.
- We don't always see things the same way.
- We can work on conflict.
- Even those with the best of intentions sometimes hurt their partner.
- I always have a choice to stay or to leave.
- I accept who my partner is.
- This isn't personal. (Usually even the worst offenses are about a deficit in the other person. Typically people act out because of their own issues and poor impulse control.)
- I take responsibility for my choice of mate.

When your partner has screwed up, but then does everything right, and you desperately want to forgive him, but can't seem to let go and move on, here are a few things you can do:

1. **Try visualization.** Visualize what it would look and feel like to move to a place of forgiveness. If you can imagine it, you can create it. Notice what feelings and resistances come up for you when you imagine this. Use that information to help you move forward.

2. **Utilize the power of prayer.** A lot of studies show that prayer can be extremely effective in the healing process. At the very least, it crystallizes what you are hoping for.

3. **Make some affirmations** (positive thinking and statements). For affirmations to be effective, they should be in the present tense and use positive words. So do not use words like "not," "no," or "never." They don't register with the unconscious mind. If you say, "I will not hold Bob's mistake against him," your unconscious will only hear "I will hold Bob's mistake against him." Instead try, "I forgive Bob" or "I let go of my anger."

4. **Journaling** can be a great tool, too. Putting a pen to paper or even fingers to a keyboard helps make the unconscious conscious and can help you work through whatever is holding you back.

5. **Talk with a close, supportive friend,** who wants the best for your relationship. Do not share something that would be a betrayal of your spouse. Sometimes a close friend can give you perspective that makes you see things differently, especially if it is someone who calls you out on your stuff.

6. **Try some thought analysis,** where you critically evaluate the facts you have gathered. Sometimes we are so entrenched in our hurt that we cannot see things objectively.

7. **Change your negative self-talk.** Divide a piece of paper in half. On the left side write down all the negative self-talk that is going on in your mind. On the right side, write down healthy responses. You can also use your healthy responses as affirmations.

8. **Write an angry letter that you don't send.** Sometimes we just need to get the rage off our chest in order to move on. I always tell my clients, when they do this exercise, to write the kind of letter that if someone found it on the street, she would be worried and would want to track you down to make sure you don't hurt the other person. People need to be given permission to express that kind of rage toward the person they love. After you've written the letter, burn it. This helps put closure on the ritual and also ensures that the other person won't read the letter, which you definitely do not want to happen.

9. **Make a gratitude list and read it out loud throughout the day.** Nothing breaks through negative energy like gratitude.

10. **Get yourself into therapy.** I recommend one year of weekly individual therapy and six months of weekly couples therapy for everyone. If you are struggling to forgive or make amends, this is a good time for you to start. Therapy is the best place to look at your resistance and figure out what is holding you back.

If you take the time to do all of these things and are still unable to move past the hurt and anger, even after your partner has made amends using the four Rs, implemented his new plan of action, shown you ongoing good behavior, and you have had plenty of time to heal, it may be time to reevaluate the relationship. If you feel that you cannot move past what has happened, you can't stay. It is not fair—to you or your partner—to stay in a relationship where you constantly feel hurt, angry, vengeful, resentful, and hostile. That is no way for either one of you to live. You always want to know that you have done absolutely everything humanly possible to heal before you leave a relationship, especially when kids are involved. But you can't stay in a relationship that is toxic and harmful, either.

Bottom Line

We all have a bottom line, a marker that separates upsetting behavior from deal-breaking behavior. It is a line that makes it impossible to stay in a relationship once it has been crossed. Sometimes we think we have a line that demarcates our limit, but once it is crossed, the line starts to move. True bottom lines are not so slippery. They come from our own morals and the way we value ourselves. While we may believe, compassionately, that the other person's bad behavior comes from a terrible childhood, poor mental health, stress, unemployment, addiction, or some other problem, we have to hold fast to the bottom line, and not let ourselves be treated in an unacceptable way. This stance comes from self-esteem, not a desire to manipulate the other person.

It is important to speak your truth and share your bottom line with your partner—but not as a threat or an ultimatum or something said in the heat of anger. I think that Harriet Lerner describes it best in her book *The Dance of Connection: How to Talk to Someone When You're Mad, Hurt, Scared, Frustrated, Insulted, Betrayed or Desperate*, ". . . a bottom line position evolves from a focus on the self, from a deeply felt awareness—which one cannot fake, pretend, or borrow—of what we need and feel entitled to, and the limits of our tolerance. We clarify a bottom line, not primarily to change or control the other person (although the wish to do so may be there) but rather to preserve the dignity, integrity, and well-being of the self."

WHAT IS YOUR BOTTOM LINE?

When trying to figure out if you should forgive your partner or walk away from the relationship, it is important to know what your bottom line is. If you answer yes to any of these questions, you should strongly consider leaving the relationship.

My partner has abused me physically. ☐ yes ☐ no

My partner threatens to hurt me. ☐ yes ☐ no

My partner is consistently verbally abusive, hypercritical, controlling, and angry with me. ☐ yes ☐ no

My partner struggles with addiction or compulsive behavior and refuses to acknowledge it or get treatment. ☐ yes ☐ no

My partner is not contributing value to our relationship or family and is unwilling to make changes. ☐ yes ☐ no

My partner has a pattern of cheating and breaking our sexual agreements, and is unwilling to address his problem in a 12-step program or therapy. ☐ yes ☐ no

My partner is unwilling to contribute financially to our family or add value in other ways. ☐ yes ☐ no

My partner is suffering from severe depression, anxiety, ADD/ADHD, or a mental illness that is hurting our relationship, but refuses to get help.   ☐ yes ☐ no

My partner has an eating disorder or is morbidly obese and refuses to get help or recognize the problem.   ☐ yes ☐ no

I have made it clear to my partner that I cannot continue in this relationship unless things change, and he is unwilling to change.   ☐ yes ☐ no

If you are seriously considering leaving your relationship, especially a marriage, you owe it to your partner to have a calm discussion about it so that he is not totally blindsided. A fair warning shows respect for the history you have shared together and should be done in a moment of calm, in private. The exception, of course, is if the other party is violent. Telling your partner that you're thinking of leaving the relationship should not be worded as a challenge or used as a way to manipulate him, and should only be shared when you are genuinely done with the relationship. Having said that, sometimes knowing that you are really going to lose your partner is just what you need to get off your butt and effect change.

Is There Really Closure?

So what if, after all this, your partner is unrepentant or you can't get past what happened and you decide that you are done with the relationship? How do you move on?

Sometimes there is no forgiveness for a partner's betrayal or other wrongdoing, but you need to accept it. Acceptance means letting go of your anger and animosity, and it is important to do it for yourself. This quote, attributed to Buddha, sums it up: "Holding on to anger is like grasping a hot coal with the intent of throwing it at someone else; you are the one who gets burned."

Anger is a healthy and important part of the grieving process of letting go of a relationship, but eventually you hit a point of diminished returns, and you have to let go of it. This is good self-care. Anger ceases to be an empowering emotion when it starts to eat away at you. It is up to you to release the other person from your hatred and desire for revenge. When you carry those feelings around for too long, it only hurts you and your ability to relate to other people. As psychiatrist and researcher Judith Herman points out in her groundbreaking book *Trauma and Recovery*, you are not responsible for the harm done to you, but you are responsible for your own recovery.

If you still have to maintain a relationship with your ex, perhaps because you share children or work in the same office, creating boundaries and keeping yourself safe is of the utmost importance. Know that acceptance does not mean you have to reconcile or have a relationship with the other person. On the contrary, most people choose not to. Acceptance is about forgiving yourself for letting the other person hurt you and developing a more neutral perspective that robs that person of his power over you. Letting go is ultimately about healing yourself.

Ignite Your Sex Life

Sex is important in marriage.
It can be the glue when things are drifting apart,
the lubrication over the rough spots, the cushioning for the bumps.

—FRANK PITTMAN, *PRIVATE LIES*

Most people underestimate the importance of sex in a relationship. If you are in a monogamous relationship, sex is something you do only with your partner. It is an activity that forges a connection and sets that person and the relationship apart, making it special. Without it, as I've said before, you are simply roommates, co-parents, or pals who spend time together. I have seen too many relationships devolve into this when sex becomes absent.

Sex bonds two people. Vasopressin and oxytocin, hormones triggered during sex in the early stages of romance, can make partners connect, feel protective of each other, and form attachments. Sexual contact is a necessary ingredient in the recipe for a connected, loving relationship. It validates you, lets you know that you are lovable, attractive, and desirable. It makes you feel noticed, relevant, and important to your partner.

Sex can be fun, exciting, passionate, crazy, and, in a healthy way, it can help you connect with your animal urges and your dark side. But when sex becomes a problem in a relationship, or if it isn't handled to each partner's satisfaction, it can create tension, stress, resentment, and anxiety. All couples go through rough patches and dry spells in their sex life. No one is immune to the complications of sex, love, and intimacy. Because sex between two partners who love each other makes them so vulnerable, feelings of pain, rejection, and resentment may result when problems are not addressed with enormous sensitivity.

Whether you are a couple in a sexual crisis or basking in the glow of passion, this chapter is for you. There is always room to up your game, expand your repertoire, and challenge your sexual beliefs in order to have more frequent and better-quality sex.

SCHTUP YOUR WAY TO GOOD HEALTH

Besides the fact that sex feels good and has many emotional benefits, it is also good for your health. Here are some ways sex promotes health:

1. **Improved immune system.** A University of Pennsylvania study analyzing the saliva of college students found that those who had sex once or twice a week had 30 percent more of the antigen immunoglobulin (IgA) than those who had sex less often. IgA is the body's first line of defense against colds and flu.

2. **Lower blood pressure.** Researchers asked healthy men and women, ages twenty to forty-seven, about their sexual frequency, and then measured their blood pressure. They found that as sexual frequency increased, blood pressure decreased.

3. **Heart health.** One study found that men who have sex at least twice a week were 45 percent less likely to develop heart disease than men who have sex once a month or less.

4. **Reduced risk of prostate cancer.** A study published in the *Journal of the American Medical Association* found that men who ejaculated twenty-one times a month (via sex, masturbation, or nocturnal emissions) in their twenties were 33 percent less likely to develop prostate cancer later in life. Science increasingly blames the development of cancer on inflammation. Another recently published study indicates that when men don't ejaculate often, inflammatory cells can gather in the seminal vesicles, which are adjacent to the prostate gland, and, over time, this inflammation may lead to cancer.

5. **Better bladder control.** Intercourse helps strengthen a woman's pelvic-floor muscles, which contract during orgasm. This, in turn, can help improve bladder control and prevent incontinence, which affects about 30 percent of women at some point in their lifetime.

6. **Lighter periods and fewer menstrual cramps.** The uterine contractions that occur during orgasm have been shown to rid the body of cramp-causing compounds and help expel blood more quickly during menstruation, helping to end a woman's period faster. Orgasms have also been shown to release endorphins, which relieve pain. Some studies have even shown that sex during menstruation has been linked to decreases in risk for endometriosis.

Mind-Blowing Sex

One of the greatest myths about sex, especially sex between two people who love each other, is that it should be effortless, easy, and instinctual.

This is simply not true. To have mind-blowing sex requires time, effort, and attention. The familiar image of a couple throwing each other up against a wall and having an orgasm in thirty seconds, which we often see depicted in movies (and porn), is inaccurate and unrealistic. Images of effortless, satisfying sex do a disservice to real couples. To have great sex, especially over the long term, couples need to put time, energy, and effort into their erotic life. Even when it starts out hot and heavy, sexual connection must be nurtured to maintain and expand it.

To have a great sex life over the long term, or to take the one you have to the next level, there are several steps you need to follow, to make it happen.

Ten Things You Need to Know Before You Blow, Kiss, Lick, or Have Sex

1. Communicate

The ability to talk about sex without inhibitions is the foundation of a passionate sex life. Everybody has their own hang-ups and anxieties that may make sexual communication challenging. We are afraid of being judged, offending our partner, or being thought of as weird or perverted. Most people talk about sex in vague terms, euphemisms, or give hints. But if you can't tell your partner what you want, you stand no chance of getting it.

Cultural myths make it even harder to ask for what you want sexually. Most women are prone to think that their partner automatically knows how to please them. As a woman, you may think that asking for what you want will appear too demanding or too sexually aggressive. On the other hand, men are typically afraid to ask for what they want because society makes them think that "real men" have no sexual needs other than having sex as much as possible.

Asking for what you want requires courage, but the benefits are huge. A study published in the *Journal of Social and Personal Relationships* found that the more comfortable people were in talking about sex, the more satisfactory their sex lives were. According to the researchers, anxiety related to talking about sex had a direct impact on whether or not partners were communicating and how satisfied they were. Couples that did communicate experienced greater satisfaction. Studies show that this correlation is particularly profound for women. Women who are able to talk about their sexual needs have higher rates of marital satisfaction, more frequent sex, more orgasms, and more multiple orgasms.

DON'T "FAKE IT 'TIL YOU MAKE IT" WHEN IT COMES TO ORGASM

I get it. Things have been going on this way for a while and it just isn't going to happen tonight. You just want to get through it, without bruising any egos. You are looking out for your lover. But really you're not. Faking orgasms does a disservice to both of you. Believe it or not, both men and women fake orgasm—it's just more common among women.

Here are a few reasons you shouldn't fake orgasm:

- **It gives sexual misinformation.** When you let your partner believe that the moves he has been doing are giving you orgasms, he will continue to do the things that he believes are producing results, and nothing will change. This is an international problem. Studies show that 90 percent of men in Brazil and 75 percent of American men are convinced their partner regularly climaxes from vaginal intercourse alone, even though research shows that only 25 percent of women can climax that way.

- **It's a lie.** Creating a safe environment for sex means being gentle but honest. It is devastating to find out that your partner has been faking it. By telling your partner what he wants to hear, instead of expressing your true sexual needs, you are disorienting him and hurting your sex life.

- **It's bad communication.** As I've mentioned before, open and clear communication is one of the core building blocks to a great sex life. By not practicing those skills, you will not develop them.

- **It prevents you from gaining clarity about what you like.** If you are unable to say, "Hey, try touching me here," you will never learn what you can really enjoy with your partner.

- **It generates resentment.** Faking it traps you both in a cycle of unsatisfying sex, which leads to resentment.

What If You Have Been Faking It All This Time?

There is no need to confess your sins and destroy your partner's sexual self-esteem. First, start pulling back on your fake O's. The things that turn us on, over time, change. Let your partner know that you have noticed a shift in your body's responses, and that you would like to try some different things. Now ask for what you really want (see the recommendations below about how to ask).

How to Ask for What You Want

We become bound by our anxieties. Falling in love with someone makes us so vulnerable because we care what the other person thinks about us so much that it makes it scary to express our needs. We worry about her opinion of us and don't want to upset her. What if I make my request and she still doesn't meet my needs? What if I tell him what

I want and he thinks I'm a freak? I have seen too many people who, rather than face their fear and talk to their partner about their needs and desires, seek sex elsewhere through an affair, with a prostitute, or by watching porn or taking a blue pill. Shame may trap us in a sexual straightjacket, but good communication can free us.

Here are some tips for asking for what you want:

- **Positive reinforcement.** Talk about the things he has done that you like. "I love the way you kissed my neck last night!" Tell him in person, text him, write him a note, have a skywriter print it in the sky, throw a parade! We all respond well to positive feedback.

- **Encore!** When your partner does something you like, let him know you would like to see that move again. Let him know in the postgame analysis: "Babe, it was so hot when you . . ." That encourages him to make what you like more of a recurring act in your sexual repertoire. Make sure to add, "I hope you'll do that to me again!"

- **Build.** Build it and she will cum, or you will. Build on something she is doing well and take it to the next level. "I love the way you licked my penis. Could you do that to my balls, too? That would be amazing!"

- **Gentle request.** A gentle request is not a command or an order. Some good ways to start one of these are the following: "I would love it if you would . . ." "Do you think you might be willing to try . . . ?" or "It would really turn me on if you . . ."

- **I had a dream.** Sydney Biddle Barrows, known as the Mayflower Madam, recommends telling your partner that you had a dream about trying a certain activity that you want, but are too embarrassed to request directly. She suggests something like this: "Honey, I had this crazy dream that you tied me up and spanked me. That is why I was all over you this morning. There was something really hot about it." See how your partner reacts. If he seems open to it, you may want to suggest trying it in real life.

- **Instead of.** It can be touchy telling your partner to stop doing something that you don't like, especially if he has been doing it for a long time and you haven't said anything. Try the "instead of" technique: "Instead of . . . , I'd love it if you . . ."

- **The moan or groan.** Letting your partner know he is doing something you like with some sexy sounds can be very helpful. This less direct method can be misinterpreted, though, especially when there is more than one thing going on at a time ("Did she like the motions I was doing with my right hand or was it what I did with my left finger that she was responding to?").

- **Helping hand.** Take your partner's hand and guide it where you would like her to touch you. This is even more effective if you can show the amount of pressure, speed, and rhythm you most enjoy.

- **One-word corrections.** Less is more. It is generally better to give feedback postmortem, but if you must do it during the act, stick to one word suggestions like "harder," "higher," or "gentle." Sometimes you need a little more description. Again, keep your words to a minimum, ideally two to three words like "further left," "circular motions," or "don't stop" all work.

- **Gottman ratio.** Remember John Gottman and his magic ratio? (See page 75.) Use it with sex, too. For every bit of negative feedback, try to give five positive ones. This ratio will keep your partner feeling positive, inspired, and appreciated, which we all like in bed.

While giving feedback and asking for what you want are very important, make sure *not* to do the following:

- **Criticize.** Sex makes us sensitive, so be sure you proceed with kindness. Criticism hurts, discourages, and makes people withdraw.
- **Condescend.** Don't talk down to your partner or lecture him. This comes across as condescending and is likely to discourage your partner from trying at all.
- **Be demanding.** Asking for what you want is good but acting entitled is not. Neither are long lists of performance requirements. Make this a collaborative experience.
- **Threaten.** Telling someone that you are going to leave her if she doesn't agree to a certain act, or that you will find someone who will, is totally out of bounds.
- **Compare.** Don't compare your partner's performance to that of your past partners. Most people are not virgins when they come to their adult relationships, but we don't need to be reminded of our partner's previous lovers.
- **Get wordy.** Getting too descriptive, being verbose, or getting into lengthy explanations during sex can be distracting and pull you both out of the moment. Save lectures, charts, and graphs for the next day.
- **Be vague.** Being vague is not going to get results. Comments like "I don't know; just be more passionate," are too general and set your lover up to fail.
- **Get frustrated.** No matter how annoyed or frustrated you get, be patient with your partner. Don't roll your eyes or let out exasperated sighs. Be patient and keep in mind that this is someone who loves you and is trying to please you.

Because asking for what you want is so hard for most people, and because our needs, fantasies, and the things that turn us on change over time, I recommend that couples communicate about sex on a regular basis. Without that kind of ongoing communication, small sexual desires may slip through the cracks or you may be too nervous to express something big that you want to try. As a result, I created a sexual inventory for couples to take together once a year. You can find it in Appendix B. Putting together this inventory gives couples a great opportunity to practice sexual communication skills. I recommend choosing a date, maybe your anniversary, to share your inventory together every year. It is crucial to keep the experience loving, nonjudgmental, and positive.

2. Master Technique

We want sex to be effortless and instinctual. We want to be able to give and receive orgasms without textbooks or instructions. But the truth is that great sex lives are created over time, and take effort and energy. Most people are not born knowing how to perfectly locate a G-spot, understanding what it takes to give a great prostate massage, knowing the best way to deep-throat without gagging, or having any idea what a U-spot is.

NEGLECTED BODY PARTS

To be a great lover you need to know anatomy. You have to be part-gynecologist, part-urologist, part-proctologist, and always very open-minded! Be open and willing to touch, lick, massage, and play with things you have never played with before and to allow your partner to do the same.

- **Anus.** This area of the body is very sensitive because of the high concentration of nerves there and can bring many men and women pleasure through touch or penetration. Not everyone likes to be stimulated in this area, so it important to communicate with your partner about his preferences. There are three things to keep in mind with anal play: (a) This is not a self-lubricating area, so you will need to use lubricant (lots of it!); (b) in order for it to be a pleasurable experience, the sphincter muscles must be relaxed first, which can be accomplished by starting slowly with your fingers; and (c) because the area is so fragile, it can tear easily. Make sure to trim your nails or wear gloves and, keep in mind that anal sex is a high-risk activity when it comes to HIV transmission. Make sure to discuss risks together and take safe-sex precautions.

- **Clitoris.** The clitoris has eight thousand nerve endings, which is double the nerve endings in the glans of a penis. The clitoris is made purely for pleasure and has nothing to do with reproduction. Only about a quarter of the clitoris (including the clitoral head, the hood, and the shaft) is visible to the naked eye. It is actually about four inches (10 cm) in length, three-quarters of which (the urethral sponge, erectile tissue, glands, vestibular bulbs, and the clitoral legs) are not visible. As much as I love Sigmund Freud's work, he was way off base when he claimed that the clitoral orgasm is an "immature orgasm," and the G-spot orgasm is a "mature one." All orgasms are good orgasms and many women enjoy clitoral ones the best.

- **Frenulum.** This is the elastic band of tissue located on the underside of the penis. It is the attachment point for the vernal mucosa and, for most men, it is highly responsive. It looks like a "V" and typically responds well to touch.

- **Grafenberg spot.** Known as the G-spot, this is a small pleasure point usually located a few inches (5–10 cm) deep. It is above the vaginal wall on the belly button side of her body. It is easiest to find using a well-lubricated finger, when a woman is already highly aroused and has emptied her bladder. About two-thirds to a full finger length inside the vaginal canal there is a ridge of slightly rough, engorged tissue. This is the G-spot. For some women, it is the Holy Grail, and for others it hardly responds to stimulation at all. Experiment with different kind of strokes, touch, and pressure to find out where your partner falls on the spectrum.

- **K-point.** I have to admit, I had never even heard of the K-point until reading one of sex guru Lou Paget's books. According to her, the K-point consists of two small bumps, the size of half-grains of rice, on either side of the clitoral hood. In her book, *365 Days of Sensational Sex,* she gives some explicit directions to make good use of this point.

- **Nipples.** Often mistreated, sometimes ignored, both men and women have them. For some people, a nipple is a highly sensitive erogenous zone, but for others, it is not. Many men feel that their nipples get overlooked, because they are not expected to enjoy stimulation in those areas. But men's nipples have the same nerve-packed receptors that women's have, and some men are turned on by a little nipple action.

- **Perineum.** This sensitive area, which is full of nerve endings and spongy erectile tissue, is located between a man's scrotum and anus. It can be found on a woman between the vagina and the anus. This is where the pelvic-floor muscles crisscross one another, making it a big hot spot. Stroking or tickling this area can activate the pudendal nerve, which runs through the pelvic-floor muscles and lets your brain know that you are aroused.

- **Prostate.** The prostate is a small, walnut-sized gland located just beneath a man's bladder. It surrounds the urethra like a doughnut. When a man becomes sexually excited, it swells up with the fluid that makes up semen, sending pleasurable sensations throughout his loins as he nears orgasm. The "P-Spot," as some call it, can be located and stimulated by putting a well-lubricated finger two to three inches (5–8 cm) into a man's anus. Stimulating, massaging, or milking the prostate can result in orgasms that are 33 percent stronger than average, according to some sex experts. Some men even report multiple orgasms and full-body orgasms. According to Christine Fawley of PleasureMechanics.com, "Prostate massage is the hottest trend in male sexuality, as straight men all around the world are waking up to the potential pleasures of anal play and prostate stimulation."

- **Testicles.** Balls tend to be overlooked and neglected, but can bring most men a lot of pleasure. Testicles are more rugged than you might imagine. They get banged around quite a bit during intercourse. But if you flick them with your finger, you might have to peel your lover off the ceiling. Many sex educators recommend focusing on the scrotum, or the pouch that surrounds the balls. Ask for lots of feedback while you experiment with touching, licking, massaging, or caressing this area. Once you have a sense of mastery, try doing these things while touching or sucking other body parts.

- **U-spot.** This is a small patch of sensitive erectile tissue located between the clitoral glans and the vaginal opening. It is the opening where urine exits the body. It's erotic potential is just starting to make news. Sex researchers have found that when this region is gently caressed with a finger, the tongue, or the tip of the penis there is a powerful sexual response. This makes sense, since the urethra is lined on three sides by the body of the clitoris.

As Dr. Patricia Love and Jo Robinson say in their book *Hot Monogamy*, "We want sex to be exciting, romantic, spiritual, mutually pleasurable—fulfilling enough to keep us satisfied and faithful. This more passionate, intimate, and enduring lovemaking requires sophisticated technique." To become a great partner, it takes time to become a sexual expert for your partner.

High-level technique requires study. When you were in school, if you wanted to get an A on a test, you studied for it. To get an A as a lover is no different. Many people have a hard time putting their ego aside to learn about sex and anatomy. "Why should I? I already know how to make my lover climax," you may think to yourself. The answer is this: You can always heighten your partner's pleasure, give better orgasms and learn new things. When it comes to technique, no matter how much you know, it is best to put your ego aside and approach this learning process from a place of openness and humility. Allow yourself to know what you don't know. Have no shame.

So how do you learn advanced techniques? Where do you get the information? Fortunately, in this day and age, we have lots of great resources available to us! A big part of sexual learning is about becoming sexually literate (meaning learning about it, reading about it, and becoming fluent in talking about sex). Here are some terrific resources:

- **Books, magazines, and blogs.** Books are among the best resources you can find on sexual technique. They give you access to experts, whom you might never meet, and you can download or order their books discreetly by mail. These books often include pictures, diagrams, and instructions that are invaluable. Magazines (from *Cosmo* to *Men's Health* to *Hustler*), either in print or online, may be great resources as well. Blogs can also be terrific resources, as long as you are not getting misinformation. Also, if discretion is not an issue, following experts on social media can give you the latest information, from sex toy reviews to book recommendations to techniques.

- **Videos.** Instructional videos can be extremely helpful. Sometimes it is easier to understand a technique that is being demonstrated, rather than reading about it. It just might turn you on, too! These kinds of videos vary in terms of nudity. Some don't show real people engaging in sex, offering clinical illustrations or animation instead. I do not recommend pornography as a way to learn about sex. While it can be fun and exciting to watch, pornography generally presents sexual fantasies, usually from the male director's perspective, and does not provide you with realistic learning tools.

- **Practice.** Yes, practice makes perfect! I recommend that couples take time away from their fail-safe techniques to experiment with new techniques. It can be scary to step out of your sexual comfort zone to try something new. Make a commitment to each other to be open-minded, nonjudgmental—and to kid with each other. Have fun with whatever happens!

- **Classes or seminars.** Yes, there are adult classes! You can take a sexual technique class in person or online. Classes are offered for individuals or couples. Adult stores, places like the Learning Annex, or sexpert seminars are great places to learn. These classes vary widely in terms of nudity, participation, and touching, so make sure you are clear on what you are getting into before you go.

- **Private instruction.** Many experts offer in-home instruction. For example, one of my favorites is author and sex expert Lou Paget, who is well-known in the Los Angeles area for oral

and manual sex instruction. There is no nudity whatsoever—
everything is demonstrated on a brand-new toy that is given to
everyone who takes the class. Paget answers questions, teaches
amazing techniques, and helps ease people's sexual anxieties.
She also offers group classes.

- **Podcasts.** Podcasts can give you all kinds of valuable
  information. Some of them include interviews with authors,
  porn stars, sex workers, doctors, and other experts. You can get
  a lot of information from multiple sources in one podcast.

- **Sex stores.** Sex stores are sex education heaven. If you are
  courageous enough to ask questions, the salespeople are usually
  well-versed in the most popular toys, classes, videos, lubricants,
  trends, and tricks, and they give great advice. The people who
  work in these stores have heard everything, and tend to be very
  sex-positive and nonjudgmental.

- **Sex therapists.** Find your own personal Dr. Ruth. You don't
  have to have a sex problem or dysfunction to have a consultation
  with a sex therapist and get some questions answered. Just make
  sure you are meeting with a qualified, licensed professional.
  A therapist should never be sexual with you. He or she should
  never touch you, come on to you, or take off his or her clothes—
  or yours. That is a violation of the therapist-client relationship,
  and should be reported to the licensing board immediately.

I recommend that couples set sex education goals every year. One
couple I worked with agreed to read two new sex books, watch one
instructional video, and try two new sex toys a year, which kept things
new and interesting for them. These goals were not too overwhelming
and gave them an opportunity to stretch. Make sure that whatever
goals you set as a couple are in line with both of your boundaries. For

example, don't set a goal to go to a group class if privacy is important for one of you. And, of course, make sure to share information and what you learned—not only about new techniques, but about what turns you on—with your partner.

3. Know Your Partner Well

You can have the greatest technique on the planet, but unless you tune in to your partner and become an expert in his particular arousal patterns and preferences, you will not be a great lover. Everybody—and every body—is different.

Most people make assumptions about what their partners like, based on what their previous partners liked, what they think men and women like in general, and what they prefer themselves. But tuning in to your partner is a whole different thing.

It's easy to become so absorbed by your own excitement that you forget about your partner's state. But refining the skill of honing in on your partner's reactions has great payoffs. Remaining attentive and focused on your partner's pleasure will make you a more skilled lover than someone who may have learned more moves but can't read his lover well. Ideally, you will develop both skill sets.

This is another area where it is advisable to become an expert on your partner. Learn what makes him tick, both physically and emotionally. Know what makes him relax, what words and phrases turn him on, what power dynamics get him hot, what his fantasies are, and use all this knowledge to please him. When you understand, without judgment, what turns your lover on, you can work from this starting point and get really creative. Know his body—every inch of it. Where is he the most sensitive? Does he like to have his nipples touched? Where does he most like to be kissed? With what speed, rhythm, and pressure does he like to be stroked? Be detail-oriented.

Where is she the most sensitive? Does she like to have her earlobe nibbled? What are her favorite sexual fantasies?

There are many ways to figure these things out. Here are a few of them:

- **Heart rate.** Try putting your head on your lover's chest while exploring his body with your hands. Listen to his heart rate. Notice what makes it speed up or slow down.
- **Breathing.** Listen closely to her breathing patterns. What make her breathing speed up, slow down, and become shallower?
- **Questions.** This is no time to be shy! Ask lots of questions about preferences. Many people are too shy to volunteer but, when asked, most are happy to share information. Your job is to gather those details and become an expert in your partner's sexual reactions.
- **Responses.** Focus closely on bodily responses. What words, touch, or activities make him hard or make her wet? Pay close attention.
- **Trial and error.** Have fun together experimenting and exploring each other's bodies. Try different things. Not everything you try is going to be a home run, but you need to find out what you both don't like to figure out what you do like. Have fun with it!
- **Focus.** Be present in the here and now. If you find your mind wandering (the problem at work can wait, so can the kids and the dishes), bring your focus back to the moment. Stay completely focused on your partner and your experience.
- **Postgame analysis.** Most people are too vulnerable right after sex to talk about it, so it is better to have a chat the next day. Ask, "What worked?" "What would you like me to do differently?" "Was there anything you really didn't like?" "What would you like me to add to the repertoire?"

4. Own It

Know your sexual self. You can't have great sex if you don't know what you enjoy. I can't tell you how many times I've received calls on my radio show from people, usually women, who are not satisfied in bed, and want their partner to magically know what they want, when they themselves don't know. My friend Taylor Strecker, host of the radio show *Wake Up! with Taylor*, did a great interview with sex expert Dr. Ruth Westheimer. During the interview Dr. Ruth said that women are responsible for their own orgasms and for telling their partners how to give them what they need to have them.

Masturbation is the key to knowing what you like, what your body responds to, and what will get you off. If you know what it takes to accomplish this alone, then you and your partner can create ideal circumstances in the bedroom together. Too many people have grown up in homes where they were taught that self-pleasure is distasteful, unacceptable, or, worse, sinful. One male client I worked with was so ashamed about it that he wouldn't touch himself. He mistakenly believed that not only was it shameful, but it was something that teenage boys did only because they couldn't get the real thing. That is not true. Masturbation is an important part of adult sexuality, regardless of your gender or how much sex you are getting with your partner.

I encourage partners to masturbate in front of each other. This serves many purposes.

- **Everyone has her own way to get off by herself.** If your lover is able to see the nuances of what you do and what works for you, he will be able to do some of the same handiwork.
- **Many people are turned on by watching their partners get off by themselves.** Adding this activity to your repertoire only expands your horizons.

235

- **It allows you to both explore your voyeuristic/exhibitionist tendencies.**
- **It shows your partner what you are into.**
- **It builds trust and intimacy.**
- **It opens new doors.** If you can do it while your partner is watching you, you can do it during intercourse, during phone sex, on video chat, and in other fun situations.

To ensure that this experience is a positive one, make sure that you commit to creating a safe, supportive, loving atmosphere. Take turns being the performer and the watcher. Save comments and feedback for the next day and keep it positive. Because of cultural taboos surrounding women and sexuality, many women feel that masturbating is shameful. It is important to be sensitive to this. Masturbation is a great way to learn about, and understand, the connections between our minds and bodies.

Studies show that women are less aware of their own sexual responses than men are. In a study done by sex researcher Meredith Chivers, women wore a plethysmograph, a miniature bulb, and a light sensor that measures blood flow to the vagina, as well as vaginal wetness, while watching ninety seconds of various types of erotic movies (between each clip they watched a video that sent the plethysmograph's reading back to a baseline). Regardless of sexual orientation, gay or straight, the women's self-reports of what turned them on totally conflicted with their physiological reactions. Their minds were not in sync with their bodies.

The researchers came up with several hypotheses to account for this disparity. One theory was that men tend to have more of an awareness of their physiological arousal because their penis is on the outside, and when men are aroused, the penis presses against clothing, creating a feedback loop between sexual arousal and awareness. Another theory is that women consciously or unconsciously diminish or block what excites them. But why? Many believe that society makes women feel ashamed of their sexuality and the things that arouse them.

But there are men who don't know what they like in bed, either. Some are ashamed to admit what they would like because they think it is not masculine or have misconceptions about sex acts and sexual orientation. Some fear their own dark side and worry that if they get in touch with their fantasies or desires they will be considered deviant. Others have experienced sexual abuse and have not worked through that trauma. Regardless of the reasons, it is important to do the work to move past them. Therapy can be very helpful here.

It is important to own your own desires and be in touch with your most animalistic urges. It is from this intensity that passion grows. Allow yourself to approach sex with enthusiasm and pleasure. Make friends with your sexual self.

Our sexual desires, preferences, and fantasies are not politically correct. When we love someone, we feel a sense of responsibility to nurture and protect that person, to treat him with kindness and care. But, oftentimes, great sex is not about that. It is raw, intense, and overpowering. It plays with power.

Psychotherapist Esther Perel describes this struggle exceptionally well in her book *Mating in Captivity*. She says, "The poetics of sex . . . are often politically incorrect, thriving on power plays, role reversals, unfair advantages, imperious demands, seductive manipulations, and subtle cruelties. American men and women, shaped by the feminist movement and its egalitarian ideals, often find themselves challenged by these contradictions. We fear that playing with power imbalances in the sexual arena, even in a consensual relationship between mature adults, risks overthrowing the respect that is essential to human relationships."

"I can't do that to my wife!" . . . "If my husband knew what I really wanted, he would never think of me the same way again!" These are things I have heard many of my clients say. It is scary to share that primitive, lustful part of ourselves with someone we are so invested in loving and approving of us. But who better to cut loose with? We have to learn to objectify each other sometimes.

As clinical psychologist David Schnarch points out in his classic book *Passionate Marriage*, "Women don't want to be used poorly—but many love to be used well. They want to be the object of their partner's carnality—but they want it to be personal!" The difference between "I'm so horny, I want to do you!" and "I'm so hot for you, I want to do you!" is huge. The first statement makes the partner interchangeable with anyone and the second makes her feel desired and sexually objectified in a good way.

A study published in *Archives of Sexual Behavior: The Official Publication of the International Academy of Sex Research*, found that, in the right circumstance, women like being sexually objectified. The right circumstance is being with a highly committed partner. The study found that being sexually valued by a highly committed sexual partner positively influenced women's relationship satisfaction.

What we want and how we want it often contradict the way we see ourselves and our ideological beliefs. What turns us on may offend our sense of self and run counter to our philosophical beliefs. But to have great sex we have to make peace with every facet of who we are. This does not mean engaging in nonconsensual sex, infidelities, or acting out our every fantasy; it means that we should allow the things that turn us on to turn us on, judgment-free. Great sex over the long term means owning our fantasies, desires, and preferences and finding ways to incorporate them safely into a rich sex life with a loving partner.

5. Vary Your Moves

As the story goes, President Calvin Coolidge and his wife, Grace Coolidge, were getting separate tours of an experimental government farm, when the First Lady noticed a rooster that was mating frequently and asked how often it happened. The farmer told her, "dozens of times each day," to which she responded, "Tell that to the president when he comes by." When this information was shared with him he asked, "Same hen every time?" The farmer responded, "Oh, no, Mr. President, a different hen every time." The president then replied, "Tell that to Mrs. Coolidge." Thus, the Coolidge Effect was born, the concept that novelty, or new sexual partners, has an invigorating effect on sexual desire. This effect has been shown to be particularly significant for men. There is a lot of literature showing that females have significant responses to sexual novelty as well.

It is impossible to keep up the level of sexual excitement that we start out with in the beginning of a relationship. If we did, nobody would ever accomplish anything. The crazy mix of phenylethylamine, or PEA (which causes feelings of elation, exhilaration, and euphoria), dopamine (which creates increased energy, a rush of pleasure, focused attention on the new love), norepinephrine (which prompts the adrenalin rush, gets the heart racing, and creates focused attention on the love object), and lower levels of serotonin (which help create that obsessive quality that we have in the beginning of a relationship) make the early stages a hot and heavy ride. Many researchers have compared the effect of the combination of those chemicals that occur in early infatuation to cocaine addiction or obsessive-compulsive disorder. Brain scans support this concept.

Our brains are not made to stay in a heightened state over the long term. Evolutionary psychologists and anthropologists estimate that the biology of infatuation can only last eighteen months to three years.

According to Dr. Michael Liebowitz of the New York Psychiatric Institute, "If you want a situation where you and your long-term partner can still get very excited about each other, you will have to work on it, because in some ways you are bucking a biological tide."

So here is the good news: It can be done! I am a big believer in monogamy. I do not recommend bringing third parties into a relationship, infidelities, or open relationships (more about all of these later). I believe that conscious couples who invest in themselves and their relationship can have incredible sex lives for many decades.

Too many couples figure out the moves that work for each other and then stick to them for years on end. Their sex life totally lacks variety. As a client of mine once complained, "He touches me in the same order for about seven minutes, I touch him in the same order for about five, he puts it in, and then we go for about ten. Then it's over. We both get there, but it just isn't very exciting." It is great when couples know what each other likes, but to maintain passion, we have to continually expand the intimate and erotic boundaries of the relationship.

SEXUALLY SATISFIED COUPLES

A recent study, called "What Keeps Passion Alive? Sexual Satisfaction Is Associated with Sexual Communication, Mood Setting, Sexual Variety, Oral Sex, Orgasm, and Sexual Frequency in a National U.S. Study," examined 38,747 married or cohabitating heterosexual couples (the same researchers are currently re-creating the study with same-sex couples), many of whom had been together for two decades or more. Of the subjects, 32 percent reported that their sex lives were just as passionate now as they had

IGNITE YOUR SEX LIFE

been in the first six months of their relationships. When researchers looked at the sexually satisfied long-term couples, they found some significant trends, which you can incorporate into your own relationship. The sexually satisfied couples were more likely to have done the following:

- Given and received more oral sex
- Had more consistent orgasms
- Incorporated more variety into their sexual repertoire
- Explored sexual fantasies together by talking about them or acting them out
- Set the mood for sex with soft lighting, candles, music, and the like
- Practiced effective sexual communication
- Read self-help books and articles and tried new ideas
- Engaged in more intimate behaviors, such as cuddling, kissing, and laughing together during sex
- Said "I love you" during their last sexual encounter
- Used text messaging to send a sexual or teasing text
- Described their last sexual encounter as "passionate," "loving and tender," or "playful"
- Had sexual encounters that lasted more than thirty minutes.
- Tried new sex positions
- Worn sexy lingerie
- Taken a bath or shower together
- Given or received a massage
- Gone on a romantic getaway
- Tried anal stimulation
- Made a date night to have sex
- Used a sex toy together

It is important to develop a broad menu of sexual options that you, as a couple, are constantly expanding. Stepping outside your sexual comfort zone has huge benefits. Understand that I am not talking about doing something that is morally offensive to you, threatening to your relationship, or traumatizing. I am, however, talking about shaking things up. You need to strike a balance. Keep in mind what authors Dr. Patricia Love and Jo Robinson say in their book *Hot Monogamy: How to Achieve a More Intimate Relationship with Your Partner*: "There is often a fine line between what turns you on and what you avoid. Your most passionate experiences may lie just outside your comfort zone."

In the study of long-term sexual satisfaction among couples, mentioned above, researchers found that the single most significant predictor of long-term satisfaction is willingness to try new things. Interestingly, about half the couples studied—both satisfied and dissatisfied couples—read sexual self-help literature, but, according to lead researcher David Frederick, "What set sexually satisfied couples apart was that they actually tried some of the ideas." So hop to it!

Here are some suggestions to add variety to your sexual repertoire:

- **Try new positions.** Pick up a book or download a sexual position app and try something new! Take turns picking new positions. This is an especially good starting point for more conservative couples.
- **New touch.** Challenge yourself to touch your partner in a new way every time you have sexual contact. Experiment with different pressures, using different parts of your hands or nails, props, different combinations of touch, or using saliva or lubricant in places you haven't touched before. Instead of making a straight line, try a less predictable zigzag.

- **Have fun with lingerie.** A survey of a thousand men who were asked what turned them on the most—dirty talk, porn, female masturbation, sexy lingerie, or "other"—92 percent said they were most turned on by sexy lingerie. Seventy-three percent of those men also reported that they relied on this kind of stimulation to keep them interested in a long-term relationship. While it is important to know what kind of lingerie your partner likes and use it to your advantage, this is also an opportunity for you to get turned on yourself. I wait for the best Victoria's Secret coupons to come out and keep a basket of special goodies for Eric. Nothing graduates out of the basket and into the drawer until it has had a successful run in the bedroom. This is a fun, easy way to add novelty to our sex life. When I walk out of the closet, he never knows what he is going to see next.

- **New techniques.** Spice things up with new techniques. Try "Ode to Bryan" (*365 Days of Sensational Sex*), the "Come-Hither" (*She Comes First*), the "Butterfly Flick" (*The Sensual Woman*), the "Princeton Belly Rub" (*Sex Tips for Straight Women from a Gay Man*), or the "Pearl Necklace" (*How to Be a Great Lover*). Try the "Sexhalation Method" (*How to Bottom Like a Porn Star: The Ultimate Guide to Gay Sex*) and the "Classy Chassis" (*Lesbian Sex Positions: 100 Passionate Positions from Intimate and Sensual to Wild and Naughty*). The more you both know and are willing to try, the more fun you can have together! Some techniques will be terrible failures and others will be home runs. Have fun experimenting together and keep it light.

- **Experiment with fantasy.** Pick up a book by Nancy Friday, a best-selling author who is known for her collections of sexual fantasies. Each story is about one to three pages long. Her books are like going to a sexual buffet. The variety is great. You will read things that you hate or love, and that will shock, arouse, or disturb you. You may be surprised by some of the things that turn you on.

- **Location, location, location.** Doing the same thing in the same place can get stale. Take it outside of the bedroom. Try a different room in the house, go outside, and get adventurous. Just be careful! I once had a friend, a well-known child star, who, as an adult, was driving cross-country with her boyfriend and decided to give him head. Apparently, she did such a good job that his driving became a bit erratic and they got pulled over. When she looked up at the police officer, he said, "Aren't you the little girl from that show?" They didn't get a ticket, but she was mortified! Have fun! Be a little risqué! But if you get arrested, don't call me!

- **Role-play.** Role-playing gives you the opportunity to play a game of seduction in which you and your partner enact different characters. This can be anything from being a different person in bed to putting on an elaborate act—dressing up and taking the show on the road, so to speak. A great example of that was Samantha Jones and her actor boyfriend, Smith Jerrod, in the television show *Sex and the City*. The two would meet up and pretend they were different characters (the agent and "secret service slut," the doctor and patient) or dress up at home (the housewife and burglar). When you are playing a character, it may help you overcome inhibitions because you can always blame it on the character.

- **Toys.** In the olden days, all we had were vibrators and dildos. Men were left out of the mix entirely. Fortunately, we are in a new era! There are great sex toys for men like the male masterbators, guybrators, cock rings, penis sleeves, vibrating nipple clamps, and prostate massagers. Women have so many new options like clitoral vibrators, g-spot vibrators, rabbits, personal massagers, bullet vibrators, dildos, and ben wa balls, to name a few. Toys for couples have exploded, especially teledonics (electronic toys that can be controlled on a phone), remote-controlled vibrators, and wearable vibrators that both people can enjoy at the same time.

• **Style.** It is important for lovers to know how to vary their style. I believe everyone should know how to make love, have sex, fuck, and everything in-between! Sometimes people think it is not okay to try certain styles with the person they love. Move past that.

Explore it all! As long as both partners are game, it's worth a shot.

Many people are afraid to experiment because they don't want to take a risk. They are fearful of looking silly or incompetent. I encourage you to take a different approach. We are all students. We must put our egos aside and practice humility to become the great lover our partner deserves.

6. Cultivate the Art of Seduction

The French philosopher Voltaire said, "It's not enough to conquer, one must know how to seduce." Some couples think that seduction is too much work once they are in a committed relationship and have moved in together or are married. They think it is unnecessary or unimportant. But the reverse is actually true. The deeper you go into a relationship, the more important seduction becomes. As Esther Perel points out, "There's an assumption . . . that we need only to pursue what we don't yet possess. The trick is that in order to keep our partner erotically engaged we have to become more seductive, not less."

When we are in the courting stage, we take the time to plan exciting creative dates, wear sexy lingerie, cook gourmet meals, buy flowers, light candles, buy thoughtful gifts, plan romantic getaways, give massages, flirt, wear sexy outfits, write personal cards, and send suggestive text messages. We pay attention to detail. We show our partner that we are invested in him and the relationship with our time, energy, resources, and focused attention. During the honeymoon phase we are constantly paying attention to him and demonstrating that we care. Too often, long-term couples stop doing that. At some point the neurological chemical honeymoon comes to an end, but seduction never has to stop.

Take time for seduction. First, carve out time for it in your day-to-day life. Make seduction a priority. Parenting, your favorite TV programs, work, friends, hobbies, and the like can eat up your romantic time together if you let them. If you don't create boundaries and protect your erotic space, it disappears. Second, recognize that seduction itself is a process. It is a layered process, both psychologically and physically, that is meant to be savored, not rushed.

The professionals understand this. They create suspense. As former madam Sydney Biddle Barrows points out, "A call girl usually doesn't initiate sex. She is charging by the hour, she's motivated to keep her clients with her as long as possible, and sex usually signifies the end of the evening." If she does her job right, not only will the evening last a long time, she will also have repeat customers. This extended time serves multiple purposes. The client feels tended to and doted on, as if the call girl cares to spend time with him. We all want that. Seduction requires emotional foreplay to be effective.

Great seduction typically involves what I call the four A's:

- **Appreciation.** This can occur on many levels. We show appreciation for what our partner is bringing to the table.

Who doesn't want to be appreciated physically, emotionally, intellectually, and sexually? Acknowledgment of our strengths, personality, physical attributes, and sexiness makes us ripe for the picking (or licking!). Feeling desired is an important part of this. It is hot to be wanted and lusted after.

- **Attention.** We are all hungry for focused attention. The focused gaze is a powerful thing. As I mentioned in step 1, on page 220, the person who expresses interest and a desire to get into our mind and understand us is incredibly provocative. Remembering the details of the other person's life demonstrates care and investment in the relationship. Thoughtful gifts, regardless of the amount spent, are an extension of this attention. They are designed to please your partner and show the time and attention you are paying to him.

- **Acceptance.** A big part of seduction is creating an atmosphere that affirms the other person enough so she can lower her guard and cut loose. Acceptance is about giving the go-ahead to share desires, animal urges, and passions. Deep down we all want permission to cut loose and be accepted or, better yet, embraced, for our lust. Seducers understand the power of that moment of surrender. As relationship writer Eric Charles points out in his article "Ask a Guy: Exactly How to Turn a Guy On (How to Seduce a Guy, Part 2)," ". . . a lot of psychological seduction is affirming to the other person—it makes him feel good, validated, safe-to-explore, accepted, wanted, appreciated, etc. Men in our society are starved for these feelings, and you can use that to your massive advantage." The truth is, women are just as starved for this kind of acceptance and affirmation.

- **Aesthetic.** Seducers provide pleasure. Part of that pleasure is visual. Often the eyes are the first body part involved in a seduction. We look at our partner prior to having the opportunity to touch, speak to, or taste her. Being visually appealing to our partner—knowing his preferences with regard to our hairstyle, clothes, undergarments, makeup, and the like and reflecting those preferences—is an important part of the seduction process. Flashing a bicep, showing a little cleavage, or modeling how well that new suit fits you—these are all part of seduction. You don't have to be a supermodel—male or female—to make yourself into eye candy. It is, however, important to be the healthiest, hottest version of you that you can be.

As Eric Charles points out, the mechanics of seduction occur on three planes.

- **Physical.** These are the things you do with your body: touching your partner, dressing in a sexy way, showing skin, making physical contact during conversation, sprucing up your makeup, doing your hair in a special way, and making the tone of your voice particularly appealing.
- **Behavioral.** These are the actions you take, including being carefree with regard to sex; showing interest with physical gestures, facial expressions, and body language; flashing skin; casting seductive looks (what evolutionary anthropologists call the "copulatory gaze"), making sexy sounds, texting suggestive messages, sharing pictures, how you take off your clothes, and, of course, overtly sexual behavior.
- **Psychological.** These are the mental and emotional strategies you use in your interactions with your partner, such as sexual innuendo, drawing out your partner's preferences, getting him to express desires, talking dirty, expressing your arousal, talking

about how good in bed your partner is, and describing what you like in bed.

If you do a Google search about how to seduce your partner, you will be bombarded with suggestions ranging from the ridiculous to the absurd. Instead of giving you specific suggestions that may not fit with your style or personality, I offer you some broad conceptual suggestions, so you can come up with your own specific techniques:

- **Keep your focus on your partner.** Seducers are not self-absorbed. Their concentration is on the other person. They get inside the other person's mind and skin.
- **Know yourself.** Know what is seductive about you. Know your own strengths and weaknesses. Seduction comes from within the seducer. It is an inside job. The things that turn us on most make us attractive to others.
- **Provide pleasure.** Seducers are providers of pleasure and they understand, on a core level, that people are waiting for pleasure. They never get enough of it. Your job in seduction is to penetrate your partner's defenses and cause her to surrender to pleasure.
- **Be unpredictable.** Create suspense. If your partner finds himself thinking, "What is she up to now?" or "What is she going to do next?" you are on the right track. As Esther Perel points out, familiarity is the enemy of seduction. Knowing the outcome of the seduction lessens the tension. She says, ". . . eroticism thrives on the unpredictable. Desire butts heads with habit and repetition." Shake things up.
- **Stay in your lane.** Pat Allen and Sandra Harmon, authors of *Getting to "I Do,"* talk a lot about masculine and feminine energy. They say that, regardless of gender and sexual orientation,

we all have masculine and feminine energy. Masculine energy is protective, provides leadership and security, and is giving. Feminine energy is focused on listening, feelings, and sensuality, and is receptive. They point out that there must be a masculine energy person and a feminine energy person in every relationship for it to work. A man may *embody* the feminine energy and a woman may *embody* the masculine energy or vice versa. Whatever your role in your relationship, revel in it. Use it to your seductive advantage. Your partner will find this attractive and seductive.

- **Play the mental game.** Seduction is a game of psychology. Regardless of gender, you probably thought your power was between your legs. But the truth is, there's greater power between your ears. Seduction requires knowing what the other person is missing and providing it. Use what you know about your partner to practice seduction.

- **Communicate on all levels.** Utilize all the strategies—physical, behavioral, psychological—to seduce. Send your message of seduction with words, actions, and body language.

- **Give permission.** We all have our sexual hang-ups and anxieties. We worry about what our partner will think of us if we really let ourselves go. This is particularly common among women. According to erotic filmmaker Candida Royalle, "Most women need permission to express themselves sexually and allow themselves pleasure." The seducer must clearly welcome sexual expression.

- **Use your words.** Use language to express your sexual desires. We all love to be told what someone wants to do to us and how irresistible we are. Verbalizing your desires forces you to own them and puts you in charge of the sexual situation.

- **Touch.** As I mentioned in my last book, *SuperBaby: 12 Ways to Give Your Child a Head Start in the First 3 Years*, we are born with 320 touch receptors per square inch (6.5 cm2), totaling approximately five million altogether. There are over 100 different types of receptors that allow human beings to respond to different types of touch, such as pain, pressure, temperature, and vibration. As Tiffany Field, director of the Touch Research Institute aptly puts it, "because skin cannot shut its eyes or cover its ears, it is in a constant state of readiness to receive messages—it is always on." Take advantage of that state of readiness with your partner.

- **Be in the moment.** When we are able to set aside all our distracting thoughts, anxieties, and concerns, we are better able to tune in to our partner and proceed with seduction. Really being in the moment and giving our partner our total focus is seductive in and of itself, not to mention the benefits we get, such as picking up on subtleties that we might not otherwise notice.

- **Keep your ego in check.** It is important for us to practice seduction for the right reasons. When we are seductive to get validation, because we feel insecure or unattractive, and want to feel better about ourselves, it taints the interaction. It can also hurt our self-esteem when things don't go as we hoped. Your sense of self should never be attached to the outcome of a seduction.

- **Use evolutionary psychology.** Studies of human seduction have taught us a few things. We know that looking directly into your lover's eyes will create a shot of adrenaline that creates excitement. Your amygdala, the part of the brain that processes emotion, lights up with activity, and produces dopamine, a "feel-good" neurotransmitter associated with passion, and oxytocin, which promotes bonding. If you can get your lover to gaze back, he's likely to experience the same reactions. A smile goes a long way, too. Studies reveal that the "open smile," where the lips are completely drawn back showing both upper and lower teeth, is effective at signaling interest. Body synchrony, where couples start to move in tandem and mirror each other's movements, is a common part of the courting and seduction process. As we are drawn to the other person, we start to keep a common rhythm.

7. Make Space for Sex

Create a life that includes sensual time together. Set limits on the outside world—technology, children, in-laws, houseguests, friends, work, household chores, and the like—to protect your erotic space together. Make sex a priority. If you don't, it will disappear. And when it does, your relationship will be in jeopardy.

One of the greatest challenges to a romantic life is parenthood. It is ironic that children, usually conceived from sex, are the biggest killers of sex. Lack of sleep, privacy concerns, hormones, and new roles as parents, throw water on the flames of desire. When you add in the overall stress of caring for children, the division of resources, parenting conflicts that inevitably come up, and resentments over who is doing what, it's amazing that parents ever have sex at all. As kids get older and more independent, their homework, extracurricular activities, late hours, and visiting friends close in on a couple's ability to have intimate time together.

Lack of boundaries with kids is one of the biggest sex killers. I will never forget a conversation I had with my friend Suzanne. Out of exhaustion, not philosophical beliefs, she had allowed her daughter to sleep in bed with her and her husband. Every time they tried to get the little girl to sleep in her own bed, she cried. They couldn't handle the tears so they let her stay. Five years later, when they were trying to conceive a second child, she confessed to me, "We're having sex in the bathroom because we don't have our bed to ourselves." This is a perfect example of not making the marital bed a sanctuary for adults, as it should be. Adults need that alone time not only for sex, but also for connection and private conversations.

As much as I like many of the philosophies of attachment parenting, I am not a fan of the "family bed." It sends the wrong messages to a child: that the world is not safe enough for him to be alone in his bedroom; that he cannot handle being separate from his parents; that his crying will determine parenting choices; and that his parents' intimate relationship is not a high priority. If you are not sure how to get your child out of your bed, I recommend reading Jill Spivack and Jennifer Waldburger's book *The Sleepeasy Solution: The Exhausted Parent's Guide to Getting Your Child to Sleep from Birth to Age 5*. They present a very gentle and humane approach to sleep training that is also highly effective.

Here are some other tips for making space for sex:

- **Send a message to your children that your relationship is a priority.** Make it clear to the kids that you are not to be disturbed during "adult time." Put a lock on your door and use it, even if you are not having sex during that time. None of us have great sex when we are worried that a kid is going to barge into the room! Have a regular date night so your kids see that you work to keep your relationship romantic and connected. All parents should have three babysitters they trust on speed dial.

- **Create bedroom boundaries.** Don't do work in the bedroom. Let that be your romantic space. Get the computer, office files, and work stuff out of the room. Every time you look at them you are going to feel as if there is something else you should be doing instead of connecting with your partner. The same goes for household chores. Don't keep piles of laundry to be folded, newspapers that have to be recycled, or cleaning products in your bedroom. These reminders of unfinished chores sap sexual energy. Kid stuff does not belong in your room, either. From diapers to dolls to comic books, all these belong in your child's room. Your bedroom is your sacred space.
- **Restrict technology in your bedroom.** Limit any TV and movie watching you do there. Have some social media blackout time that you spend focused on each other. Do any necessary work in a different room, and try to avoid taking work calls in the bedroom.

Making space for connection, private time, and sex is the only way it will happen. If you don't make the time, effort, and room for that connected time in a long-term relationship, your sex life will shrivel up. As Esther Perel says, "Committed sex is intentional sex." Plan it, schedule it, make room for it, and make it happen.

8. Keep Up Your Libido

I get a lot of calls on my radio show from both men and women who are frustrated by a diminished libido. Sometimes they are resigned to the belief that because they have been married for many years, are a certain age, or have kids, they won't want sex any more. Other times, the call comes from someone younger, who recognizes that something is wrong, but isn't sure what to do. Neither of these kinds of callers has to suffer. It doesn't have to be that way. We can have great sex throughout our lives. As a matter of fact, a Baylor University study found that couples who have been married for half a century have an increase in sexual activity.

The great thing about libido issues is that there is a lot you can do to turn them around. After decades of clinical experience, here is what I have found to be most effective:

- **Go to the doctor.** You always want to rule out medical problems first. Get a physical and have your hormone levels checked. A thirty-something couple once came into my office after a decade of struggles due to the husband's low libido. This was a young, attractive couple. After listening to them, I suggested that he get his hormone levels tested, because I was concerned that his testosterone levels might be low. His wife had been begging him to go for years. When he finally went to the doctor, he found out that his levels were very low. The doctor prescribed testosterone shots and his libido came back. But years of sexual rejection had injured his wife and his marriage. She had suffered needlessly for ten years and now she was, understandably, resentful.

Research suggests that one in four men over the age of thirty has low testosterone, but only one in twenty will exhibit clinical symptoms. Over the last decade, I have noticed a huge increase in young men with low testosterone in my practice.

- **Look at your meds.** What medications are you taking? Some, such as birth control pills, antidepressants, antihistamines, blood pressure medication, hair growth medication, medical marijuana, anti-seizure drugs, opioid painkillers, medication to treat enlarged prostates, beta blockers, benzodiazepines, and cholesterol-lowering medications (like statins and fibrates) can all *reduce* libido. Sometimes a simple change in medication can solve the problem. Just because you have side effects from one birth control pill doesn't mean you are going to have them with another prescription.

- **Go back to basics.** When I asked Sally, a working mom of four, what she did to get ready for dates when she and her husband first met, she gave me a long list: She got her nails done, had a bikini wax, shaved her legs, wore sexy matching bras and panties, and picked out special, provocative outfits. She would fantasize about their last sexual encounter and anticipate their next one. She would get excited thinking about some new sexual position she wanted to try with him. In her preparation for their dates, she was getting herself turned on. She thought it was all about being a great girlfriend, but the secondary gain was that all that date prep got her own juices flowing. When I asked her how much of that she was currently doing, she honestly responded, "None." She admitted she had let it all go because it didn't seem as important as her kids, she was wearing granny panties and sweats to bed, and she hadn't shaved or waxed in months. Who feels sexy in that state?

- **Get yourself in the mood.** Read sexy books, take time to fantasize, and watch movies or porn that gets you hot. The romance novel genre is a $1.5 billion a year business, with 91 percent of purchases by women. As I write this, the erotic romance series *Fifty Shades of Grey* has surpassed 100 million in copies sold. Readers reap many benefits. A study came out recently that reported that erotic novel readers have sex 74 percent more frequently and are more satisfied with sex than their non–erotica reading counterparts.

A few years ago I got a call on my radio show from a woman who just wasn't feeling much desire. She would get into bed next to her husband and feel as if her sexual light switch had been turned off. I gave her an assignment: Read one story a night from Nancy Friday's collections of women's sexual fantasies. She agreed and promised to call me back in a week to let me know how the experiment was going. She called me a week later to report that she was so turned on that she was waking her husband up in the middle of the night to have sex! Her light switch was on again!

- **Stop Spectatoring**. Spectatoring is a term coined by Masters and Johnson. It is the process of being overly self-aware or hyper-conscious of your partner during sex. This is usually in the form of distracting thoughts, self-consciousness, or critical internal dialogue instead of focusing on your own or your partner's sensations. Spectatoring takes you out of the sexual experience and creates anxiety, fear, and sexual dysfunction. It is a libido killer. Research shows that women who engage in spectator sex are less satisfied, have fewer real orgasms, and fake more orgasms.

In order to break the habit, you have to practice mindfulness. This means quieting the destructive and distracting voices in your head and being totally in the moment. Completely immerse yourself in the feelings and sensations. Pay attention to what gives you pleasure or arouses you the most. Focus on what is feels like to be in your body, not what if looks like to look at your body. Worrying about your body will destroy sexual desire.

- **Have sex.** Have it with your partner. Have it with yourself. I know, when you're not feeling it, the last thing you want to do is have sex. But here's the thing: Sex begets sex. The more you have, the more you want. Both men and women have testosterone. When you don't have sex for a while, your testosterone levels drop. Since testosterone is a big contributor to sex drive, your level of desire goes down. Set a sex goal for yourself. Try making a commitment to have sex twice a week (at least once with your partner, as opposed to solo) for a month and see how you feel.

9. Get Healthy

Being or becoming sexually fit is a multidimensional process. You go to the gym (hopefully!) to train your body, so why wouldn't you do as much for your sex life? Keeping yourself in the best shape possible, in terms of weight, fitness, grooming, sexual health, and lifestyle choices, has a significant impact on your partner and your sex life.

We have a fantasy that our partner is supposed to love us and be attracted to us no matter what. But when we make a commitment to be someone's only sexual partner, we should also make a commitment to be healthy and to take care of ourselves. Getting complacent is unacceptable.

The best example of this is a call I got on my radio show, a few years ago, from a woman named Molly, who was very upset because her husband had not been interested in having sex with her for about a year. I asked if she knew what accounted for the change. She said she had put on a few pounds and that he was upset about it. "How much weight?" I asked. I get a lot of calls from both men and women who are either frustrated by their own or their spouse's weight gain. Typically, when I ask this question, the answer is in the ten- to twenty-pound (4.5– 9 kg) range, occasionally as high as forty pounds (18 kg). I almost fell off my chair when Molly responded with "one hundred pounds [45.5 kg]," which she had gained in about one year! Her weight gain had not been caused by a medical condition. She was simply eating compulsively and was mad at her husband for not being attracted to her! To gain one hundred pounds (45.5 kg) and expect your partner to want to tear your clothes off is unrealistic. It is counter to our biological drives and it is unhealthy.

A study examining preferences of men of various races and ethnicities showed that they prefer women to be a healthy average weight, with a body mass index between 18.25 and 24.9. Some men are outliers and prefer either a woman with more "meat on her bones" or one with a very thin body. Despite the pressure that many women feel to be super-thin, not all men are looking for that. The same goes for men, most of whom believe that women want them to be far more muscular than women actually want them to be. A Harvard study found that men believed that women want a male body that has twenty to thirty pounds (9–14 kg) more muscle mass than their own and the male average, but, when women were asked to pick their preferred body type from a lineup, they picked the one that was toned, but not as brawny as the men had thought the women would want. In my clinical experience, gay men are the most demanding when it comes to body expectations of partners. A study called "Muscularity and the Gay Ideal" found that gay men view thin and muscular as ideal, making them more susceptible to eating disorders. A study by Adam Cohen and Ilana Tannenbaum found that when lesbians and bisexual women were asked to rate different figures, they found the heavier figure to be more attractive. Find out your partner's preferences and do your best to be your own healthy version of that.

Letting yourself go is not okay. Unfortunately, studies show that many couples do anyway. Married couples are notorious for letting the weight creep on. A study titled "Marital Satisfaction Predicts Weight

Gain in Early Marriage" found that couples who are more satisfied with their marriage are more likely to gain weight. Other studies have found that, in a two-year period, married women are 46 percent more likely to gain a large amount of weight (twenty pounds [9 kg] or more); married men are 25 percent more likely to be obese; nearly half of women are carrying ten extra pounds (4.5 kg) and 25 percent had kept on an extra twenty or more pounds (9+ kg) after childbirth; and men who become fathers are more likely to gain weight. It doesn't have to be this way! And it shouldn't!

The bottom line is that we need to develop and maintain healthy habits that allow us to be the best we can be, given our own genetics. Eating compulsively and not working out, as Molly did, is negligent to our partners and ourselves. We have a responsibility to ourselves and our partner to look as good as we can.

I am not talking about the hypercritical partner who has unrealistic expectations. Suzette called my radio show because her husband was complaining about her weight. She had gained five pounds and he was giving her regular lectures about how he preferred "a woman who keeps herself up," despite the fact he had gained sixty pounds (27 kg) himself! When someone keeps finding fault, you have to look at what else is going on. Is he using weight criticisms to create distance and avoid intimacy?

We all want to have a hot partner. As politically incorrect as it is to say, our partner is a status symbol. We want to be with someone we can be proud of. When one of my clients in private practice, Marissa, married Tyler, he was a gainfully employed investment banker. A few years into the marriage, he lost his job and started gaining weight. She knew he was under a lot of stress and she didn't want to add to it, but his weight gain affected her attraction to him. After five years of unemployment and sixty pounds (27 kg), she came to him and said, "I am working hard to support us both. I have shown this by getting help for you from experts and therapists, and yet you are not getting work and you're continuing to gain weight. Pick one or the other: Either be a trophy husband or find a job and be as heavy as you want. I can't deal with both any more." Marissa's husband didn't change his behavior and their marriage didn't make it. We tend to think of men as "visual" creatures, but women like something nice to look at, too.

When your partner does not take care of herself, you may feel that she does not care about the relationship or you. This is particularly true for men. In a survey of more than sixteen hundred men, ages twenty-one to seventy-five, Shaunti Feldhahn, a social researcher and the best-selling author of *For Women Only*, found that when asked how they would feel if they had an overweight wife who wore baggy sweats and only put on makeup or did her hair to go out, only 12 percent of the men said, "It doesn't bother me at all." The majority said they would be upset by that behavior, followed by "I want her to make an effort to take care of herself—not just for her, but also for me."

What Feldhahn found was that the men in her survey reported feeling that when they saw their wives making an effort to look good for them, it made them feel loved. The converse is true as well. The men reported that when their wives did not keep up with their own self-care, the men felt unvalued and unhappy. As one twenty-seven-year-old husband pointed out, ". . . women need to realize that their doubling in size is like a man going from being a corporate executive to a minimum-wage slacker and assuming it has no effect on his spouse. A woman's appearance is a simple yet important part of happiness in a marriage."

So what can you do? Here are some suggestions:

- **Address your eating issues.** If you are overeating, yo-yo dieting, bingeing, eating-disordered, or just not paying attention to your body's signals, deal with the issue. You may need the help of a therapist to address the underlying issues. I get it; I've been there. I was once fifty pounds (23 kg) heavier than I am now.

- **Do not diet.** Diets have been shown to have a 95–98 percent failure rate. Studies have shown that dieting leads to loss of control over food and binge-eating. But most dieters are quick to blame themselves for their loss of control around food. I recommend the nondiet approach that teaches people how to tune in to their body's signals of hunger and satiety and lose weight without restricting. I wrote my doctoral dissertation on this approach and have used it myself. I weigh less now in my forties, after two kids, than I did in my twenties, and I don't restrict. You may want to check out my No More Diets app., which is based on my dissertation, and will give you the tools you need to lose weight in a healthy way. You can find the iPhone or iPad version of No More Diets in the app store and the Android version in the Google Play store.
- **Set yourself up to succeed.** Make your health a priority. Set aside time to go grocery shopping, so you have the food you like in the house and fresh fruits and vegetables are an option. Schedule the things you need to do. If you don't put exercise, grocery shopping, or other self-care activities on your calendar, you are unlikely to do them.
- **Set process-oriented goals.** Make goals for which you can actually control the outcome. For example, set a goal to walk one mile (1.5 km), which you can choose to do, instead of setting a goal to lose ten pounds (4.5 kg), since you cannot control how your body will react to your new level of activity. Make goals that are both achievable and controllable.

- **Find exercise you enjoy.** You don't have to go to the gym if that is not your thing. Going for walks or hikes, or finding someplace to swim can be great options.
- **Change the way you think about yourself.** If you have a history of failing to meet your goals, you start to think of yourself as someone who does not keep her word, even to herself. This erodes your self-esteem. To have faith in yourself again, you must develop a pattern of meeting your goals. Instead of making a promise to go to the gym every day, make a promise to go for a twenty-minute walk once a week. Once you have the experience of success, you can add another small and manageable goal to your list. Again, keep it process-oriented.

Maintaining your physical health promotes a healthy sex life. Here's what you need to do:

- **Get regular checkups.** Depending on your gender and age, this may include annual visits to the gynecologist, the urologist, or the proctologist, and regular mammograms.
- **Get checked for sexually transmitted diseases.** This is especially crucial if you are new to a relationship or have any kind of open arrangement, where you are sexually involved with more than one person.
- **Use birth control.** You can't have great sex if you are worried about an unwanted pregnancy. Make sure you and your partner are on the same page.
- **Do your Kegels.** Kegel exercises strengthen the pelvic-floor muscles, which support the bladder and the bowel. Strengthening these muscles can improve bladder functioning but, even more exciting, they can increase the strength and

intensity of your orgasms. We tend to think of Kegels as an exercise for women only, but men have pelvic muscles, too, and can benefit from strengthening them as well. Kegel exercises can be done anywhere, any time, and involve contracting and releasing the muscles. To get suggestions on the best Kegel regimen for you, ask your doctor, read about Kegels, or check out a Kegel app.

- **Stop smoking.** Besides being a smelly, disgusting habit that will kill you, smoking harms your sex life. Smoking has been shown to cause impaired sexual performance, diminished sexual desire, and infertility. According to Dr. Richard Milsten, urologist and coauthor of *The Sexual Male*, "Smoking causes damage to smooth muscle inside the penis that interferes with erectile functioning." Smokers are far less satisfied with the sex they are having. When asked to rate their sexual satisfaction on a scale of one to ten, nonsmoking couples averaged 8.7, while couples with male smokers fared far worse, with an average of only 5.2.

- **Minimize your intake of alcohol.** Alcohol may increase sexual desire, but it inhibits sexual performance. And while alcohol can reduce performance anxiety and make you more open to trying new things, it can impact sexual function if is chronically consumed over a long period. Alcohol is a depressant, and using it heavily can dampen mood, decrease sexual desire, and make it difficult for a man to achieve erections or climax while under the influence. Excessive drinking is a common cause of erectile dysfunction. High blood alcohol content (BAC) levels have been associated with delayed orgasm and decreased sensitivity for both men and women. Alcohol can impair the coordination between your genitals and the central nervous system.

10. Work through Your Issues

We bring all of our unresolved issues into the bedroom. They impact our ability to be free, open, and communicative, all of which has an impact on our partners and our relationships. We have a responsibility to work toward healing. Here are a few of the most common unresolved issues that hurt couples and keep them from achieving a fulfilling intimate life together. Therapy, ideally with a specialist, is recommended for all of these:

- **Sexual abuse and rape.** It has been estimated that one in five girls and one in six boys have been the victim of sexual abuse. In situations where one or both partners in a relationship have experienced childhood sexual abuse, it usually takes a lot of therapy to work through the trauma. Because sexual abuse involves unwanted or inappropriate touch or exposure, usually from trusted people, it can create a host of other problems down the line. It is not uncommon for survivors of sexual abuse to act out by engaging in casual sex. When sex and intimacy come together, that can trigger many unresolved issues. This is particularly true for male survivors. Some common responses to sexual abuse that affect intimacy include:

  - Flashbacks
  - Discomfort with certain areas of the body or certain sex acts
  - Hypersexual behavior or low arousal
  - Difficulty reaching orgasm
  - Disassociating or disengaging emotionally during sex
  - The need to be in control
  - Difficulty trusting a partner

Rape has similar long-term effects. According to the Department of Justice, 82 percent of rape survivors were assaulted by someone they knew. According to the Rape, Abuse & Incest National Network, 3 percent of men have been raped. Members of the LGBT community are fifteen times more likely to be raped than others. Getting professional support is of the utmost importance.

- **Sex addiction.** "Sexual addiction" (which is not an actual diagnosis in the Diagnostic and Statistical Manual) is a term used by lay people to describe what therapists call compulsively acting out or out-of-control sexual behavior. This type of acting out does terrible damage to a relationship. I think of the line between a bad impulsive choice and compulsive behavior this way: The sexually compulsive person is willing to do things that violate his own sense or morals and ethics, and is willing to jeopardize what is most important to him (spouse, family, career, reputation, and the like) in order to act out sexually. He feels compelled to repeatedly make the same destructive choices. He alternates between denial, rationalization, guilt, and shame. He vows to stop these hurtful behaviors, but is unable to. Typically this comes in the form of compulsively engaging in hookups, conducting affairs, patronizing prostitutes, watching porn, going to massage parlors, surfing sex websites, and, sometimes, engaging in lascivious and illegal acts.

At their core, sexually compulsive people do not see themselves as people worthy of love. Because of their poor self-esteem, even addicts who are highly accomplished believe that other people would not love or take care of them if they knew everything about them. They focus on their need for sex and steer clear of meaningful relationships in an unconscious attempt to avoid intimacy, vulnerability, and potential rejection.

The shame of living with sexual compulsivity is like an invisible wall between partners. You cannot be close to someone when you are living a secret life and breaking promises and vows. Even if you think your partner does not know you are cheating, on some level, she does. For the partner who has been cheated on, trust has been decimated. Usually that person becomes obsessed with her partner's behavior and experiences tremendous anxiety and depression. She may also doubt her attractiveness and her sexuality, as well as fear abandonment and public embarrassment. These threats to the relationship make it feel unsafe, and when people feel unsafe, they don't have great sex.

If you or your partner struggle with this issue, I recommend therapy with a licensed therapist specializing in sexually compulsive behavior. The sex-related 12-step programs are controversial and it is best to work with a therapist to determine if they are the right option for you.

- **Eating disorders.** It has been estimated that twenty million women and ten million men in the United States suffer from clinically significant eating disorders, which makes these disorders even more common than breast cancer or Alzheimer's disease. The staggering number of people who have been diagnosed with an eating disorder doesn't even include those who have subclinical eating disorders. These are disorders that don't meet the criteria to qualify as anorexia nervosa, bulimia nervosa, or binge eating disorder, but sufferers experience symptoms that affect their lives in negative ways nonetheless. This group includes people who yo-yo diet, struggle with their weight, and are preoccupied with food, as well as those obsessed with their bodies, have body dysmorphia, exercise compulsively, or experience huge fluctuations in their weight.

A person who has subclinical issues may experience body shame that impacts sex. For example, she may not want to try certain positions or she may need to have the lights off or on low during sex. Obsession with food, weight, or exercise can make a person less present and able to connect with her partner or experience the full range of sexual pleasure. For those who have full-blown eating disorders, the effects may be even more significant, including:

- Low sexual desire
- Sexual anxiety
- Fear of intimacy
- Sexual inhibition
- Detached relationship
- Avoidance of sex

If you struggle with these issues, you owe it to yourself and your partner to get help. It is particularly important to work with a licensed therapist who has a specialty in eating disorders.

- **Religious hang-ups.** It is always interesting to me to discover which religious rules people internalize and which ones they don't. For example: Premarital sex is okay, but masturbation is not. Divorce is unacceptable, but an affair isn't so bad. Marital sex is acceptable, but talking dirty about it isn't. It's a sin to have sex with someone who is the same gender as you, but it's a good idea to live a lie and be with someone with whom you don't want to be, and lie about your sexual orientation. These are real examples from my treatment room.

I think religion has a lot to offer individuals and couples. Studies show that religious married couples have more satisfying sex lives. I frequently recommend prayer and attendance at religious services in houses of worship. I also refer patients to religious counselors and recommend that clients read religious literature. That said, I have seen religion do a lot of harm when it comes to free expression of sexual desires, sexual orientation, and sexual exploration. In my practice, I have counseled too many people racked with guilt and shame for normal urges and desires.

I regularly get calls on my radio show from people who struggle to enjoy sex because of religious guilt. Ideas about what is and isn't sexually acceptable get implanted at a young age and make it incredibly difficult for us to communicate our sexual desires, try new things, masturbate, have a healthy sex life, or make love with the person we love, if he or she is the same gender. In his book *Sex & God: How Religion Distorts Sexuality*, psychologist Darrel Ray says, "Many beliefs and assumptions came from your religious upbringing and environment—assumptions that you may have unknowingly picked up from your devout grandmother, a prudish Sunday School teacher, or a religious gym coach. Religious sexual ideas can infect you, especially when you are young and unable to think critically."

When it comes to religion, guilt and shame are the main reasons people aren't having better sex. In the study "Sex and Secularism," by Darrel Ray and Amanda Brown, it was found that the more conservative religions and denominations have more harmful effects on people's sex lives than more moderate or progressive ones in terms of guilt, sex education, sexual information, the ability to accept one's sexual identity, and more.

If your religious upbringing is preventing you from having a fun, healthy sex life with your partner, it is important to find a way to leave the guilt at the bedroom door. Work with a therapist, meet with a sex-positive leader who belongs to your religion, and do some reading to inform yourself about sex-positive ideas, so that you can enjoy a sensual connection with your partner.

- **Mental health.** Mental health has a huge impact on your ability to be close and sexual with your partner. The single most common mental health issue affecting couples' sex lives today is depression. An estimated 15.7 million adults have experienced a major depressive episode in the last year. Depression can kill desire, undermine sexual confidence, make it take longer to reach orgasm, and make sex less enjoyable.

Sexual desire starts in the brain, and the genitals rely on the chemicals in the brain to promote libido, as well as changes in blood flow necessary for sex. When depression disrupts the balance of these brain chemicals, it can have a major impact on the ability to perform. To make matters worse, antidepressants, which can be very helpful in treating depression, may have side effects that impair sexual functioning.

When it comes to treatment, talk therapy is generally the first line of defense. Oftentimes, a therapist will recommend working with a psychiatrist to get evaluated for medication to see if that is needed. The US Department of Health and Human Services reports that six out of ten people struggling with depression will feel better with the first antidepressant they are prescribed. Psychiatry is not a perfect science. Different people have different responses to medications, and it is not uncommon to have to experiment with a few different ones before finding the right option for you. If you go that route, it is not a replacement for therapy, and you should make sure you are working with an experienced, licensed psychiatrist or psychopharmacologist. I am strongly opposed to getting psychotropic medications from internists, gynecologists, or other types of doctors. You wouldn't go to an oncologist to treat your heart condition. You would consult a specialist. The same goes for your mental health.

HELP FOR THE SIDE EFFECTS OF ANTIDEPRESSANTS

Antidepressants, especially selective serotonin reuptake inhibitors (SSRIs), can work wonders on depressive symptoms. But it's been estimated that anywhere from 12 percent to 60 percent of people experience sexual side effects from SSRI treatment. A study published in the *Journal of Sex and Marital Therapy* found the use of ginkgo biloba (60–120 mg) to be 84 percent effective in treating antidepressant-induced sexual dysfunction predominantly caused by SSRIs. Ninety-one percent of the women and 76 percent of the men in the study saw positive results with this treatment. The use of ginkgo biloba showed positive effects on all four phases of the sexual desire response cycle: desire, excitement (erection and lubrication), orgasm, and resolution. It is important to work with your prescribing doctor to see if the use of ginkgo biloba is appropriate for you, and also to do your homework to make sure that you are getting quality ginkgo biloba, since standards may vary.

In Defense of Monogamy

I believe in monogamy. I don't think it is easy, but I do think it is the gold standard. Monogamy requires maturity, impulse control, and high levels of communication, self-awareness, and commitment. In general, I am not someone who believes in taking the easy way out, as demonstrated by the recommendations in my parenting books. I believe that working through difficult times, overcoming temptation, and investing in our mate only makes us value her and the relationship more.

I *suspect* that some people will read this and think that I am a prude. Nothing could be further from the truth. I make no judgments about who sleeps with whom. I have even encouraged single clients or radio callers to act out fantasies with two or more partners. I am all for sexual exploration, but I believe that the sex lives of couples who love each other are compromised when they open their relationship to others. Sex is not exciting, bonding, or romantic when partners are only having sex with each other because their preferred partner isn't available. I believe there is something very valuable about relying on each other for sexual intimacy. This takes the relationship to another level. As a couples therapist, my job is to look out for the well-being of intimate relationships and recommend what I believe is in the best interest of the couple in the long term.

I recognize that monogamy has experienced a dip in popularity in recent years. More and more couples are opening up their relationships. I have been in private practice for two and a half decades and I have yet to see an open relationship enhance a couple's relationship over the long term. I have counseled plenty of couples who have enjoyed an open relationship, especially in the beginning. I get why. But in my clinical experience, these arrangements eventually backfire. People get slippery about the agreements they make, develop bonds with nonprimary partners, start telling lies, become jealous, and hurt each other's feelings. Also in this scenario, preferences for people change, and intimacy gets diluted.

A perfect example of this is a call I got a couple of years ago from a man named Owen. I appreciated that he started the conversation by saying, "I'm calling you because you are so open-minded and nonjudgmental, especially about sex." Owen was a heterosexual guy who had always wanted to watch his wife have sex with another man. When he told his wife Darcy about this desire, she was excited by the prospect of cuckolding. Cuckolding is when a husband derives pleasure from watching his wife have sex with another man, usually someone with a bigger penis. Depending on the arrangement, the wife has sex with the other man while her husband watches, or sometimes she has sex with the other man without him there and then shares details or video later, depending on the agreement.

Owen's best friend James had recently gone through a divorce. His work was going to require him to spend one week a month in their town, and he needed someplace to stay. Owen loved and trusted James and felt that this was a great option, especially since Darcy was onboard with it. Thus the arrangement began. For one week a month, James lived with the two of them and had sex with Darcy while Owen watched. I asked Owen if he was ever sexually involved with James, with or without Darcy, but he reported he was not. For him, the excitement came from watching his friend get his wife off. At the end of the week, James went home and the married couple shared their hot secret together. It seemed to bring them closer.

But eight years into the relationship, Owen noticed that Darcy was looking at James differently. He was sure she was falling in love with James. Why wouldn't she? James was a cool enough guy that Owen considered him a best friend, and Darcy enjoyed having sex with him. With eight years of oxytocin being released, sharing meals and bodies, it was not shocking that Darcy fell for him. When Owen confronted her and told her that he didn't want to continue their arrangement, she freaked out, cried hysterically, and ran out of the house. She made it extremely clear that she didn't want to stop. When Owen called me, Darcy was next door at a friend's house and was refusing to come home. Their marriage was on the rocks.

And then there was Chloe, who decided to fulfill her husband Noah's lifelong fantasy of a threesome on his fortieth birthday. She wanted to make him happy and give him the gift of a lifetime. They found a young woman on a website that helps people hook up in situations like this. When Britney arrived at the hotel, they were stunned to see that she was as attractive as her online profile, which is often not the case. They had a few glasses of wine and got down to business. Noah couldn't have been more thrilled! What Chloe had not anticipated was how into Britney Noah would be. He was clearly more responsive and more excited by this new woman (hello, Coolidge Effect!) than he was with her. In addition to being younger, thinner, and perkier, it appeared that Britney was a more skilled lover than Chloe was. While Noah enjoyed watching the two women together, he was clearly most excited about being with Britney. In addition to all the touching, stroking, and oral excitement, somehow Noah managed to have intercourse with Britney three times that night! He had never done that with Chloe. She was devastated. Noah was so over the moon with the whole thing that he didn't pick up on Chloe's reaction.

When Noah suggested that they make this a more regular event, Chloe called me to make an appointment for couples therapy. She couldn't get the images out of her head. She never expected to feel so jealous and resentful. She hadn't really wanted to do the threesome, but she thought it would satisfy her husband's desire. Instead, it opened a door, she realized, that she didn't want open, and now, every time she had sex with her husband she was haunted by the images of him and the other woman having sex. She felt like a second choice sexual partner. Noah did nothing wrong by expressing his desires and enjoying the sexual experience. It's just that Chloe could not have imagined that the reality of a threesome would feel so devastatingly different than the fantasy.

When my new friend Hillary caught wind of what I was writing about, she pulled me aside to tell me her story. Hillary works as a development executive. She is a smart professional in her early thirties, who never wears makeup and is always struggling to lose twenty pounds (9 kg). Apparently, her last boyfriend, Todd, was adamant about having an open relationship. She was in her late twenties at the time and was afraid of losing him, so she agreed to go along with the plan. Initially, Todd was on the hunt and Hillary didn't take advantage of the setup. She wasn't looking to sleep with other people. She only wanted to be with Todd. Todd was not having as much luck getting women to sleep with him as he had expected. At some point Hillary decided that she was going to give their open relationship a shot. Hillary's success rate was a hell of a lot better than Todd's. Within a few months, men were beating down her door. She was having a lot of fun with these guys and felt pretty disconnected from Todd, who now wanted to change the rules. But it was too late. Hillary left the relationship.

I know there are couples who rave about the open-relationship model and say it works for them. After over two and a half decades of being a therapist, however, and having seen open relationships in all their permutations, there are a half a dozen reasons why I do not recommend that you bring a third party (or more) into your bedroom:

- **Dilution.** Bringing a third (or more) party into your relationship creates a distraction from the emotional connection between the two of you. It dilutes the intimacy in your relationship, when you spread yourself thinner.
- **Jealousy.** Eventually, someone has feelings toward someone. I have seen way too many jealousy issues arise and emotional bonds form *as a result of* what was supposed to be meaningless sex.
- **Detachment.** We are wired to covet what we value, to protect what we care most about. Jealousy is a normal human emotion. In order not to feel that way about someone you are truly in love with, there has to be some emotional disconnection. In her

book *Romantic Jealousy: Causes, Symptoms, Cures,* psychologist Ayala Malach Pines nails it, when she says, "In Freud's view, if you don't experience jealousy when an important relationship is threatened, something is not altogether right about you. It is akin to not feeling grief when someone you care deeply about dies."

- **Lack of sacrifice.** Sacrifice creates trust. Resisting the normal urge to have sex with other people shows a level of commitment and sacrifice that makes the relationship stronger.

- **Lack of creativity.** Bringing a new person into the mix prevents you from putting energy and creativity into your sex life and relationship with your partner. You're no longer working to up your game and figure out new fantasies to explore, techniques to try, and preferences your partner may have that you haven't yet probed. While the addition of others in your relationship may be exciting initially, it does not solve the longer-term, bigger issue of how to keep things fresh in your relationship and how to become a better lover to your partner.

- **Avoidance of issues.** Opening your relationship to other people is a band aid for intimacy issues (or unresolved childhood issues), and prevents personal growth from happening. Typically, when someone has intimacy issues (and most people are challenged to have an emotionally and sexually connected relationship on some level), those issues play out in the bedroom. For example, a man may be used to meaningless sex with women he doesn't care about; a woman may have undergone a sexual trauma; an adult might have had an emotionally unavailable parent. Our issues affect our intimate life and they are also opportunities to grow.

In case I did not make myself clear, I do not recommend opening your relationship to other people. But if you choose to ignore my advice, make sure that you and your partner clearly define the rules, limits, and boundaries of your arrangement. Communication is of the utmost importance. In situations like this, faithfulness is defined by honoring those commitments and boundaries. Keep your promises, but also leave room to renegotiate, in case either one of you has different reactions than you expected. Understand that both partners must agree to whatever is agreed upon. Consent under pressure does not count as a collaborative agreement.

Monogamy, Not Monotony

Monogamy is hot. It is singular in its focus. It is concentrated emotional and sexual attention. It is about knowing each other's body, fantasies, quirks, and turn-ons. It is constantly looking for new ways to turn each other on, because you don't want to rest on your laurels. It is relaxing in the familiarity of each other's body, scents, skin texture, and voice. And yet, it is being surprised at how great the sex can be after so many years. It is about loving someone so much that her pleasure is yours and vice versa. It is being able to share your darkest moments and wipe away each other's tears, when needed. It is about being vulnerable, in bed and out. It is getting to make love with your best friend, your confidant, your greatest supporter and ally.

Happy Endings

Amazing sex requires effort. It doesn't just happen. It is the dividend from a great investment that can only occur in a safe environment that encourages open communication, continued sexual education, and willingness to both give and take feedback. It requires you to take responsibility for your own pleasure by knowing your mind and body, and sharing that information with your lover. Couples who want long-term passion make the time for sex and seduction and protect their erotic connection by creating boundaries with the outside world. They keep themselves in good health, physically and emotionally, so they can bring their "A game" to the bedroom. Doing these things is not viewed as a chore, but instead, as an opportunity to achieve a whole new level of intimacy for a lifetime. If you do the things I suggest in this chapter, and in this book, I promise that it will not only change your sex life and your relationship, it will change your life.

Appendix A

36 Questions

The following questions are those used in Arthur Aron's study *The Experimental Generation of Interpersonal Closeness: A Procedure and Some Preliminary Findings.* You and your partner may want to try asking them to one another as an exercise in closeness. To get the full effect, try the recommended four-minute eye gaze without speaking at the end.

Set I

1. Given the choice of anyone in the world, whom would you want as a dinner guest?
2. Would you like to be famous? In what way?
3. Before making a telephone call, do you ever rehearse what you are going to say? Why?
4. What would constitute a "perfect" day for you?
5. When did you last sing to yourself? To someone else?
6. If you were able to live to the age of 90 and retain either the mind or body of a 30-year-old for the last 60 years of your life, which would you want?
7. Do you have a secret hunch about how you will die?
8. Name three things you and your partner appear to have in common.
9. For what in your life do you feel most grateful?
10. If you could change anything about the way you were raised, what would it be?

11. Take four minutes and tell your partner your life story in as much detail as possible.

12. If you could wake up tomorrow having gained any one quality or ability, what would it be?

Set II

13. If a crystal ball could tell you the truth about yourself, your life, the future, or anything else, what would you want to know?

14. Is there something that you've dreamed of doing for a long time? Why haven't you done it?

15. What is the greatest accomplishment of your life?

16. What do you value most in a friendship?

17. What is your most treasured memory?

18. What is your most terrible memory?

19. If you knew that in one year you would die suddenly, would you change anything about the way you are now living? Why?

20. What does friendship mean to you?

21. What roles do love and affection play in your life?

22. With your partner, alternately share something you consider a positive characteristic of each other. Share a total of five items.

23. How close and warm to each other is your family? Do you feel your childhood was happier than most other people's?

24. How do you feel about your relationship with your mother?

Set III

25. Make three true "we" statements each. For instance, "We are both in this room feeling . . ."

26. Complete this sentence: "I wish I had someone with whom I could share . . ."

27. If you were going to become a close friend with your partner, please share what would be important for him or her to know.

28. Tell your partner what you like about him or her; be very honest this time, saying things that you might not say to someone you've just met.

29. Share with your partner an embarrassing moment in your life.

30. When did you last cry in front of another person? By yourself?

31. Tell your partner something that you like about him or her already.

32. What, if anything, is too serious to be joked about?

33. If you were to die this evening with no opportunity to communicate with anyone, what would you most regret not having told someone? Why haven't you told them yet?

34. Your house, containing everything you own, catches fire. After saving your loved ones and pets, you have time to safely make a final dash to save any one item. What would it be? Why?

35. Of all the people in your family, whose death would you find most disturbing? Why?

36. Share a personal problem and ask your partner's advice on how he or she might handle it. Also, ask your partner to reflect back to you how you seem to be feeling about the problem you have chosen.

The source of the information in this Appendix is Brooke C. Feeney, "A Secure Base: Responsive Support of Goal Strivings and Exploration in Adult Intimate Relationships," *Journal of Personality and Social Psychology* 87, no. 5 (November 2004): 631–648.http://dx.doi. org/10.1037/0022-3514.87.5.631.

Appendix B

Sexual Inventory

We can't meet each other's needs if we don't know what they are or if we are unclear about the specifics. This exercise is an opportunity to listen and get clarity about your partner's desires, share your own needs, talk about things you may never have talked about—or even thought about—and become more intimate, emotionally and sexually.

Even the most sexually open person can sometimes struggle to communicate her wants. Shame—concerns about what it is okay (or not okay) to share or do with a long-term partner or spouse—can get in the way. So can the day-to-day grind: the deadline at work, the kids' soccer practice, doing the laundry, etc., can take you away from sexual exploration and the opportunity to give intimacy the time, energy, and attention it needs. It is easy to let those things keep you from sexual communication. It is easier to talk about the bills than it is to say, "Honey, I'd really like you to bend me over and spank me." So we allow distractions to keep us from sharing our secret desires.

I recommend that couples take the following sexual inventory once a year. Find a special date, maybe an anniversary, the first Saturday of August, or winter Solstice. It doesn't matter what date it is, only that you do the sexual inventory once a year and make it a positive experience.

What turns us on changes over time. There are many different things—exposure to new ideas, movies, books, working on ourselves in therapy, and developing a comfort level with our own sexuality— that affect our preferences as we age, and as our bodies and hormones change. Sharing this shifting information with our partner is an important part of staying sexually connected.

The questions in the inventory below cover a lot of ground and are extremely personal. Most of the questions are open-ended, in order to facilitate communication and openness. Answers should never be shared with anyone but your partner.

You may notice that while there are questions about fantasies, there are no questions about third parties or open relationships. Please see page 272 to understand why.

Use the questions in the inventory as an opportunity to learn about your partner. It is a chance to know how to give well. Not everyone is going to get his or her every need met as a result of this exercise, but it will give each of you a great starting point. As Mort Fertel points out in his book *Marriage Fitness*, "The main purpose of asking for what you want is not so you get what you want; it's so your spouse can give you what you want. Giving creates love."

Here are my recommendations for doing this exercise.

- Make a commitment to be nonjudgmental and open-minded.
- Plan to take at least two hours to complete the inventory.
- Find a quiet place and time where you will not be interrupted (and the kids won't disturb you). Minimize disruptions: don't answer phones, turn off the TV, etc.
- Pay close attention to each other.
- Take turns being the interviewer and the interviewee, ideally on separate nights, and don't let more than a week pass between interviews.

- If possible, ask all the questions on the list and feel free to add your own. If you are a same gender couple and a question is not relevant to you, just skip over it.
- Be sensitive to your partner's hot button issues. Feel free to leave out something that you know will really trigger him. But don't avoid asking a question just because it is difficult to share the information.
- Look for opportunities to make your partner feel more comfortable.
- Take notes and confirm with your partner that your understanding of what she has said is accurate.
- Be detail oriented and as specific as possible. If you partner does not volunteer details, ask for them.
- Create the right mood to talk about sex. Light a candle, have a glass of wine (but not so many that you are not present or connected), and make sure that you have privacy.
- Keep everything that is discussed totally confidential.

Before beginning, remind yourselves that this is an opportunity to be vulnerable, intimate, and become better partners and better lovers.

Dr. Jenn's Sexual Inventory for Couples
All of the questions below are for the interviewer to ask the interviewee. Keep in mind that these are not general questions; they are sex specific.

Aesthetics and Health
Dress

- Which clothes do you feel sexiest in?
- Which of my clothes (the ones that I wear) get you in the mood?
- Of the outfits I wear, which are your favorites?
- What do you wish I would wear?
- Is there anything that I wear that is a real turn off for you?

- What underwear do you like to see me in? Colors? Cuts?
- Of the lingerie I've worn for you, which are your favorites?
- What lingerie do you like best in general?
- Is there anything I haven't worn that you would like me to wear or wear more often?
- What do you like me to wear in bed?
- Is there anything that I wear in bed that is a big turn off?
- What shoes do you find sexiest?

Makeup

- Please complete the sentence: I feel sexiest when my makeup is _____.
- I like your .makeup best when _____.
- My favorite lipstick color is _____.

Hygiene

- What are your preferences when it comes to my body hair? Shaved back? Armpits? Legs? Chest hairs?
- What are your pubic hair preferences? Trimmed? Shaven clean? Wild? Do you prefer short in one place and long in another? Be specific.
- Some people like the smell of sweat and think there is nothing sexier than going down on their partner after a sweaty workout. Others prefer a freshly showered partner. What is your preference? Is it different for different acts? If so, please be specific.

Body Modification

- How to you feel about tattoos?
- Piercings?

- Branding?
- Corsets?
- Plastic surgery?

Health

- When was your last check up?
- Have you been tested for STDs?
- Are you on any medications that may affect your sex drive or performance? See page 256 for a list.
- When was your last mammogram? Visit to the proctologist? Urologist? Gynecological check up?
- What kind of birth control are you using? How do you feel about it?
- Are there any safe sex practices that you think we should be following but are not?

Health

- Have you had any procedures or surgeries that have left any part of your body sensitive, in pain, or numb?
- Have you had any medical conditions that affect you in bed?

Communication
Expressing Needs

Please complete these sentences:

- The things I have the hardest time expressing to you are _____.
- I have a hard time asking for _____.
- Please fill in the blanks: Instead of _____, I would love it if you would _____.
- Asking for more sex makes me feel _____.

- It would make it easier for me to talk to you about sex if you

  _____.

Favorites

- What are your three favorite sexual memories that we have shared this year?
- What is your single, most favorite sexual memory of our relationship?
- What are your three favorite things that I do to you in bed?
- What are your three favorite sexual activities?
- Please complete this sentence: You're so good at _____.
- Tell me something we used to do more of, but don't do now, and you would like to bring back?
- Three things I value about you as a lover are _____.
- Three things I enjoy about your body are _____.
- My three favorite parts of your body are _____.
- What is your favorite order of activities?
- Do you prefer to be a top or a bottom? Are you at all flexible on this?

Word Choice

The words we like in to say or hear in bed can be dramatically different from what is acceptable out of bed. In order for couples to be able to turn each other on, they need to know what words work and which ones are like a cold shower.

According to Patricia Love, there are four types of sex words that we use:

1. Clinical terms, example *sexual intercourse*
2. Dirty talk, example *fucking*
3. Slang, example *doing it*
4. Romantic terms, example *making love*

It is important to know what is most effective when we are together. What words are acceptable, unacceptable or exciting? For each of the following, please let me (the interviewer) know your favorite words to use in bed for the following and any words that you really don't like.

Female:	*Male:*
Anus	Anus
Breasts	Buttocks
Buttocks	Ejaculation
Clitoris	Erection
G Spot	Nipples
Labia	Penis
Nipples	Prostate
Pubic Hair	Pubic Hair
Vulva	Scrotum
	Testicles

Activities:

Analingus	Manual stimulation of female genitals
Anal Sex	Manual stimulation of male genitals
Cunnilingus	Masturbation
Digital penetration	Oral Sex (in general)
Digital stimulation	Sexual intercourse
Fellatio	
Kissing	

• Overall, what are your three favorite words during sex?
• What are your three favorite phrases during sex?

Being Sensitive
Sensitivities

All couples have sensitive areas. It is important to know your partner's. Perhaps the idea of a threesome or the mention of your college boyfriend, Bob, makes your partner upset. In order to avoid stepping on landmines, we should know and respect these sensitivities. If your partner is feeling hot and heavy, this is not the time to mention that thing Bob did to you in bed—it will pull your partner out of a sexual headspace.

- Are there any things, people, or places that you would prefer I not mention when we are in a sexual space?

Rejection

- What is the best way for me to reject sex with you if I am not in the mood?
- What things make you not want to have sex?
- If you say you are not interested, is there room for me to convince you?
- When you are sexually rejected by me, how does it make you feel? Please note, the question is not "what does it make you want to do?"

Trauma

- Have you ever been forced to do something sexual against your will?
- Are there any words, smells, touches, or sexual activities that are triggering for you?
- What can I do to make sex feel safe for you?

Safety

- What would you like your safety word to be? If used, all activity must come to a halt.
- What makes you feel sexually unsafe?
- What can I do to make you feel safer?

Challenges

- What are our biggest sexual challenges?
- What do you think we can do to overcome them?
- How can I support you?
- What would be helpful to me is _____.

Getting In the Mood
Ideal Conditions

While we don't always get to have ideal conditions for sex, it is always good to know what your partner's preference is:

- What is your ideal time of day for sex?
- How do you feel about morning sex? Afternoon sex? Nighttime sex?
- How do you feel about being woken up in the middle of the night for sex?
- How would you feel if you woke up to me giving you oral sex?
- What is your favorite day of the week to have sex?
- What temperature is ideal for you when we have sex?
- How does having kids in the house affect you and your sexual desire?
- What can we do to prevent having children in the house from having a big impact on our sex life?
- What kind of lighting do you prefer for sex?

- Name one place in our home that we have never had sex and where you would like to have it.
- What are you favorite places to have sex?
- Where have we never had sex that you would like to try?
- How do you feel about sex in public places?
- What do you think about sex in a Jacuzzi? Shower? Bathtub? The ocean?
- How to you feel about having sex while you are menstruating? Oral sex? Anal sex? Intercourse?
- How to you feel about having sex with me when I am menstruating? Oral sex? Anal sex? Intercourse?
- When in your cycle are you the most horny?
- What is the best way for me to know when you have your period?
- Do you want to know when I have my period or would you prefer not to?
- What is your favorite type of sex?
- How do you feel about quickies?
- How do you feel about marathon sex?
- How do you feel about noise during sex? Dirty talk?
- How do you feel about moans, groans, panting, screaming, or yelling?
- How do you feel when I am loud?
- How do you feel about your own sex sounds?
- Do you worry about the neighbors or kids? Does this hold you back?

Kissing

- What is your favorite kind of kissing?
- Do you like deep kisses? Soft kisses?
- How much tongue do you like in your mouth?
- Do you like to have my lips rub up against yours?
- Do you like to have your lip sucked? Bit?
- Do you like to have your tongue sucked on?
- What do you wish I would do more of? Less of?

Foreplay

- How much foreplay is ideal for you?
- Would you like more than I am doing? Less than I am doing?
- What would you like me to add to the foreplay repertoire?
- How would you like for me to ask for more foreplay? Less foreplay?
- What foreplay are you most responsive to?
- What foreplay do you like doing to me the most?

Seduction

- What is the difference between romance and seduction to you?
- What activities are romantic to you?
- Do you prefer it when you initiate sex or when I do?
- How do you like to be approached?
- What is the most effective way to seduce you?
- What are your favorite phrases or sexual words when being seduced?

Expanding Knowledge
Books

- Would you like to read an erotic novel together?
- Are there any books that you would like to share that turn you on?
- How would you like to incorporate erotic literature into our sex life?

Pornography

- Philosophically, how do you feel about porn?
- Do you watch porn?
- What kind of porn do you watch? Are there any themes?
- How do you feel about watching porn together?

Education

- How do you feel about instructional sex books?
- Are you open to reading them together?
- How do you feel about instructional videos? Would you be willing to watch one together?
- How do you feel about sex workshops or classes? Is that something that interests you?
- How do you feel about instructional television shows, podcasts, or online videos? Are you open to sharing those together?
- What could we do as a couple to help us take our sex life to the next level this year?

Turn-Ons and Turn-Offs
Arousal

- What arouses you?
- What things that I say or do get you excited?
- What are your three biggest sexual hot spots, physically?

Masturbation

- What are you favorite masturbation techniques?
- Are you willing to show me?
- How has your sexual technique, with yourself, changed over time?
- What helps you get excited when you are taking care of yourself sexually?
- What do you watch, fantasize about, or read?

The Act . . . Or Acts
Touch

- How do you like to be touched?
- What parts of your body are most sensitive?
- Is there an order you prefer?
- Do you like to be touched throughout your body before the genitals?
- How do you like to be touched or kissed on the following body parts? Arms? Legs? Thighs? Neck? Ears? Face? Shoulders? Feet? Hands? Chest? Back? Breasts? Buttocks region? Vaginal area? On and around your penis and testicles?

Orgasms

- What are your orgasms like?
- How have they changed over time?
- What makes them vary?
- What is the easiest way for you to have an orgasm?
- How do you feel after you have an orgasm with me? Physically? Emotionally?
- How do you feel when you have trouble having an orgasm with me? What can I do to make that easier on you?
- What is your favorite type of orgasm?
- Please complete this sentence: I would like you to get me to orgasm by _____.
- When I am experiencing an orgasm, I would like you to _____.

Positions

- What are your three favorite positions?
- Are there any positions that we haven't done that you would like to try?
- Are you open to looking at a book or app of sexual positions and picking out some new ones?
- Are there any positions that you are really opposed to?
- Are there any positions you would like to do, but are concerned that I may have feelings about them?

Sex of the Mind
Emotion

- How do you feel after we have sex?
- What would you like from me after sex? Physically? Emotionally?
- What does sexual intercourse mean to you?

- What does oral sex mean to you? Giving? Receiving?
- What does anal sex mean to you? Giving? Receiving?
- How do you feel about eye contact during sex? Is it different for different sex acts? For different moods? What are your preferences?
- What are the sexual things that make you feel most connected?

Fantasy

- What are your three biggest fantasies?
- Do you fantasize when you masturbate?
- Please share your favorite fantasy in as much detail as possible.

Power and Aggression

As discussed in Chapter 6, power plays a role in sex and sexual fantasies. There is an element of domination and submission in most sexual interactions, even with the most egalitarian couple. When you make peace with the power exchange involved in erotic life, you can play with it and enjoy it more. Hot sex in not usually egalitarian sex. You can be respectful in your erotic disrespect.

Most couples aren't aware of the power dynamics in their sex life. The following questions will help open the door to discussing, enjoying, and playing with the power dynamics in your relationship.

- Do you like to dominate or be dominated?
- How do you feel about being submissive?
- Do you feel the need to stick to one role? Why?
- How do you feel about passionate, throw-each-other-against-a-wall sex?
- Are there things that you wouldn't do with me sexually because we love each other?
- Do you like to be ordered around during sex? If so how?

Stepping Out of Your Comfort Zone
Experimentation

- Name three things that we have never done that you would like to try.
- How do you feel about pornography? About watching it together?
- Are you open to _____ (fill in the blank)?

Toys

- How do you feel about bringing toys in to the bedroom? Toys to use on you? Toys to use on me?
- What are you favorite toys to use on yourself?
- What are you favorite toys for me to use on you?
- What toys have you always wanted to try but haven't?
- Are you open to going to a sex store or visiting an online store together to pick out some new things?
- Are there any toys that you are really opposed to my using or using yourself?
- How do you feel about toys during intercourse?
- Are some toys more acceptable than others when we use them as a couple?
- Do you have any fears or concerns about using toys together?

Kinky Sex

How do you feel about experimenting together with any of the following:

- How to you feel about food play, as in eating food off each other's body?
- How do you feel about temperature play? Using hot wax? Ice cubes?

- How do you feel about wearing a blindfold or if I wear one?
- How do you feel about being constrained with ropes?* Handcuffs? Velcro cuffs? Under bed restraints? Ties? Bondage tape? Door jam cuffs?
- How do you feel about spanking me or if I spank you?
- How do you feel about flagellation? With a paddle? Slapper? Crops? Canes? Floggers?
- How do you feel about wearing—or having me wear—ball gags?
- How do you feel wearing—or having me wear—nipple clamps?
- How do you feel about pain during sex?
- How do you feel about dog collars and leashes?
- Are there any costumes that you would find sexy? For me? For you?
- What should we be for Halloween?
- How do you feel about role-playing?
- What kind of role might you be interested in playing?
- How do you feel about fisting? Vaginal? Anal?
- How do you feel about play with urine or feces?

Looking Ahead
Goals

- What sex goals would you like to make this year for yourself?
- For me?
- For us as a couple?

---

*Please note: When experimenting with bondage, it is important to observe safety precautions. Never leave someone tied up while he or she is unattended. Keep scissors nearby. No matter what, if any part of your partner's body turns blue, purple, numb, or cold, he or she must be released immediately. When in doubt, seek medical help.

References

STEP 1: Create Connection

Books

Burns, Jim. *Creating an Intimate Marriage: Rekindle Romance through Affection, Warmth & Encouragement.* Minneapolis: Bethany House Publishers, 2006.

Chapman, Gary. *The Five Love Languages: How to Express Heartfelt Commitment to Your Mate.* Chicago: Northfield Publishing, 1995.

Cohen Praver, Fran. *The New Science of Love.* Naperville, Ill.: Sourcebooks, 2011.

Fertel, Mort. *Marriage Fitness: 4 Steps to Building & Maintaining PHENOMENAL LOVE.* Baltimore: MarriageMax, Inc., 2004.

Gottman, John M., PhD. *The Relationship Cure: A 5 Step Guide to Strengthening Your Marriage, Family and Friendships.* New York: Harmony, 2001.

———. *The Science of Trust: Emotional Attunement for Couples.* New York: W.W. Norton & Company, 2011.

Hendrix, Harville, PhD, and Helen LaKelly Hunt, PhD. *Making Marriage Simple: 10 Relationship Saving Truths.* New York: Harmony, 2013.

Johnson, Sue. *Hold Me Tight: Seven Conversations for a Lifetime of Love.* New York: Little, Brown and Company, 2008.

Jourard, Sidney M. *The Transparent Self: Self-Disclosure and Well-Being.* Princeton, N.J.: D. Van Nostrand Company, Inc., 1964.

Kuchinskas, Susan. *The Chemistry of Connection: How the Oxytocin Response Can Help You Find Trust, Intimacy, and Love.* Oakland, Calif.: New Harbinger Publications, Inc., 2009.

Lerner, Harriet, PhD. *The Dance of Connection: How to Talk to Someone When You're Mad, Hurt, Scared, Frustrated, Insulted, Betrayed, or Desperate.* New York: HarperCollins, 2002.

Levine, Amir, MD, and Rachel S. F. Heller. *Attached: The New Science Of Adult Attachment and How It Can Help You Find And Keep Love.* New York: Penguin Group, 2011.

Neuman, Gary M. *The Truth about Cheating: Why Men Stray and What You Can Do to Prevent It.* Hoboken, N.J.: John Wiley & Sons Inc., 2008.

———. *Connect to Love: The Keys to Transforming Your Relationship.* Hoboken, N.J.: John Wiley & Sons, Inc., 2011.

Page, Susan. *Why Talking Is Not Enough: 8 Loving Actions That Will Transform Your Marriage.* San Francisco: Jossey-Bass, 2006.

Pincott, Jena. *Do Gentlemen Really Prefer Blondes? Bodies, Behavior, and Brains—The Science Behind Sex, Love & Attraction.* New York: Delta, 2008.

Pines, Ayala M., PhD. *Romantic Jealousy: Understanding and Conquering the Shadow of Love.* New York: St. Martin's Press, 1992.

Stone, Douglas, Bruce Patton, and Sheila Heen. *Difficult Conversations: How to Discuss What Matters Most.* New York: Penguin Books, 1999.

Tatkin, Stan, PsyD. *Wired for Love: How Understanding Your Partner's Brain Can Help You Defuse Conflict and Spark Intimacy.* Oakland, Calif.: New Harbinger Publications, Inc., 2011.

Turkle, Sherry. *Alone Together: Why We Expect More from Technology and Less from Each Other.* New York: Basic Books, 2011.

Articles and Studies

Alden, Scott. "3 Reasons Why Sex Really Does Change Everything." The Date Report (November 2011). http://www.thedatereport.com/dating/science/972-why-sex-changes-everything.

Amen, Daniel, MD "Understand What Sex Does to Your Brain." *Men's Health* (April, 2013). http://www.menshealth.com/sex-women/understanding-sex-and-brain.

Aron, Arthur, Edward Melinat, Elaine N. Aron, Robert Darrin Vallone, Renee J. Bator. "The Experimental Generation of Interpersonal Closeness: A Procedure and Some Preliminary Findings." *Personality and Social Psychology Bulletin 23*, no. 4 (April 1997): 363–377. http://psp.sagepub.com/content/23/4/363.refs.

Brower, Naomi. "Have Fun! The Importance of Play in Couple Relationships." Utah State University Cooperative Extension (April 2011). https://extension.usu.edu/files/publications/publication/FC_Relationships_2012–01 pr.pdf.

Carey, Benedict. "For Couples, Reaction to Good News Matters More Than Reaction to Bad." New York Times (December 5, 2006). http://www.nytimes.com/2006/12/05/health/psychology/05marr.html.

Catron, Mandy Len. "To Fall in Love with Anyone, Do This." *New York Times* (January 11, 2015). http://mobile.nytimes.com/2015/01/11/fashion/modern-love-to-fall-in-love-with-anyone-do-this.html.

Cluff Shade, Lori, Jonathan Sandberg, Roy Bean, Dean Busby, and Sarah Coyne. "Using Technology to Connect in Romantic Relationships: Effects on Attachment, Relationship Satisfaction, and Stability in Emerging Adults." *Journal of Couple & Relationship Therapy 12* (2013): 314–338. http://www.tandfonline.com/doi/abs/10.1080/15332691.2013.836051?journalCode=wcrt20.

Dick Jones Communication. "What the 'Silent Treatment' Says about Your Relationship." *Science Daily* (August 4, 2014). https://www.sciencedaily.com/releases/2014/08/140804122903.htm.

Drigotas, Stephen M., Caryl E. Rusbult, Jennifer Wieselquist, and Sarah W. Whitton. "Close Partner as Sculptor of the Ideal Self: Behavioral Affirmation and the Michelangelo Phenomenon." *Journal of Personality and Social Psychology* 77, no. 2 (1999): 293–323.

The Editors of *Prevention*. "10 Little Things Connected Couples Do." *Prevention* (December 27, 2014). www.prevention.com/sex/good-habits-for-a-happy-relationship.

Estroff Marano, Hara. "A Male Thing." *Psychology Today* (March/April 2015): https://www.psychologytoday.com/articles/201503/unconventional-wisdom-male-thing.

"Eye Contact Part 3: The Look of Love." Evolution: Male (August 2011). https://evolutionmale.wordpress.com/2011/08/22/eye-contact-part-3-the-look-of-love.

Feeney, Brooke C. "A Secure Base: Responsive Support of Goal Striving and Exploration in Adult Intimate Relationships." *Journal of Personality and Social Psychology* 87, no. 5 (November 2004): 631–648. http://psycnet.apa.org/journals/psp/87/5/631.

Fogarty, Thomas F., MD "The Distancer and the Pursuer." Center for Family Learning—Compendium II—The Best of the Family (1978–1983): 45–50. http://cflarchives.org/images/The_Distancer_and_The_Pursuer.pdf.

Gable, Shelly L., Gian C. Gonzaga, and Amy Strachman. "Will You Be There for Me When Things Go Right? Supportive Responses to Positive Event Disclosures." *Journal of Personality and Social Psychology* 91, no. 5 (November 2006): 904–917. http://psycnet.apa.org/journals/psp/91/5/904.

Godson, Suzi. "'Spending Time Together Isn't Enough.' The Legendary Arthur Aron on How to Make Love Last Forever." Suzi Godson (April 2014). http://suzigodson.com/2014/04/arthur-aron-on-how-to-make-love-last-forever.

A GoodTherapy.org News Summary. "An Attitude of Gratitude Helps Maintain Loving Relationships." (August 2012). http://www.goodtherapy.org/blog/attitude-of-gratitude-helps-maintain-loving-relationships-0813121.

Gordon, Amie M., PhD. "Is Gratitude the Antidote to Relationship Failure?" *Psychology Today* (March 2013). https://www.psychologytoday.com/blog/between-you-and-me/201303/is-gratitude-the-antidote-relationship-failure.

Gordon, Amie M., Emily A. Impett, Aleksandr. Kogan, Christopher Oveis, and Dacher Keltner. "To Have and to Hold: Gratitude Promotes Relationship Maintenance in Intimate Bonds." *Journal of Personality and Social Psychology* 103, no. 2 (2012): 257–274. Socrates. berkeley.edu/~keltner/publications/GordonEtAl_2012_JPSP.pdf. doi: 10.1037/a0028723.

Gray, Emma. "From Sex to Love: Emotional Attachment and Sexual Desire Originate in Overlapping Parts of the Brain (STUDY)." *Huffington Post* (July 9, 2012). http://www.huffingtonpost.com/2012/07/09/from-sex-to-love-emotional-attachment-sexual-desire-originate-in-overlapping-parts-of-the-brain.

Huston, Ted L. "What's Love Got To Do With It? Why Some Marriages Succeed and Others Fail." *Personal Relationships*. Vol 16, issue 3, pp. 301–327 (September, 2009). Wiley Online Library. http://onlinelibrary.wiley.com/doi/10.1111/j.1475-6811.2009.01225.x/abstract.

Jayson, Sharon. "'We-Time' Key to a Happy Marriage." ABC News. (July 2008). http://abcnews.go.com/Health/Family/story?id=5387217.

Johnson, Sue. "Say Something I'm Giving Up on You." Dr. Sue Johnson (January 2015). http://www.drsuejohnson.com/relationships/say-something.

Jones, Daniel. "No. 37: Big Wedding or Small." *New York Times* (January 11, 2015). http://mobile.nytimes.com/2015/01/11/fashion/no-37-big-wedding-or-small.html.

Kubacka, Kaska E., Catrin Finkenauer, Caryl E. Rusbult, and Loes Keijsers. "Maintaining Close Relationships: Gratitude as a Motivator and a Detector of Maintenance Behavior." *Personality and Social Psychology* Bulletin XX, no. X (2011): 1–4.

Laurenceau, Jean-Philippe, Lisa Feldman Barret, and Paula R. Pietromonaco. "Intimacy as an Interpersonal Process: The Importance of Self-Disclosure, Partner Disclosure, and Perceived Partner Responsiveness in Interpersonal Exchanges." *Journal of Personality and Social Psychology 74,* no. 5 (1998): 1238–1251.

Mikulincer, Mario. "Adult Attachment Style and Individual Differences in Functional Versus Dysfunctional Experiences in Anger." *Journal of Personality and Social Psychology* 74, no. 2 (February 1998): 513–524. http://www.ncbi.nlm.gov/pubmed/9491590.

Mikulincer, Mario. "Attachment Style and the Mental Representation of the Self," 69, no. 6 (1995): 1203–1215.

Murphy, Kate. "Psst. Look Over Here." *New York Times* (May 17, 2014). http://www.nytimes.com/2014/05/17/sunday-review/the-eyes-have-it.html?_r=0.

Niehuis, PhD, Sylvia, PhD, Linda Skogrand, PhD, Ted L. Huston, Ph.D. "FFCI: When Marriages Die: Premarital and Early Marriage Precursors to Divorce." *Forum for Family and Consumer Issues* (FFCI) (June 2006). http://ncsu.edu/ffci/publications/2006/v11-n1-2006-june/fa-1-marriages-die.php.

Northwestern University. "Partners Sculpt Each Other to Achieve Their Ideal Selves: If Successful, Relationship Goes Well." *Science Daily* (December 31, 2009). http://www.sciencedaily.com/releases/2009/12/091216144143.htm.

Parker-Pope, Tara. "The Science of a Happy Marriage." *New York Times* (May 10, 2010). http://well.blogs.nytimes.com/2010/05/10/tracking-the-science-of-commitment.

———. "The Happy Marriage Is the 'Me' Marriage." *New York Times* (December 31, 2010). http://www.nytimes.com/2011/01/02/weekinreview/02parkerpope.html.

Patz, Aviva. "Will Your Marriage Last?" *Psychology Today* (January 1, 2000). https://www.psychologytoday.com/articles/200001/will-your-marriage-last.

Perina, Kaja. "The Success of a Marriage." *Psychology Today* (May 1, 2003). https://www.psychologytoday.com/articles/200305/the-success-marriage.

Sands, Briana. "Sex and Glue: The Emotional Bond of a Physical Act." Wordpress. (June 2013). http://bryanasands.wordpress.com/2013/06/23/sex-and-glue-the-emotional-bond-of-a-physical-act.

Schrodt, Paul, Paul L. Witt, and Jenna R. Shimkowski. "A Meta-Analytical Review of the Demand/Withdraw Pattern of Interaction and Its Associations with Individual, Relational, and Communicative Outcomes." *Communication Monograms* 81, no. 1 (2014): 28. doi: 10.1080/03637751.2013.813632.

Selig, Meg. "Can the 'Novelty Habit' Boost a Couple's Commitment?" *Psychology Today* (May 2010). https://www.psychologytoday.com/blog/changepower/201005/can-the-novelty-habit-boost-couples-commitment.

Simon, Harvey B., MD "Giving Thanks Can Make You Happier." *Harvard Health Publications—Harvard Medical School* (November 2011). http://www.health.harvard.edu/healthbeat/giving-thanks-can-make-you-happier.

Vilibert, Diana. "5 Ways Having Sex Makes a Couple Stronger." Your Tango (2010). https://www.google.com/?gws_rd=ssl#q=Vilibert%2C+Diana.+%E2%80%9C5+Ways+Having+Sex+Makes+a+Couple+Stronger.%E2%80%9D+Your+Tango+ (2010).

Winch, Guy, PhD. "Harm from a Handheld?" Psychology Today (March/April 2015): 37.

STEP 2: Fight Fair
Books

Baker, James A. *The Anger Busting Workbook: Simple, Powerful Techniques for Managing Anger & Saving Relationships.* Houston: Bayou Publishing, 2005.

Chapman, Gary, and Jennifer Thomas. *The Five Languages of Apology: How to Experience Healing in All Your Relationships.* Chicago: Northfield Publishing, 2008.

Downs, Tim, and Joy Downs. *Fight Fair: Winning at Conflict without Losing at Love.* Chicago: Moody Publishers, 2003.

Dreyfus, Nancy. *Talk to Me Like I'm Someone You Love: Relationship Repair in a Flash.* New York: Tarcher, 2013.

Fisher, Helen. *Anatomy of Love: A Natural History of Mating, Marriage, and Why We Stray.* New York: Ballantine Books, 1994.

——. *Why We Love: The Nature and Chemistry of Romantic Love.* New York: Henry Holt & Co., 2004.

Fruzzetti, Alan E. The *High-Conflict Couple: A Dialectical Behavior Therapy Guide to Finding Peace, Intimacy & Validation.* Oakland, Calif.: New Harbinger Publications, 2006.

Gentry, W. Doyle. *Anger Management for Dummies.* Hoboken, N.J.: Wiley, 2006.

Gottman, John M. *The 5 Love Languages: The Secret to Love That Lasts.* Chicago: Moody Publishers, 2015.

——. *The Relationship Cure: A 5 Step Guide to Strengthening Your Marriage, Family, and Friendships.* New York: Harmony, 2002.

——. *The Science of Trust: Emotional Attunement for Couples.* New York: W.W. Norton & Company, 2011.

——. *Ten Lessons to Transform Your Marriage: America's Love Lab Experts Share Their Struggles for Strengthening Your Relationship.* New York: Harmony, 2007.

——. *Why Marriages Succeed or Fail: And How You Can Make Yours Last.* New York: Simon & Schuster, Inc., 1994.

Gottman, John, and Julie Schwartz Gottman. *And Baby Makes Three: The Six-Step Plan for Preserving Mental Intimacy and Rekindling Romance After Baby Arrives.* New York: Crown/Three Rivers Press, 2007.

Gottman, John M., and Nan Silver. *The Seven Principles for Making Marriage Work: A Practical Guide from the Country's Foremost Relationship Expert.* New York: Crown Publishing Group, 1999.

Gray, John. *Men Are from Mars, Women Are from Venus: The Classic Guide to Understanding the Opposite Sex.* New York: HarperCollins Publishing, 1993.

Hendrix, Harville. *Couples Companion: Mediations & Exercises for Getting the Love You Want: A Workbook for Couples.* New York: Atria Books, 1994.

————. *Getting the Love You Want: A Guide for Couples.* New York: Henry Holt & Co., 2007.

Lerner, Harriet. *The Dance of Intimacy: A Woman's Guide to Courageous Acts of Change in Key Relationships.* New York: Harper Perennial, 1990.

————. *Marriage Rules: A Manual for the Married and the Coupled Up.* New York: Gotham Books, 2012.

McKay, Matthew, and Peter Rogers. *The Anger Control Workbook.* Oakland, Calif.: New Harbinger Publications, 2000.

Page, Susan. *Why Talking Is Not Enough: 8 Loving Actions That Will Transform Your Marriage.* San Francisco: California: Jossey-Bass, 2007.

Puhn, Laurie. *Fight Less, Love More: 5-Minute Conversations to Change Your Relationship without Blowing Up or Giving In.* Emmaus, Pa.: Rodale Books, 2012.

Rivkin, Sharon M. *Breaking the Argument Cycle: How to Stop Fighting Without Therapy.* Guilford, Conn.: Globe Pequot Press, 2009.

Robinson, Jonathan. *Communication Miracles for Couples: Easy and Effective Ways to Create More Love and Less Conflict.* Newburyport, Mass.: Conari Press, 2012.

Salazar, Linda. *Parents in Love: Reclaiming Intimacy after Your Child Is Born.* Rolling Hills Estates, Calif.: Kystar Publishing, 1998.

Smalley, Greg. *Fight Your Way to a Better Marriage: How Healthy Conflict Can Take You to Deeper Levels of Intimacy.* New York: Howard Books, 2013.

Stutz, Phil, and Barry Michels. *The Tools: Transform Your Problems into Courage, Confidence, and Creativity.* New York: Spiegel & Grau, 2012.

Tannen, Deborah. *You Just Don't Understand: Women and Men in Conversation.* New York: HarperCollins Publishing, 2013.

Walker, Lenore E. *Battered Woman.* New York: William Morrow Paperbacks, 1980.

Zweig Connie, and Jeremiah Abrams. *Meeting the Shadow: The Hidden Power of the Dark Side of Human Nature.* New York: Tarcher, 1991.

Articles and Studies

Anwar, Yasmin. "Couples who say 'we' have a better shot at resolving conflicts." *Berkeley News* (January 27, 2010). http://news.berkeley.edu/2010/01/27/couple_we_ness.

Birnbach, Lawrence, and Beverly Hyman. "9 Ways Couples Must Agree: A Quick Guide for Solving the Most Common Problems in a Marriage." *Hitched.* http://www.hitchedmag.com/article.php?id=897.

Borenstein, Seth. "'Hangry'" Spouses More Likely to Lash Out On Each Other, Study Says." *Huffington Post* (April 16, 2014). http://www.huffingtonpost.com/2014/04/16/fighting-with-spouse-stud_n_5160699.html.

Brigham Young University. "Online role-playing games hurt marital satisfaction, experts say." *Science Daily* (February 14, 2012). http://www.sciencedaily.com/releases/2012/02/120214100932.htm.

Buck, A. A., and L. A. Neff. "Stress Spillover in Early Marriage: The Role of Self-Regulatory Depletion." PubMed (2012). http://www.ncbi.nlm.nih.gov/m/pubmed/22866931.

Brigham Young University. "Online role-playing games hurt marital satisfaction, experts say." *Science Daily* (February 14, 2012). http://www.sciencedaily.com/releases/2012/02/120214100932.htm.

Chatel, Amanda. "The Real Reason Facebook Causes One-Third of Divorces." *Your Tango* (January 28, 2012). http://www.yourtango.com/2012128108/Facebook-divorce.

Colons, Susie, and Otto Collins. "Why Time Alone Is the Key to a Successful Marriage." *Huffington Post* (December 2, 2013; updated January 23, 2014). http://m.huffpost.com/us/entry/4326246.

Connelly, Sherryl. "For a happier marriage just say 'we.'" *NY Daily News* (January 29, 2010.) http://www.nydailynews.com/life-style/couples-refer-happier-study-article-1.457634.

Dew, Jeffrey. "Financial Disagreements and Marital Conflict Tactics." *Journal of Financial Therapy*: Vol. 2: Issue 1, Article 7. Utah State University, 2011. http://digital commons.usu. edu/cgi/viewcontent.cgi?article=1069&context=fchd_facpub.

Dick Jones Communications. "What the Silent Treatment Says About Your Relationship." *Science Daily*. August 4, 2014. http://www.sciencedaily.com/releases/2014/08/140804122903.htm.

Effron, Lauren. "I Love You, But Get Off My Facebook: Social Media Prenups." ABC News (June 3, 2014). https://abcnews.go.com/Lifestyle/love-perfect-watch-facebook-social-media-prenups/story?id=23977608.

"Fighting Fairly." University of Wisconsin–Platterville, Counseling Services (1995–2015). http://www.uwplatt.edu/counseling-services/fighting-fairly.

Goleman, Daniel. "Study Defines Major Sources of Conflict between Sexes." *New York Times* (June 13, 1989). www.nytimes.com/1989/06/13/science/study-defines-major-sources-of-conflict-between-sexes.html?pagewanted=all.

Grohol, John. "Stress Hurts Relationships." *World of Psychology* (2009). http://psychcentral.com/blog/archives/2009/08/31/stress-hurts-relationships.

"Had a Row with Your Partner Today? That Will Be One of the 2,455 You Will Have This Year." *Daily Mail* (May 20, 2011). http://www.dailymail.co.uk/news/article-1389002/Fallout-Couples-argue-average-seven-times-day.html.

Heitler, Susan. "Does Gratitude Matter in Marriage?: Gratitude Is an Essential Ingredient of the Glue That Keeps Couples Bonded." *Psychology Today* (July 14, 2012). https://www.psychologytoday.com/blog/resolution-not-conflict/201207/does-gratitude-matter-in-marriage.

Hill, Heather. "Time, Gender, and Distrust: Why Couples Argue about Leisure." Northwestern University (September 26, 2003). paa2004.princeton.edu/papers/40837.

"Holmes and Rahe Stress Scale." Wikipedia. http://en.m.wikipedia.org/wiki/Holmes_and_Rahe_stress_scale.

"It's Good to Argue with Your Spouse." Intelligence for Your Life (2015). http://www.tesh.com/story/love-and-relationships-category/its-good-to-argue-with-your-spouse/cc/13/id/16139.

Kaminer, Wendy, Carolina Izquierdo, and Thomas N. Bradbury. "The Difference between a Happy Marriage and Miserable One: Chores." *The Atlantic* (March 1, 2013). http://www.theatlantic.com/sexes/archive/2013/03/the-difference-between-a-happy-marriage-and-miserable-one-chores/273615.

Katie, M. "Fair Fighting—Lectures." University of Texas at Austin. StudyBlue Communication Studies (December 3, 2010). https://www.Study.blue.com/notes/note/n/fair-fighting-lecture/deck/152009.

Masi, Alessandria. "New Study Claims Facebook Is Linked to Increase in Divorce Rate." *IBT Times* (July 8, 2014). http://www.ibtimes.com/new-study-claims-facebook-linked-increase-divorce-rate-1622492.

Miller, Anna. "Can this marriage be saved?" *American Psychological Association* 44, no 4, Print Version: 42 (April 2013). http://www.apa.org/monitor/2013/04/marriage.aspx.

Nauert, Rick. "Angry Partner May Also Be Sad." Psych Central (May 22, 2012). http://psych central.com/news/2012/05/22/angry-partner-may-also-be-sad/39044.html.

———. "Couples Fight Over Power, Relationship Investment." Psych Central (July 10, 2013). http://psychcentral.com/news/2013/07/10/couples-fight-over-power-relationship-investment.

———. "Facebook can damage your relationship." Psych Central (June 10, 2013). http://psychcentral.com/news/2013/06/10/Facebook-can-damage-your-relationship/55846.

———. "Perceived Emotions Can Intensify a Quarrel between Lovers." *Live Science* (January 13, 2011). http://m.livescience.com/9284-perceived-emotions-intensify-quarrel-lovers.html.

Neff, L. A., and B. R. Karney. "Stress and Reactivity to Daily Relationship Experiences: How Stress Hinders Adaptive Processes in Marriage." *Journal of Personality and Social Psychology* 97, no. 3 (2009): 435–450.

Northwestern University. "Twenty-one minutes to marital satisfaction: Minimal intervention can preserve marital quality over time." *Science Daily* (February 5, 2013). http://www. sciencedaily.com/releases/2013/02/130205123702.htm.

Nowinski, Joseph. "Do You and Your Spouse Argue Over Drinking? How to Avoid Armageddon." *Huffington Post* (April 16, 2013; updated June 16, 2013). http://www. huffingtonpost.com/joseph-nowinski-phd-alcohol-abuse-relationships_b_3076888.html.

Parker-Pope, Tara. "Is Marriage Good for your Health?" *The New York Times Magazine* (April 14, 2010). http://www.nytimes.com/2010/04/18/magazine/18marriage-t. html?pagewanted=1&sq=marriage.

Peterson, Andrea. "So Cute, So Hard on a Marriage: After Baby, Men and Women are Unhappy in Different Ways; Pushing Pre-Emptive Steps." *Wall Street Journal* (April 28, 2011). http://www.wsj.com/articles/SB10001424052748704099704576288954011675900.

Pines, A. M., and C. F. Bowes. "Romantic Jealousy: How to Recognize Where Jealousy Comes from and How to Cope with It." *Psychology Today* (March 1, 1992). https://www. psychologytoday.com/articles/200910/romantic-jealousy.

Rampell, Catherine. "Money Fights Predict Divorce Rates." *New York Times* (December 7, 2009). http://economix.blogs.nytimes.com/2009/12/07/ money-fights-predict-divorce-rates/?_=1.

Rebecca. "Free Time: Husband vs. Wife." Moms Alive: Blog, *Just for You, Love and Marriage, Mother, Rebecca* (November 10, 2010). www.momsalive.com/2010/11/ free-time-husband-vs-wife.

Rosenfeld, Everett. "Social networking linked to divorce, marital unhappiness." CNBC (July 8, 2014). http://www.cnbc.com/2014/07/08/social-networking-linked-to-divorce-marital-unhappiness.html.

Rutgers University. "A wife's happiness is more crucial than her husband's in keeping marriage on track." *Science Daily* (September 12, 2014). http://www.sciencedaily.com/ releases/2014/09/140912134824.htm.

Sanford, Keith. "Hard and Soft Emotion During Conflict: Invested Married Couples and Other Relationships." *Personal Relationships* 14, issue 1 (March 2007): 65–90. Wiley Online Library. http://onlinelibrary.wiley.com/doi/10.1111/j.1475-6811.2006.00142.x/ abstract.

Schneider, Barbara, & Waite, Linda J. "The 500 Family Study (1998–2000 United States)." Child Care & Early Education Research Connections. ICPSR. http://www.csun. edu/~vcsoc00i/classes/s680f13/04549-Description.pdf.

Slater and Gordon. "Social Media is the New Marriage Minefield." Slater and Gordon Lawyers (April 30, 2015). http://www.slatergordon.co.uk/media-centre/press-releases/2015/04/ social-media-is-the-new-marriage-minefield.

"Sleep Study Reveals Couples Fight More After A Bad Night's Sleep." *Huffington Post* (July 9, 2013). http://www.huffingtonpost.com/2013/07/09/sleep-study_n_3569613.html.

Spike, W. S., and Norbert Schwartz Lee. "Framing Love: When It Hurts to Think We Were Made for Each Other." *Journal of Experimental Social Psychology* 54 (September 2014): 61–67. http://www.sciencedirect.com/science/article/pii/S0022103114000493?via%3Dihub. doi: 10.1016/j.jesp2.

Stout, Hilary. "The Key to a lasting marriage: combat." *The Wall Street Journal* (November 4, 2004). http://www.wsj.com/articles/SB109952103084364089.

Taylor and Francis. "When TV and marriage meet: TV's negative impact on romantic relationships." *Science Daily* (September 18, 2012). http://www.sciencedaily.com/ releases/2012/09/120918121322.htm.

Telegraph Reporters. "Writing a quarterly report is the trick to saving a marriage." *Telegraph* (February 6, 2013). http://www.telegraph.co.uk/lifestyle/9852207/ Writing-a-quarterly-report-is-the-trick-to-sa.

University of Illinois College of Agricultural, Consumer and Environmental Sciences. "When newlyweds believe in sharing household chores, follow-through is everything." *Science Daily* (May 6, 2014). http://www.sciencedaily.com/releases/2014/05/140506190740.htm.

University of Minnesota. "You benefit if your romantic partner recovers well from spats." *Science Daily* (February 14, 2011). http://www.sciencedaily.com/releases/2011/02/1102111143.htm.

Weaver, Nicole. "5 Ways Facebook Can (and Sometimes Does) Cause Divorce." *Your Tango* (May 13, 2015). http://magazine.foxnews.com/love/5-ways-Facebook-can-and-sometimes-does-cause-divorce.

Wilcox, W. Bradford. "Unequal, Unfair, and Unhappy: The 3 Biggest Myths about Marriage Today: Most Married Couples with Children Are Satisfied with Their Relationships." *The Atlantic* (June 3, 2013). www.theatlantic.com/sexes/archive/2013/06/unequal-unfair-and-unhappy-the-3-biggest-myths-about-marraige-today/276468.

Wilde, Cathy. "Heavy Drinking Is Bad for Marriage If One Spouse Drinks, But Not Both." University of Buffalo—News Center (November 21, 2013). www.buffalo.edu/news/releases/2013/11/031.html.

Wong, Brittany. "Stay Off Social Media (Or Risk Divorce), New Survey Says." *Huffington Post* (April 30, 2015). http://www.huffingtonpost.com/2015/04/30/way-to-ruin-marriages-facebook_n_7183296.html.

STEP 3: Negotiate

Books

Barbach, Lonnie, and David L. Geisinger. *Going the Distance: Finding and Keeping Lifelong Love*. New York: Plume, 1991.

Beck, Aaron T., MD. *Love Is Never Enough: How Couples Can Overcome Misunderstandings, Resolve Conflicts, and Solve Relationship Problems through Cognitive Therapy*. New York: Harper Perennial, 1988.

Diamond, Stuart. *Getting More: How to Negotiate to Achieve Your Goals in the Real World*. New York: Crown Business, 2010.

Fisher, Roger, and William Ury. *Getting to Yes: Negotiating Agreement Without Giving In*. New York: Penguin Group, 2011.

Fraenkel, Peter, PhD. *Sync Your Relationship, Save Your Marriage: Four Steps to Getting Back on Track*. New York: Palgrave Macmillan, 2011.

Goleman, Daniel. Emotional Intelligence: Why It Can Matter More Than IQ. New York: Bantam, 1995.

Gottman, John. *Why Marriages Succeed or Fail: And How You Can Make Yours Last*.

Harley, Willard F., Jr. *He Wins, She Wins: Learning the Art of Marital Negotiation*. Grand Rapids, Mich.: Revell, 2013.

Kirshenbaum, Mira. *Too Good to Leave, Too Bad to Stay: A Step-by-Step Guide to Help You Decide Whether to Stay in or Get out of Your Relationship*. New York: Dutton, 1996.

Lerner, Harriet, PhD. *The Dance of Anger*. New York: Harper Perennial, 1985, 1997.

———. The Dance of Intimacy.

Love, Patricia, EdD, and Steven Stosny, PhD. *How to Improve Your Marriage without Talking About It*. New York: Harmony, 2007.

Lowndes, Leil. *How to Talk to Anyone: 92 Little Tricks for Big Success in Relationships*. New York: McGraw-Hill, 2003.

Patterson, Kerry, Joseph Grenny, Ron McMillan, and Al Switzler. *Crucial Conversations: Tools for Talking When Stakes Are High*, 2nd ed. New York: McGraw-Hill, 2012.

Scarf, Maggie. *Intimate Partners: Patterns in Love and Marriage*. New York: Ballantine Books, 1987.

Sills, Judith, PhD. *A Fine Romance: The Passage of Courtship from Meeting to Marriage*. New York: Random House Ballantine Publishing Group, 1987.

Solomon, Marion, and Stan Tatkin. *Love and War in Intimate Relationships: Connection, Disconnection, and Mutual Regulation in Couple Therapy.* New York: W. W. Norton & Company, 2011.

Stone, Douglas, Bruce Patton, and Sheila Heen. *Difficult Conversations: How to Discuss What Matters Most.* New York: Penguin Group, 2010.

Ury, William. *The Power of a Positive No: Save the Deal Save the Relationship.* New York: Bantam, 2007.

Wheeler, Michael. *The Art of Negotiation: How to Improvise Agreement in a Chaotic World.* New York: Simon & Schuster, 2013.

Zweig, Connie, PhD, and Steve Wolf, PhD. *Romancing the Shadow: A Guide to Soul Work for a Vital, Authentic Life.* New York: Ballantine Wellspring, 1997.

Articles and Studies

Coutu, Diane. "Making Relationships Work." *Harvard Business Review* (December 2007). https://hbr.org/2007/12/making-relationships-work.

Haskins, Suzan, & Prescher, Dan. "We Call it the Rashomon Effect." *Huffington Post.* November 8, 2013. http://m.huffpost.com/us/entry/4235194.

Salmansohn, Karen. "Good Compromise vs. Bad Compromise." OWN (December 17, 2014). http://www.oprah.com/relationships/Good-Compromise-vs-Bad-Compromise.

Salovey, Peter, and John D. Mayer. "Emotional Intelligence." Baywood Publishing Co., Inc. 1990. http://www.unh.edu/emotional_intelligence/EIAssets/EmotionalIntelligenceProper/EI1990%20Emotional%20Intelligence.pdf.

Van Lange, Paul A. M., Caryl E. Rusbult, Stephen M. Drigotas, Ximena B. Arriaga, Betty S. Witches, and Chante L. Cox. "Willingness to Sacrifice in Close Relationships." *Journal of Personality and Social Psychology* 72, no. 6 (1997): 1373–1375.

White, Mark D., PhD. "How Much Should You Compromise for Your Relationship?" *Psychology Today* (June 24, 2011). http://www.psychologytoday.com/blog/maybe-its-just-me/201106/how-much-should-you-compromise-your-relationship.

STEP 4: Resolve Childhood Issues
Books

Abrams, Jeremiah, ed. *Reclaiming the Inner Child.* Los Angeles: Jeremy P. Tarcher, Inc., 1990.

Adams, Kenneth M. *Silently Seduced: When Parents Make Their Children Partners, revised and updated.* Deerfield, Fla.: Health Communications, Inc., 2011.

Bradshaw, John. *Family Secrets: The Path from Shame to Healing.* New York: Bantam Books, 1995.
———. *Bradshaw On: The Family: A New Way of Creating Solid Self-Esteem.* Deerfield, Fla.: Health Communications, Inc., 1996.

Brown, Brené. *Daring Greatly: How the Courage to Be Vulnerable Transforms the Way We Live, Love, Parent and Lead.* New York: Avery Publishing, 2015.

Brown, Emily. *Patterns of Infidelity and Their Treatment.* London: Routledge, 2011.

Brown, Eva Marian. *My Parent's Keeper: Adult Children of the Emotionally Disturbed.* Oakland, Calif.: New Harbinger Publications, Inc., 1989.

Farmer, Steven. *Adult Children of Abusive Parents: A Healing Program for Those Who Have Been Physically, Sexually, or Emotionally Abused.* New York: Random House, 1989.

Faulkner, William. *Requiem for a Nun.* New York: Random House, 1951.

Ford, Arielle. *Turn Your Mate into Your Soulmate: A Practical Guide to Happily Ever After.* New York: HarperCollins Publishers, 2015.

Forward, Susan, with Craig Buck. *Toxic Parents: Overcoming Their Hurtful Legacy and Reclaiming Your Life.* New York: Bantam Books, 1989.

Gottman, John M. *The Relationship Cure: A 5 Step Guide to Strengthening Your Marriage, Family, and Friendships.* New York: Crown Publishers, 2001.

Goleman, Daniel. *Emotional Intelligence: Why It Can Matter More Than IQ.* New York: Bantam, 1995.

Hendrix, Harville. *Getting the Love You Want: A Guide for Couples.*

Hendrix, Harville, and Helen LaKelly Hunt. *Making Marriage Simple: 10 Relationship Saving Truths.* New York: Harmony Books. 2014.

Johnson, David, and Jeff Van Vonderen. *The Subtle Power of Spiritual Abuse: Recognizing and Escaping Spiritual Manipulation and False Spiritual Authority within the Church.* Minneapolis: Bethany House Publishers, 1991.

Kendall-Tackett, Kathleen. *The Hidden Feelings of Motherhood: Coping with Mothering Stress, Depression and Burnout.* Oakland, Calif.: New Harbinger, 2001.

Lerner, Harriet. *The Dance of Deception: A Guide to Authenticity and Truth-Telling in Women's Relationships.* New York: HarperCollins Publishers, 1993.

———. *The Dance of Connection: How to Talk to Someone When You're Mad, Hurt, Scared, Frustrated, Insulted, Betrayed, or Desperate.* New York: HarperCollins Publishers, 2002.

Mann (Berman), Jenn. *SuperBaby: 12 Ways to Give Your Child a Head Start in the First 3 Years.* New York: Sterling, 2010.

Miller, Alice. *The Drama of the Gifted Child: The Search for the True Self.* New York: Basic Books, 2008.

Minuchin, Salvador, and Michael P. Nichols. *Family Healing: Tales of Hope and Renewal from Family Therapy.* New York: The Free Press, 1993.

Napier, Augustus Y., with Carl Whitaker. *The Family Crucible: The Intense Experience of Family Therapy.* New York: HarperCollins Publishers, 1978.

Nathiel, Susan. *Daughters of Madness: Growing Up and Older with a Mentally Ill Mother.* Westport, Conn.: Praeger, 2007.

Neuharth, Dan. *If You Had Controlling Parents: How to Make Peace with Your Past and Take Your Place in the World.* New York: HarperCollins, 1998.

Neuman, Gary M. *The Truth about Cheating: Why Men Stray and What You Can Do to Prevent It.* Hoboken, N.J.: John Wiley & Sons, Inc., 2008.

———. *Connect to Love: The Keys to Transforming Your Marriage.* Hoboken, N.J.: John Wiley & Sons, Inc., 2010.

Neuman, Gary M., with Patricia Romanowski. *Helping Your Kids Cope with Divorce: The Sandcastles Way.* New York: Random House, 1998.

Schuurman, Donna. *Never the Same: Coming to Terms with the Death of a Parent.* New York: St. Martin's Griffin, 2004.

Spring, Janis Abrahms, with Michael Spring. *After the Affair: Healing the Pain and Rebuilding Trust When a Partner Has Been Unfaithful.* New York: HarperCollins Publishers, 2012.

Stapp, Scott, with David Ritz. *Sinner's Creed: A Memoir.* New York: Tyndale House Publishers, Inc., 2012.

Straus, Murray A., Emily M. Douglas, and Rose Anne Medeiros. *The Primordial Violence: Spanking Children, Psychological Development, Violence, and Crime.* New York: Routledge, 2013.

Van Der Kolk, Bessel. *The Body Keeps the Score: Brain, Mind, and Body in the Healing of Trauma.* New York: Viking, 2014.

Wallerstein, Judith S., Julia M. Lewis, and Sandra Blakeslee. *The Unexpected Legacy of Divorce: The 25 Year Landmark Study.* New York: Hyperion, 2000.

Woititz, Janet. *Adult Children of Alcoholics.* Deerfield, Fla.: Health Communications, Inc., 1990

Zweig, Connie, and Steve Wolf. *Romancing the Shadow: A Guide to Soul Work for a Vital, Authentic Life.* New York: The Ballantine Publishing Group, 1997.

Articles and Studies

Aber, J. Lawrence, and Joseph P. Allen. "Effects of Maltreatment on Young Children's Socioemotional Development: An Attachment Theory Perspective." *Developmental Psychology* 23, no. 3 (1987): 406–414. "Adult Children of Those with Mental Illness." The Band Back Together Project (n.d.). http://www.bandbacktogether.com/adult-child-of-those-with-mental-illness.

"Adult Survivors of Childhood Sexual Abuse." Sexual Trauma Services of the Midlands (n.d.). https://www.stsm.org/get-information/about-sexual-assault/adult-survivors-childhood-sexual-abuse.

Afifi, Tracie O., Natalie P. Mota, Patricia Dasiewicz, Harriet L. MacMillan, and Jitender Sareen. "Physical Punishment and Mental Disorders: Results from a Nationally Representative US Sample." *Pediatrics* 130, issue 2 (August 2012). http://pediatrics.aapublications.org/content/130/2/184.

Amato, Paul R. "The Consequences of Divorce for Adults and Children." *Journal of Marriage and Family* 62, issue 4 (November 2000): 1269–1287. http://onlinelibrary.wiley.com/doi/10.1111/j.1741-3737.2000.01269.x/abstract. doi: 10.1111/jomf.2000.62.issue-4/issuetoc.

Amato, Paul R., and Juliana M. Sobolewski. "The Effects of Divorce and Marital Discord on Adult Children's Psychological Well-Being." *American Sociological Review* 66, no. 6 (December 2001): 900–921. http://www.jstor.org/stable/3088878?seq=1#page_scan_tab_contents.

APA PsychNET (2015). http://psycnet.apa.org/journals/bul/99/1/66.

Arkowitz, Hal, and Scott O. Lilienfeld. "Is Divorce Bad for Children?: The Breakup May Be Painful, But Most Kids Adjust Well Over Time." *Scientific American MIND* (March 1, 2013). http://www.scientificamerican.com/article/is-divorce-bad-for-children.

Bartlett, Carolyn. "Bowen Family Model." Insight for Change (n.d.). http://www.insightforchange.com/enneagram_bowen.html.

Beitchman, Joseph H., Kenneth J. Zucker, Jane E. Hood, Granville A. DaCosta, Donna Akman, and Erika Cassavia. "A Review of the Long-Term Effects of Child Sexual Abuse." *Child Abuse & Neglect* 16, no. 1 (1992): 101–118. http://www.sciencedirect.com/science/article/pii/014521349290011F. doi: 10.1016/0145–2134(92)90011–F. 1992.

Bernstein, Elizabeth. "Are You Likely to Have an Affair? Risk Factors for Cheating Are Age, Gender and Relationship Satisfaction." *Wall Street Journal* (January 26, 2015). http://www.wsj.com/articles/are-you-likely-to-have-an-affair-1422295888.

Brooks, Andree. "Experts Find Extramarital Affairs Have a Profound Impact on Children." *New York Times* (March 9, 1989). http://www.nytimes.com/1989/03/09/us/health-psychology-experts-find-extramarital-affairs-have-profound-impact.html.

Brown, Brené. "How Vulnerability Holds the Key to Emotional Intimacy: And Shame Sabotages Our Desire for Closeness." *Spirituality & Health* (November/December 2012). http://spiritualityhealth.com/articles/brené-brown-how-vulnerability-holds-key-emotional-intimacy.

Browne, Angela, and David Finkelhol. "Impact of Child Sexual Abuse: A Review of the Research." *Psychological Bulletin* 99, no. 1 (January 1986): 66–77. http://dx.doi.org/10.1037/0033-2909.99.1.66.

Cherlin, Andrew J., Lindsay P. Chase-Lansdale, and Christine McRae. "Effects of Parental Divorce on Mental Health throughout the Life Course." *American Sociological Review* 63, no. 2 (April 1998): 239–249. http://www.jstor.org/stable/2657325?seq=1#page_scan_tab_contents.

"Child Abuse and Neglect Statistics." American Humane Association (2013). http://www.americanhumane.org/children/stop-child-abuse/fact-sheets/child-abuse-and-neglect-statistics.html.

"Child Abuse Statistics & Facts." Childhelp (n.d.). https://www.childhelp.org/child-abuse-statistics/.

"Child Abuse Statistics & Resources." Speak Up Now—Voices for Children (n.d.). https://www.speakupnow.org/child-abuse-statistics-resources/?gclid=CMfW5cWbtMkCFYZBfgodjfkFVQ.

"Child Neglect." American Humane Association (2013). http://americanhumane.org/children/stop-child-abuse/fact-sheets/child-neglect.html.

"Child Neglect." *Psychology Today* (last updated on December 27, 2015). https://www.psychologytoday.com/conditions/child-neglect.

"Child Sexual Abuse Statistics." National Center for Victims of Crime (2012). https://www.victimsofcrime.org/media/reporting-on-child-sexual-abuse/child-sexual-abuse-statistics.

"Children Divorce Statistics." Children-and-Divorce.com (2013). http://www.children-and-divorce.com/children-divorce-statistics.html.

"Couples Therapy with Dr. Jenn/Janice Dickinson & Joe Budden Argue Over Beating Their Kids/VH1." Video posted on YouTube by VH1 (comment by Sharon Evans). (November 2015). https://m.youtube.com/watch?v=E2OBiHqjPCc.

Doares, Leslie. "Is My Marriage Doomed If My Parents Got Divorced When I Was a Kid?" PsychCentral: World of Psychology (November 9, 2012). http://psychcentral.com/blog/archives/2012/11/09/is-my-marriage-doomed-if-my-parents-got-divorced-when-i-was-a-kid/.

Dube, Shanta R., and Robert F. Anda, Vincent J. Felitti, Valerie J. Edwards, and Janet B. Croft. "Adverse Childhood Experiences and Personal Alcohol Abuse as an Adult." Science Direct 27, no. 5 (September–October 2002): 71–725. http://www.sciencedirect.com/science/article/pii/S0306460301002040. doi:10.1016/S306-4603(01)00204-0.

Durrant, Joan, and Ron Ensom. "Physical Punishment of Children: Lessons from 20 Years of Research." Canadian Medical Association Journal (February 6, 2012). doi: 10.1503/cmaj.101314 http://www.cmaj.ca/content/early/2012/02/06/cmaj.101314.citation.

"Effects of Child Sexual Abuse on Victims." National Center for Victims of Crime (2012). https://www.victimsofcrime.org/media/reporting-on-child-sexual-abuse/effects-of-csa-on-the-victim.

Figes, Kate. "How to Ruin Your Child's Chance of a Happy Love Life: Have an Affair—and the Damage Is WORSE the Older They Are When You Stray." Daily Mail (April 22, 2013). http://www.dailymail.co.uk/femail/article-2313246/How-ruin-childs-chance-happy-love-life-have-affair-damage-WORSE-older-stray.html.

Finkelhor, David, and Angela Browne. "The Traumatic Impact of Child Sexual Abuse: A Conceptualization." Originally published in American Journal of Orthopsychiatry 55, no. 4 (October 1985). Retrieved from Trainer's Resource Handout—Center for Sex Offender Management. "The Role of the Victim and Victim Advocate in Managing Sex Offenders." (March 24, 2010). http://www.csom.org/train/victim/resource/the%20traumatic%20impact%20of%20child%20sexual%20abuse.pdf.

Fleig, Jessica. "Controlling Parents 'Cause Long-Term Mental Damage to Their Children'—And the Trauma Is as Bad as Losing a Loved One." Daily Mail (December 7, 2015). http://www.dailymail.co.uk/health/article-3222078/Controlling-parents-cause-long-term-mental-damage-children-trauma-bad-losing-loved-one.html.

Friedman, Richard A. "When Parents Are Too Toxic to Tolerate." New York Times (October 19, 2009). http://nytimes.com/2009/10/20/health/20mind.html?_r=0.

Gaspard, Terry. "Vulnerability: The Secret Key to a Long-Lasting Relationship." Your Tango (2015). http://www.yourtango.com/experts/terry-gaspard/5-top-reasons-why-being-vulnerable-leads-intimacy.

Gershoff, Elizabeth T. "Corporal Punishment by Parents and Associated Child Behaviors and Experiences: A Meta-Analytic and Theoretical Review." Psychological Bulletin 128, no. 4 (2002): 539–579. https://www.endcorporalpunishment.org/assets/pdfs/reference-documents/Gershoff-research-2002.pdf.

———. "Spanking and Child Development: We Know Enough Now to Stop Hitting Our Children." Child Development Perspectives (July 10, 2013). http://www.ncbi.nlm.nih.gov/pmc/articles/PMC3768154/.

Hobart, Pamela J. "Children of Controlling Parents Are Less Happy as Adults, Study Shows, But Here's What You Can Do About It." Bustle (September 6, 2015). http://www.bustle.com/articles/108857-children-of-controlling-parents-are-less-happy-as-adults-study-shows-but-heres-what-you-can.

Hudson, Paul. "The Pain of Being in Love with Someone You Can Never Be with." *Elite Daily* (March 25, 2014). http://elitedaily.com/dating/sex/means-love-someone-can-never.

Hughes, Robert Jr. "The Long-Term Effects of Divorce on Young Adult's Intimate Relationships." *Huffington Post* (October 27, 2011; updated December 26, 2011). http://www.huffingtonpost.com/robert-hughes/the-longterm-effects-of-d_b_1027162.html.

"The Issue of Child Abuse." Child Help. http://www.childhelp.org/child-abuse.

"Impact of Child Abuse." ASCA—Adults Surviving Child Abuse. http:/www.blueknot.org.au/WHAT-WE-DO/Resources/General-Information/Impact-of-child-abuse.

Johnson, Jeffrey G., Patricia Cohen, Elizabeth M. Smailes, Andrew E. Skodol, Jocelyn Brown, and John M. Oldham. "Childhood Verbal Abuse and Risk for Personality Disorders During Adolescence and Early Adulthood." *Science Direct* 42, no. 1 (January 2001): 16–23. http://www.sciencedirect.com/science/article/pii/S0010440X01668895. doi: 10.1053/comp.2001.19755.

Kovac, Sarah. "Spanking the Gray Matter Out of Our Kids." CNN Health (July 23, 2014). http://www.cnn.com/2014/07/23/health/effects-spanking-brain/.

LaBeir, Douglas. "Why the Impact of Child Abuse Extends Well into Adulthood: Research Finds That Child Abuse Harms Mental and Physical Health in Adulthood." *Psychology Today* (October 19, 2013). https://www.psychologytoday.com/blog/the-new-resilience/201310/why-the-impact-child-abuse-extends-well-adulthood.

"Laundry List." Adult Children of Alcoholics World Service Organization (2015). http://www.adultchildren.org/lit-Laundry_List.

"The Lifelong Effects for a Child After the Death of a Parent." A Goodtherapy.org News Summary (October 24, 2011). www.goodtherapy.org/blog/parent-death-during-childhood/.

Lisak, David. "The Psychological Impact of Sexual Abuse: Content Analysis of Interviews with Male Survivors." *Journal of Traumatic Stress* 7, no. 4 (1994): 525–548.

"Long-Term Consequences of Child Abuse and Neglect." Child Welfare Information Gateway (July 2013). https://www.childwelfare.gov/pubs/factsheets/long_term_consequences.cfm.

Malinosky-Rummell, Robin, and David J. Hansen. "Long-Term Consequences of Childhood Physical Abuse." *Psychological Bulletin* 114, no. 1 (1993): 68–79.

McLanahan, S. S. "Father Absence and Children's Welfare." *In Coping with Divorce, Single Parenting, and Remarriage: A Risk and Resiliency Perspective, edited by* E. M. Hetherington. Mahwah, NJ: Erlbaum, 1999. http://www.apa.org/about/gr/issues/cyf/divorce.aspx.

McNulty Walsh, Karen, and Peter Genzer. "Gray Matter in Brain's Control Center Linked to Ability to Process Reward: Structure-Functions Impairments Observed in People Addicted to Cocaine." *BNL Newsroom* (November 29, 2011). http://www.bnl.gov/newsroom/news.php?a=11355.

"Multigenerational Transmission Process." The Bowen Center (September 3, 2014). http://www.thebowencenter.org/theory/eight-concepts/multigenerational-transmission-process/.

National Child Traumatic Stress Network (NCTSN). "Child Sexual Abuse Fact Sheet: For Parents, Teachers, and Other Caregivers." National Center for Child Traumatic Stress (April 2009). http://www.nctsn.org/nctsn_assets/pdfs/caring/ChildSexualAbuseFactSheet.pdf.

———. Physical Abuse Collaborative Group. "Physical Punishment: What Parents Should Know." National Center for Child Traumatic Stress (October 2009). http://www.nctsn.org/nctsn_assets/pdfs/PhysicalPunishment_Factsheet.pdf.

National Coalition against Domestic Violence (NCADV). "Domestic Violence National Statistics: What Is Domestic Violence?" (2015). http://www.ncadv.org/need-help/what-is-domestic-violence.

———. "Statistics." (2015). http://www.ncadv.org/learn/statistics.

O'Connell Corcoran, Kathleen. "Psychological and Emotional Aspects of Divorce." Mediate.com (June 1997). http://www.mediate.com/articles/psych.cfm.

Person-Ramey, Kirsten. "How Do Affairs Affect Children?" *Bounce Back from Betrayal* (June 9, 2015). http://bouncebackfrombetrayal.com/blog/how-do-affairs-affect-children.

Salario, Alizah. "How Infidelity Affects the Kids." *Daily Beast* (May 28, 2011). http://www.
thedailybeast.com/articles/2011/05/28/arnold-schwarzeneggers-affair-how-infidelity-affects-
the-kids.html.

Samakow, Jessica. "What Science Says about Using Physical Force to Punish a Child."
Huffington Post (September 18, 2014). http://www.huffingtonpost.com/2014/09/18/adrian-
peterson-corporal-punishment-science_n_5831962.html.

Smith, Anne B. "The State of Research on the Effects of Physical Punishment." Children's
Issues Centre—University of Otago (March 2006). https://www.msd.govt.nz/about-msd-
and-our-work/publications-resources/journals-and-magazines/social-policy-journal/spj27/
the-state-of-research-on-effects-of-physical-punishment-27-pages114-127.html.

Smith, Brendan L. "The Case against Spanking: Physical Discipline Is Slowly Declining As
Some Studies Reveal Lasting Harm for Children." *Monitor on Psychology* 43, no. 4 (April
2012): 60. http://www.apa.org/monitor/2012/04/spanking.aspx.

"Spanking Children Slows Cognitive Development and Increases Risk of Criminal
Behavior, Expert Says." *ScienceDaily* (December 11, 2013). http://www.sciencedaily.com/
releases/2013/12/131211103958.htm.

Spohn, William C. "The American Myth of Divorce." Santa Clara University: Markkula Center
for Applied Ethics (2014). http://www.scu.edu/ethics/publications/iie/v9n2/divorce.html.

Springer, Kristen W., Jennifer Sheridan, Daphne Kuo, and Molly Carnes. "Long-Term
Physical and Mental Health Consequences of Childhood Physical Abuse: Results from Large
Population-Based Sample of Men and Women." *Child Abuse and Neglect* 5 (May 31, 2007):
517–530. doi: 10.1016/j.chiabu.2007.01.003.

"Statistics—Child Sexual Abuse." Parents for Megan's Law: The Crime Victims Center
(2000–2015). http://www.parentsformeganslaw.org/public/statistics_childSexualAbuse.
html.

Strafford, Mai, Diana Kuh, Catherine Gale, Gita Mishra, and Marcus Richards. "Parent-
Child Relationships and Offspring's Positive Mental Wellbeing from Adolescence to
Early Older Age." *Edinburgh Research Explorer* (September 15, 2015). http://www.
research.ed.ac.uk/portal/en/publications/parentchild-relationships-and-offsprings-
positive-mental-wellbeing-from-adolescence-to-early-older-age(5f5cdffa-b169-4350-a471-
2128eaad405e).html.

Straus, Murray A. "New Evidence for the Benefits of Never Spanking" *Society* 38, issue 6
(September 2001): 52–60. http://link.springer.com/article/10.1007%2FBF02712591?LI=true.

Tomoda, Akemi, Hanako Suzuki, and Martin H. Teicher. "Reduced Prefrontal Cortical Gray
Matter Volume in Young Adults Exposed Harsh Corporal Punishment." *National Center for
Biotechnology Information.* http://www.ncbi.nlm.nih.gov/pmc/articles/PMC2896871.

Trivedi, Parul. "What Are the Long Term Psychological Effects of Death of a
Parent During Childhood?" *Quara* (December 3, 2010). https://www.quora.com/
What-are-the-long-term-psychological-effects-of-death-of-a-parent-during-childhood.

"Types of Child Abuse." ASCA—Adults Surviving Child Abuse. http://www.blueknot.org.au/
WHAT-WE-DO/Resources/General-Information/Types-of-child-abuse.

Tyrka, Audrey R., Lauren Weir, Lawrence H. Price, Nicole S. Ross, and Linda L. Carpenter.
"Childhood Parental Loss and Adult Psychopathology: Effects of Loss Characteristics and
Contextual Factors." PubMed (2008). http://www.ncbi.nlm.nih.gov/pmc/articles/PMC3580165.

"Understanding Child Maltreatment: Factsheet." US Centers for Disease Control and
Prevention, Department of Health & Human Services; National Center for Injury Prevention
and Control: Division of Violence Protection (2014). http://www.cdc.gov/violenceprevention/
pdf/understanding-cm-factsheet.pdf.

"Spanking Children Slows Cognitive Development and Increases Risk of Criminal
Behavior, Expert Says." *Science Daily* (December 11, 2013). http://www.sciencedaily.com/
releases/2013/12/131211103958.htm.

Walton, Alice G. "The Long-Term Effects of Spanking." *The Atlantic* (February 24, 2012). http://www.theatlantic.com/health/archive/2012/02/the-long-term-effects-of-spanking/253425/.

"What Is Spiritual Abuse?" Freedom Builders—Soulation (2015). http://www.soulation.org/freeatlast/spiritualabuse.

Williamson, David F., Theodore J. Thompson, Robert F. Anda, William H. Dietz, and Vincent J. Felitti. "Body Weight and Obesity in Adults and Self-Reported Abuse in Childhood: Abstract." *International Journal of Obesity* 26, no. 8 (August 2002): 1075–1082. http://www.nature.com/ijo/journal/v26/n8/full/0802038a.html.

Yerkovich, Kay, and Milan Yerkovich. "How Childhood Experiences Impact Marriage Relationships." *Thriving Family Magazine* (August/September 2012). http://www.thrivingfamily.com/Features/Magazine/2012/patterns-from-the-past.aspx.

Zaslow, Jeffrey. "Families with a Missing Piece." *Hello Grief* (June 2, 2010). http://www.hellogrief.org/families-with-a-missing-piece.

STEP 5: Forgive and Make Amends
Books

Abrahms Spring, Janis, and Michael Spring. *How Can I Forgive You?: The Courage to Forgive, the Freedom Not to.* New York: HarperCollins Publishers, 2004.

Beazley, Hamilton. *No Regrets: A Ten-Step Program for Living in the Present and Leaving the Past Behind.* Hoboken, N.J.: John Wiley & Sons, Inc., 2004.

Berger, Allen. *12 Hidden Rewards of Making Amends: Finding Forgiveness and Self-Respect by Working Steps 8–10.* Center City, Minn.: Hazelden, 2013.

Branden, Nathaniel. *Taking Responsibility: Self-Reliance and the Accountable Life.* New York: Simon & Schuster, 1996.

Campbell, Susan, and John Grey. *Five-Minute Relationship Repair: Quickly Heal Upsets, Deepen Intimacy, and Use Differences to Strengthen Love.* Tiburon, Calif.: HJ Kramer Books, published in a joint venture with New World Library, 2015.

Chapman, Gary. *Desperate Marriages: Moving toward Hope and Healing in Your Relationship.* Chicago: Northfield Publishing, 2008.

———. *The Five Love Languages: The Secret to Love That Lasts.* Chicago: Northfield Publishing, 2015.

Chapman, Gary, and Jennifer Thomas. *The Five Languages of Apology: How to Experience Healing in All Your Relationships.* Chicago: Northfield Publishing, 2006.

Coates, Christine A., and E. Robert LaCrosse. *Learning from Divorce: How to Take Responsibility, Stop the Blame, Move On.* San Francisco: Jossey-Bass, 2003.

Engel, Beverly. *The Power of Apology: Healing Steps to Transform All Your Relationships.* New York: John Wiley & Sons, Inc., 2001.

Enright, Robert D. *Forgiveness Is a Choice: A Step-by-Step Process for Resolving Anger and Restoring Hope.* Washington, D.C.: APA LifeTools, 2001.

Figes, Kate. *Our Cheating Hearts: Love & Loyalty, Lust & Lies.* London: Virago, 2013.

Freeman, Arthur, and Rose DeWolf. *Woulda, Coulda, Shoulda: Overcoming Regrets, Mistakes, and Missed Opportunities.* New York: HarperCollins, 1989.

Fruzzetti, Alan E. *The High-Conflict Couple: A Dialectial Behavior Therapy Guide to Finding Peace, Intimacy & Validation.* Richmond, B.C., Canada: Raincoast Books, 2006.

Hargrave, Terry. *Forgiving the Devil: Coming to Terms with Damaged Relationships.* Phoenix: Zeig, Tucker & Theisen, Inc., 2001.

Herman, Judith. *Trauma and Recovery: The Aftermath of Violence: from Domestic to Political Terror.* New York: Basic Books, 1997.

Lamb, Sharon, and Jeffrie G. Murphy, eds. *Before Forgiving: Cautionary Views of Forgiveness in Psychology.* New York: Oxford University Press, Inc., 2002.

Lawson, Annette. *Adultery: An Analysis of Love and Betrayal.* New York: Basic Books, 1988.

Lerner, Harriet. *The Dance of Connection: How to Talk to Someone When You're Mad, Hurt, Scared, Frustrated, Insulted, Betrayed, or Desperate.* New York: HarperCollins, 2002.

Luskin, Fred. *Forgive for Love: The Missing Ingredient for a Healthy and Lasting Relationship.* New York: HarperOne, 2007.

Lusterman, Don-David. *Infidelity: A Survival Guide.* Richmond, B.C., Canada: Raincoast Books, 1998.

MacDonald, Linda J. *How to Help Your Spouse Heal from Your Affair: A Compact Manual for the Unfaithful.* Gig Harbor, Wash.: Healing Counsel Press, 2010.

Markman, Howard J., Scott M. Stanley, Susan L. Blumberg, Natalie H. Jenkins, and Carol Whiteley. *12 Hours to a Great Marriage: A Step-by-Step Guide for Making Love Last.* San Francisco: Jossey-Bass, 2004.

Nay, Robert. *Overcoming Anger in Your Relationship: How to Break the Cycle of Arguments, Put-Downs, and Stony Silences.* New York: The Guilford Press, 2010.

Page, Susan. *Why Talking Is Not Enough: 8 Loving Actions That Will Transform Your Marriage.* San Francisco: Jossey-Bass, 2006.

Pines, Ayala M. *Romantic Jealousy: Understanding and Conquering the Shadow of Love.* New York: St. Martin's Press, 1992.

Pittman, Frank. *Private Lies: Infidelity and the Betrayal of Intimacy.* New York: W. W. Norton & Company & Company, 1989.

———. *Grow Up!: How Taking Responsibility Can Make You a Happier Adult.* New York: St. Martin's Griffin, 1998.

Puhn, Laurie. *Fight Less, Love More: 5-Minute Conversations to Change Your Relationship without Blowing Up or Giving In.* New York: Rodale, 2010.

Rivkin, Sharon M. *Breaking the Argument Cycle: How to Stop Fighting without Therapy.* Guilford, Conn.: GPP Life, 2009.

Smalley, Greg. *Fight Your Way to a Better Marriage: How Healthy Conflict Can Take You to Deeper Levels of Intimacy.* New York: Howard Books, 2013.

Smedes, Lewis B. *Forgive & Forget: Healing the Hurts We Don't Deserve.* New York: HarperCollins, 2007.

Stutz, Phil, and Barry Michels. *The Tools: Transform Your Problems into Courage, Confidence, and Creativity.* New York: Spiegel & Grau, 2012.

Truman, Karol K. *Feelings: Buried Alive Never Die . . . ,* revised and updated. St. George, Utah: Olympus Distributing, 2003.

Tutu, Desmond, and Mpho Tutu. *The Book of Forgiving: The Fourfold Path for Healing Ourselves and Our World,* edited by Douglas C. Abrams. New York: HarperOne, 2014.

Vanzant, Iyanla. *Forgiveness: 21 Days to Forgive Everyone for Everything.* Carlsbad, Calif.: Hay House, Inc., 2013.

Waldron, Vincent R., and Douglas L. Kelley. *Communicating Forgiveness.* Los Angeles: Sage Publications, 2008.

Weiner, Marcella Bakur, and Bernard D. Starr. *Stalemates: The Truth About Extra-Marital Affairs.* Far Hills, N.J.: New Horizon Press, 1989.

Wiesenthal, Simon. *The Sunflower: On the Possibilities and Limits of Forgiveness.* New York: Schocken Books, 1997.

Wile, Daniel B. *After the Fight: Using Your Disagreements to Build a Stronger Relationship.* New York: The Guilford Press, 1993.

Articles and Studies

Berg, Molly. "The Power of Thank You: UGA Research Links Gratitude to Positive Marital Outcomes." *UGA Today* (October 21, 2015). http://news.uga.edu/releases/article/research-links-gratitude-positive-marital-outcomes-1015.

Braithwaite, Scott R., Edward A. Selby, and Frank D. Fincham. "Forgiveness and Relationship Satisfaction: Mediating Mechanisms." *Journal of Family Psychology* 25, no. 4 (August 2011): 551–559. doi: 10.1037/a0024526.

Denmark, Florence, Deanna Chitayat, Harold Cook, Corann Okorodudu, Janet Sigal, Harold Takooshian, Neal Rubin, and Norma Simon. "Forgiveness: A Sampling of Research Results." American Psychological Association (2006). http://www.readbag.com/apa-international-resources-forgiveness.

Fenell, David L. "Characteristics of Long-Term First Marriages." *Journal of Mental Health Counseling* 15, no. 4 (October 1993): 446–460. http://eric.ed.gov/?id =EJ472268.

Fincham, Frank D., Steven R. H. Beach, and Joanne Davila. "Forgiveness and Conflict Resolution in Marriage." *Journal of Family Psychology* 18, no.1 (2004) 72–81. doi: 10.1037/0893–3200.18.1.72.

Firestone, Lisa. "5 Ways You Need to Build Forgiveness into Your Relationship: Don't Recreate Old Family Dynamics with Your Partner." *Psychology Today* (October 12, 2015). https://www.psychologytoday.com/blog/compassion-matters/201510/5-ways-you-need-build-forgiveness-your-relationship.

McMullough, Michael E., K. Chris Rachal, Steven J. Sandage, Everett L. Worthington Jr., Susan Wade Brown, and Terry L. Hight. "Interpersonal Forgiving in Close Relationships: II. Theoretical Elaboration and Measurement." *Journal of Personality and Social Psychology* 75, no. 6 (1998): 1586–1603. http://www.psy.miami.edu/faculty/mmccullough/Papers/Interpers%20Forgiving_II.pdf.

Murphy, Jeffrie G. "Two Cheers for Vindictiveness." *Punishment & Society* 2 (2000): 131. http://ssrn.com/abstract=1462831.

Schnur, Susan. "Beyond Forgiveness" *Lilith Magazine* (Fall 2001). http://lilith.org/articles/beyond-forgiveness.

Simon, George. "Understanding 'Splitting' as a Psychological Term." Counselling Resource. October 28, 2008. http://counsellingresource.com/features/2008/10/28/splitting-as-psychological-term.

Williamson, Marianne. Epigraph: "Until we have seen someone's darkness we don't really know who they are. Until we have forgiven someone's darkness, we don't really know what love is." http://www.goodreads.com/author/quotes/17297.Marianne_Williamson.

STEP 6: Ignite Your Sex Life
Books

Allen, Pat, and Don Schmincke. *The Truth (about Men) Will Set You Free: The Science of Love and Dating.* Newport Beach, Calif.: The Dr. Pat Allen WANT Institute, 2009.

Allen, Patricia, and Sandra Harmon. *Getting to "I Do": The Secret to Doing Relationships Right!* New York: William Morrow Paperbacks, 1995.

Amen, Daniel G. *The Brain in Love: 12 Lessons to Enhance Your Love Life.* New York: Three Rivers Press, 2007.

Anderson, Dan, and Maggie Berman. *Sex Tips: For Straight Women from a Gay Man.* New York: HarperCollins, 2008.

Arp, David, and Claudia Arp. *Love Life for Parents: How to Have Kids and a Sex Life Too.* Grand Rapids, Mich.: Zondervan Publishing House, 1998.

Bader, Michael J. *Arousal: The Secret Logic of Sexual Fantasies.* New York: Thomas Dunne Books/St. Martin's Press, 2002.

Baker, Robin. *Sperm Wars: Infidelity, Sexual Conflict, and Other Bedroom Battles.* New York: Basic Books, 2006.

Barbach, Lonnie. *For Each Other: Sharing Sexual Intimacy.* New York: A Signet Book/New American Library, 1984.

———. *For Yourself: The Fulfillment of Female Sexuality.* New York: Signet, 2000.

Bergner, Daniel. *What Do Women Want?: Adventures in the Science of Female Desire.* New York: HarperCollins, 2013.

Bering, Jesse. *Perv: The Sexual Deviant in All of Us.* New York: Farrar, Straus and Giroux, 2013.

Berkowitz, Bob, and Susan Yager-Berkowitz. *Why Men Stop Having Sex: Men, the Phenomenon of Sexless Relationships, and What You Can Do about It.* New York: HarperCollins, 2009.

Betcher, William. *Intimate Play: Playful Secrets for Falling and Staying in Love.* New York: Penguin Books, 1988.

Biddle Barrows, Sydney, and Judith Newman. *Just Between Us Girls: Secrets About Men from the Mayflower Madam.* New York: St. Martin's Paperback, 1996.

Blakeway, Jill. *Sex Again: Recharging Your Libido: Ancient Wisdom for Modern Couples: Reawaken Your Desire, Discover a Renewed Sexual Balance, Reconnect with Your Partner.* New York: Workman Publishing, 2012.

Block, Jenny. *O Wow: Discovering Your Ultimate Orgasm.* Berkeley, Calif.: Cleis Press, 2015.

Blum, Deborah. *Sex on the Brain: The Biological Differences between Men and Women.* New York: Viking, 1997.

Brizendine, Louann. *The Male Brain: A Breakthrough Understanding of How Men and Boys Think.* New York: Three Rivers Press, 2010.

Brockway, Laurie Sue. *How to Seduce a Man and Keep Him Seduced.* New York: Citadel Press, 1998.

Bryans, Bruce. *Make Him BEG for Your Attention: 75 Communication Secrets for Captivating Men to Get the Love and Commitment You Deserve.* Bruce Bryans, 2013. CreateSpace Independent Publishing Platform, 2013.

———. *The 7 Irresistible Qualities Men Want in a Woman: What High-Quality Men Secretly Look for a When a Choosing "The One."* CreateSpace Independent Publishing Platform, 2013.

Buss, David M. *The Dangerous Passion: Why Jealousy Is As Necessary As Love and Sex.* New York: The Free Press, 2000.

Calming the tempest, bridging the gorge: healing in couples ruptured by "sex addiction." https://www.researchgate.net/publication/263732501_Calming_the_tempest_bridging_the_gorge_healing_in_couples_ruptured_by_sex_addiction.

Carnes, Patrick. *Out of the Shadows: Understanding Sexual Addiction*, 3rd ed. Center City, Minn.: Hazelden, 2001.

Carroll, Aaron E., and Rachel C. Vreeman. *Don't Put That in There! And 69 Other Sex Myths Debunked.* New York: St. Martin's Griffin, 2014.

Chartham, Robert. *The Sensuous Couple.* New York: Ballantine Books, 1971.

Cox, Tracey. *The Hot Sex Handbook: The Handy Pocket Guide to Hot Sex Anywhere, Anytime!* New York: Bantam Books, 2005.

Craker, Lorilee. *We Should Do This More Often: A Parents' Guide to Romance, Passion, and Other Prechild Activities You Vaguely Recall.* Colorado Springs, Colo.: WaterBrook Press, 2005.

Cramer, Elizabeth. *131 Dirty Talk Examples: Learn How to Talk Dirty with These Simple Phrases That Drive Your Lover Wild & Beg You for Sex Tonight.* CreateSpace Independent Publishing Platform, 2013.

Davis, Kristin, and Lainie Speiser. *The Manhattan Madam's Secrets to Great Sex: Expert Advice for Becoming the Best Lover He's Ever Had.* London: Quiver Publishing, 2012.

Davis Raskin, Valerie. *Great Sex for Moms: Ten Steps to Nurturing Passion While Raising Kids.* New York: Simon & Schuster, 2002.

Donaghue, Chris. *Sex outside the Lines: Authentic Sexuality in a Sexually Dysfunctional Culture.* Dallas: BenBella Books, Inc., 2015.

Easton, Dossie, and Janet W. Hardy. *The Ethical Slut: A Practical Guide to Polyamory, Open Relationships, & Other Adventures,* 2nd ed., updated and expanded. *Berkeley,* Calif.: Celestial Arts, 2009.

Em & Lo. *150 Shades of Play: From A to Z.* New York: Better Half Books, 2012.

Erickson-Schroth, Laura, ed. *Trans Bodies, Trans Selves: A Resource for the Transgender Community.* New York: Oxford University Press, 2014.

Fegatofi, Michelle. *BDSM Basics for Beginners: A Guide for Dominants and Submissives Starting to Explore the Lifestyle.* lulu.com, 2013.

Feldhahn, Shaunti. *For Women Only: What You Need to Know about the Inner Lives of Men,* *revised and updated ed. Colorado Springs,* Colo.: Multnomah Books, 2013.

Feldhahn, Shaunti, and Jeff Feldhahn. *For Men Only: A Straightforward Guide to the Inner Lives* *of Women. Colorado Springs,* Colo.: Multnomah Books, 2013.

Fisher, Helen. *Anatomy of Love: A Natural History of Mating, Marriage, and Why We Stray.* New York: Fawcett Columbine, 1992.

———. *Why We Love: The Nature and Chemistry of Romantic Love.* New York: Henry Holt & Company, 2004.

Fletcher, Baje. *A Goal Digger's Guide: How to Get What You Want without Giving It Up!* Orlando, Fla.: Glitz & Glamour Models, Talent and Publishing: 2009.

Forleo, Marie. *Make Every Man Want You: How to Be So Irresistible You'll Barely Keep from* *Dating Yourself!* New York: McGraw-Hill Companies, 2008.

Fulbright, Yvonne K. *The Better Sex Guide to Extraordinary Lovemaking.* London: Quarto Publishing, 2009.

———. *The Best Oral Sex Ever: Her Guide to Going Down.* Massachusetts: Adams Media Corporation, 2011.

———. *The Best Oral Sex Ever: His Guide to Going Down.* Massachusetts: Adams Media Corporation, 2011.

Gottman, John, and Julie Schwartz Gottman. *And Baby Makes Three: The Six-Step Plan for* *Preserving Marital Intimacy and Rekindling Romance After Baby Arrives.* New York: Three Rivers Press, 2007.

Gray, John. *Mars and Venus in the Bedroom: A Guide to Lasting Romance and Passion.* New York: Harper Perennial, 1997.

Greene, Robert. *The Art of Seduction.* New York: Penguin Books, 2001.

Hanako. *The Geisha Secret: Ancient Dating Rituals Proven to Win a Modern Man's Heart, 2nd ed.* New York: FassFrankfurt Media, LLC, 2013.

Harley, Willard F., Jr. *His Needs, Her Needs: Building an Affair-Proof Marriage. Ada,* Mich.: Reveli, 2011.

Hartley, Nina, and I. S. Levine. *Nina Hartley's Guide to Total Sex.* New York: Avery/Penguin Group, 2006.

Harvey, Steve. *Act Like a Lady, Think Like a Man: What Men Really Think About Love,* *Relationships, Intimacy, and Commitment.* New York: Amistad; HarperCollins, 2009.

Heiman, Julie R., and Joseph LoPiccolo. *Becoming Orgasmic: A Sexual and Personal Growth* *Program for Women, revised and expanded ed.* New York: Simon & Schuster, 1988.

Hite, Shere. *The Hite Report: A Nationwide Study of Female Sexuality.* New York: Seven Stories Press, 2004.

Hubbard, Eleanor A., and Cameron T. Whitley, eds. *Trans-Kin: A Guide for Family & Friends of* *Transgender People.* Bolder Press, 2012.

J. *The Sensuous Woman.* New York: Dell Publishing, 1969.

Joannides, Paul. *Guide to Getting It On: A Book about the Wonders of Sex.* Waldport, Ore.: Goofy Foot Press, 2014.

Jones, Taylor B. *The Sugar Daddy Formula: A Sugar Baby's Ultimate Guide to Finding a Wealthy* *Sugar Daddy.* Georgia: R&D Publishing, 2014.

Kahn, Elayne, and David Rudnitsky. *Parents Who Stay Lovers: How to Keep the Magic Alive* *from Pregnancy Onward. Avon,* Mass.: Adams Media Corp., 1992.

Kahr, Brett. *Who's Been Sleeping in Your Head?: The Secret World of Sexual Fantasies.* New York: Basic Books, 2008.

Keesling, Barbara. *How to Make Love All Night: And Drive a Woman Wild.* New York: HarperCollins Publishers, 1994.

———. *All Night Long: How to Make Love to a Man Over 50.* New York: M. Evans & Company, 2000.

———. *The Good Girl's Guide to Bad Girl Sex: An Incredible Guide to Pleasure & Seduction.* New York: M. Evans & Company, 2009.

Kerner, Ian. *Passionista: The Empowered Woman's Guide to Pleasuring a Man*. New York: HarperCollins, 2008.

———. *Sex Recharge: A Rejuvenation Plan for Couples and Singles*. New York: Collins Living, 2009.

———. *She Comes First: The Thinking Man's Guide to Pleasuring a Woman*. New York: William Morrow, 2010.

Kerner, Ian, and Heidi Raykeil. *Love in the Time of Colic: The New Parents' Guide to Getting It on Again*. New York: Collins Living, 2009.

Kim Conant, Py. *Sex Secrets of an American Geisha: How to Attract, Satisfy, and Keep Your Man*. Alameda, Calif.: Hunter House Inc., 2007.

King, Kara. *The Power of the Pussy: How to Get What You Want From Men: Love, Respect, Commitment and More . . . What Do You Want?* CreateSpace Independent Publishing Platform, 2012.

Krasnow, Iris. *Sex After . . . Women Share How Intimacy Changes as Life Changes*. New York: Gotham Books, 2015.

Lambert, G. L. *Ho Tactics: How to Mindf**k a Man into Spending, Spoiling, and Sponsoring*. *Walnut*, Calif.: Viceroy, 2014.

Leiblum, Sandra R., and Raymond C. Rosen, eds. *Principles and Practice of Sex Therapy: Update for the 1990s*. New York: The Guilford Press, 1989.

Love, Patricia, and Jo Robinson. *Hot Monogamy: Essential Steps to More Passionate, Intimate Lovemaking*. Patricia Love and Jo Robinson, 2012. CreateSpace Independent Publishing Platform, 2012.

Malach Pines, Ayala. *Romantic Jealousy: Causes, Symptoms, Cures*. London: Routledge, 1998.

Mann (Berman), Jenn. *SuperBaby: 12 Ways to Give Your Child a Head Start in the First 3 Years*. *New York*: Sterling, 2010.

Margolies, Eva, and Stan Jones. *Seven Days to Sex Appeal: How to Be Sexier Without Surgery, Weight Loss, or Cleavage*. Kansas City, Mo.: Andrews McMeel Publishing, LLC, 2008.

Masters, Peter. *The Control Book*. Custom Book Publishing, 2006. CreateSpace Independent Publishing Platform, 2009.

Meston, Cindy M., and David M. Buss. *Why Women Have Sex: Women Reveal the Truth about Their Sex Lives, from Adventure to Revenge (and Everything in Between)*. New York: St. Martin's Griffin, 2009.

Metz, Michael E., and Barry W. McCarthy. *Coping with Premature Ejaculation: How to Overcome PE, Please Your Partner, & Have Great Sex*. Oakland, Calif.: New Harbinger Publications, Inc., 2003.

Michaels, Mark A., and Patricia Johnson. *Great Sex Made Simple: Tantric Tips to Deepen Intimacy & Heighten Pleasure*. Woodbury, Minn.: Llewellyn Worldwide Inc., 2012.

Michaelsen, Gregg. *To Date a Man, You Must Understand a Man: The Keys to Catch a Great Guy*. Gregg Michaelsen, 2014. [Self-Published]

Miller, Alan S., and Satoshi Kanazawa. *Why Beautiful People Have More Daughters: From Dating, Shopping, and Praying to Going to War and Becoming a Billionaire—Two Evolutionary Psychologists Explain Why We Do What We Do*. New York: Penguin Group, 2008.

Monet, Veronica. *Veronica Monet's Sex Secrets of Escorts: Tips from a Pro*. New York: Alpha Books, 2005.

Morin, Jack. *The Erotic Mind: Unlocking the Inner Sources of Sexual Passion and Fulfillment*. New York: HarperCollins Publishers, 1995.

Neustifter, Ruth. *The Nice Girl's Guide to Talking Dirty: Ignite Your Sex Life with Naughty Whispers, Hot Fantasies and Screams of Passion*. Berkeley, Calif.: Amorata Press, 2011.

Ogas, Ogi, and Sai Gaddam. *A Billion Wicked Thoughts: What the Internet Tells Us about Sexual Relationships*. New York: Plume/Penguin Group, 2012.

O'Reilly, Jessica. *Hot Sex: Tips, Tricks, and Licks: Sizzling Touch and Tongue Techniques for Amazing Orgasms*. New York: Quarto Publishing, 2013.

Paget, Lou. *How to Be a Great Lover: Girlfriend-to-Girlfriend Totally Explicit Techniques that Will Blow His Mind*. New York: Random House, 1999.
———. *How to Give Her Absolute Pleasure: Totally Explicit Techniques Every Woman Wants Her Man to Know*. New York: Broadway Books, 2000.
———. *Orgasms: How to Have Them, Give Them, and Keep Them Coming*. New York: Broadway Books, 2001.
———. *The Great Lover Playbook: 365 Sexual Tips and Techniques to Keep the Fires Burning All Year Long*. New York: Gotham Books, 2005.
———. *Hot Mamas: The Ultimate Guide to Staying Sexy throughout Your Pregnancy and the Months Beyond*. New York: Gotham Books, 2005.
———. *365 Days of Sensational Sex: Tantalizing Tips and Techniques to Keep the Fires Burning All Year Long*. New York: Gotham Books, 2003.
Pellicane, Arlene. *31 Days to a Happy Husband: What a Man Needs Most from His Wife*. Eugene, Ore.: Harvest House Publishers, 2012.
Perel, Esther. *Mating in Captivity: Unlocking Erotic Intelligence: Can We Desire What We Already Have? Does Good Intimacy Always Make for Hot Sex?* New York: Harper, 2006.
Pincott, Jena. *Do Gentlemen Really Prefer Blondes?: Bodies, Behavior, and Brains—The Science Behind Sex, Love & Attraction*. New York: Delta Trade Paperbacks, 2009.
Pittman, Frank. *Private Lies*.
Pokras, Somraj, and Jeffre Talltrees. *Female Ejaculation: Unleash the Ultimate G-Spot Orgasm*. Berkeley, Calif.: Amorata Press, 2009.
Poll Shows Sex Within Marriage More Fulfilling. http://www.imom.com/poll-shows-sex-within-marriage-is-more-fulfilling/#.V6B_za9HaK1.
Prioleau, Betsy. *Seductress: Women Who Ravished the World and Their Lost Art of Love*. New York: Penguin Books, 2003.
Ray, Darrel. *Sex & God: How Religion Destroys Sexuality*. Bonner Springs, Kan.: IPC Press, 2012.
Reanick, Stella. *The Heart of Desire: Keys to the Pleasures of Love*. Hoboken, N.J.: John Wiley & Sons, 2012.
Reiss, Ira L., and Harriet M. Reiss. *An End to Shame: Shaping Our Next Sexual Revolution*. New York: Prometheus Books, 1990.
Resnick, Stella. *The Pleasure Zone: Why We Resist Good Feelings & How to Let Go and Be Happy*. New York: MJF Books, 1997.
Ridley, Matt. *The Red Queen: Sex and the Evolution of Human Nature*. New York: Harper Perennial, 1993.
Roach, Mary. *Bonk: The Curious Coupling of Science and Sex*. New York: W. W. Norton & Company, 2008.
Ryan, Christopher, and Cacilda Jetha. *Sex at Dawn: How We Mate, Why We Stray, and What It Means for Modern Relationships*. New York: Harper Perennial, 2010.
Santagati, Steve. *The Manual: A True Bad Boy Explains How Men Think, Date, and Mate—and What Women Can Do to Come Out on Top*. New York: Three Rivers Press, 2007.
Schnarch, David. *Passionate Marriage: Keeping Love and Intimacy Alive in Committed Relationships*. New York: Henry Holt & Company, 1997.
———. *Intimacy & Desire: Awaken the Passion in Your Relationship*. New York: Beautfort Books, 2009.
Siegel, Stanley. *Your Brain on Sex: How Smarter Sex Can Change Your Life*. Naperville, Ill.: Sourcebooks Casablanca, 2011.
Spivack, Jill, and Jennifer Waldburger. *The Sleepeasy Solution: The Exhausted Parent's Guide to Getting Your Child to Sleep—from Birth to Age 5*. Florida: Health Communications, Inc., 2007.
St. Claire, Olivia. *203 Ways to Drive a Man Wild in Bed*. New York: Harmony Books, 1993.
———. *Unleashing the Sex Goddess in Every Woman*. New York: Harmony Books, 1996.

Surely, Kayt. *This Is Your Brain on Sex: The Science behind the Search for Love.* New York: Simon & Schuster Paperbacks, 2012.

Sweet, Lisa. *Expert Mind-Blowing BJs.* London: Carlton Books Limited, 2011.

Taormino, Tristan. *The Ultimate Guide to Kink: BDSM, Role Play, and the Erotic Edge.* Berkeley, Calif.: Cleis Press, 2012.

The Benefits from Marriage and Religion in the United States: A Comparative Analysis. http://www.ncbi.nlm.nih.gov/pmc/articles/PMC2614329.

Teich, Nicholas, M. *Transgender 101: A Simple Guide to a Complex Issue.* New York: Columbia University Press, 2012.

Thomashauer, Regina. *Mama Gena's Owner's and Operator's Guide to Men.* New York: Simon & Schuster, 2003.

Thorn, Clarisse. *The S&M Feminist: Best of Clarisse Thorn.* CreateSpace Independent Publishing Platform, 2012.

Verdolin, Jennifer L. *Wild Connection: What Animal Courtship and Mating Tell Us about Human Relationships.* New York: Prometheus Books, 2014.

Waxman, Jamye, and Emily Morse. *Hot Sex: Over 200 Things You Can Try Tonight.* San Francisco: Weldon Owen Inc., 2011.

Weiner Davis, Michele. *The Sex-Starved Marriage: Boosting Your Marriage Libido: A Couple's Guide.* New York: Simon & Schuster Paperbacks, 2004.

White, Ellen T. *Simply Irresistible: Unleash Your Inner Siren and Mesmerize Men, with Help from the Most Famous and Infamous Women in History.* Philadelphia: Running Press, 2007.

Wilson, Gary. *Your Brain on Porn: Internet Pornography and the Emerging Science of Addiction.* United Kingdom: Commonwealth Publishing, 2014.

Wiseman, Jay. *Tricks: More Than 125 Ways to Make Good Sex Better.* Emeryville, Calif.: Greenery Press, 1996.

———. *SM 100: A Realistic Introduction.* Emeryville, Calif.: Greenery Press, 1998.

Wray Gregoire, Sheila. *31 Days to Great Sex: For Married Couples.* Winnipeg, Manitoba, Canada: World Alive Press, 2013.

Young, Larry, and Brian Alexander. *The Chemistry between Us: Love, Sex, and the Science of Attraction.* New York: Current, 2014.

Ziglar, Stefan. *Talk Dirty: How to Talk to Get Your Man Aroused and in the Mood for Sex.* Stefan Ziglar, 2015. CreateSpace Independent Publishing Platform, 2015.

Zilbergeld, Bernie. *Male Sexuality: The First Book That Tells the Truth about Men, Sex and Pleasure.* New York: Bantam Books, 1978.

Zoldbrod, Aline P. *Sex Smart: How Your Childhood Shaped Your Sexual Life and What to Do about It: Transform Your Sex Life.* Indianapolis: iUniverse, 2009.

Articles and Studies

Alexander, Hilary. "Survey Suggests Men Prefer Black Lingerie: New Lingerie Survey Exposes the Naked Truth: That Men Favor Black Underwear." Fashion.Telegraph.co.uk. (February 10, 2010). http://fashion.telegraph.co.uk/news-features/TMG7204312/Survey-suggests-men-prefer-black-lingerie.html.

Babin, Elizabeth A. "An Examination of Predictors of Nonverbal and Verbal Communication of Pleasure during Sex and Sexual Satisfaction." *Journal of Social and Personal Relationships* (August 9, 2012). http://m.spr.sagepub.com/content/early/2012/08/08/0265407512454523. abstract. doi: 10.1177/0265407512454523.

Bernstein, Elizabeth. "What Keeps Couples Happy Long Term." *Wall Street Journal* (February 8, 2016). http://www.wsj.com/articles/what-keeps-couples-happy-long-term-1454961956.

Borreli, Lizette. "Quit Smoking and Slouching: 6 Surprising Health Problems That May Be Killing Your Sex Drive." *Medical Daily* (September 24, 2014). http://www.medicaldaily.com/quit-smoking-and-slouching-6-surprising-health-problems-may-be-killing-sex-drive-304612.

———. "What's Your Fantasy? 7 Facts about Sexual Fantasies That'll Make You

Feel Normal." *Medical Daily* (May 18, 2015). http://www.medicaldaily.com/pulse/whats-your-fantasy-7-facts-about-sexual-fantasies-thatll-make-you-feel-normal-333846.

———. "The Science of Dirty Talk and Why It Increases Sexual Pleasure." *Medical Daily* (August 27, 2015). http://www.medicaldaily.com/science-dirty-talk-and-why-it-increases-sexual-pleasure-349854.

———. "Alcohol and Sex: What Is 'Whiskey Penis' and How Does It Affect the Male Libido?" *Medical Daily* (October 15, 2015). http://www.medicaldaily.com/alcohol-and-sex-what-whiskey-penis-and-how-does-it-affect-male-libido-357278.

Brennan, Faye, and Jamie Hergenrader. "We've Come a Loooong Way: Polishing the Pearl." *Women's Health*: 128.

Brown, Jill S. "Can Being in Love Make You Fat? Plus, 10 Suggestions for Losing Marriage-Induced Love Handles." *Huffington Post* (February 10, 2015). http://www.huffingtonpost.com/Jill-s-brown/does-being-in-love-make-y_b_6675706.html.

Bushak, Lecia. "Does Marriage Make Men Fatter? Married Men 25% More Likely to Be Obese Than Their Single Counterparts." *Medical Daily* (January 16, 2014). http://www.medicaldaily.com/does-marriage-make-men-fatter-married-men-25-more-likely-be-obese-their-single-counterparts-267276.

Castleman, Michael. "8 Reasons Sex Improves Your Health." *AARP* (June 11, 2011). http://www.aarp.org/relationships/love-sex/info-06-2011/sex-improves-men-health.html.

Chapman University. "Body Satisfaction Examined in American Study of Men: Results of National Study Examining How Men Feel about Their Bodies, Attractiveness." *Science Daily* (March 8, 2016). https://www.sciencedaily.com/releases/2016/03/160308182808.htm.

Chapman University. "What Keeps Passion Alive in Long-Term Relationships?" *Science Daily* (February 25, 2016). https://sciencedaily.com/releases/2016/02/160225101244.htm.

Charles, Eric. "Ask a Guy: Exactly How to Seduce a Man (How to Turn a Man On, Part 1)." A New Mode (n.d.). http://www.anewmode.com/dating-relationships/how-to-seduce-a-man.

———. "Ask a Guy: Exactly How to Turn a Guy On (How to Seduce a Guy, Part 2)." A New Mode (n.d.). http://www.anewmode.com/dating-relationships/how-to-turn-a-guy-on.

Chemaly, Soraya. "50 Actual Facts about Rape." *Huffington Post* (December 8, 2014). http://m.huffpost.com/us/entry/2019338.html.

Cherney, Kristeen. "Depression & Sex: How Depression Can Affect Sexual Health." *Health Line* (January 11, 2016). http://www.healthline.com/health/depression/sexual-health#Overview1.

Chiarella, Tom. "The Missionary Position." *Esquire* (April 2012): 98–99.

"Child Sexual Abuse Statistics." National Center for Victims of Crime.

Chivers, M.L., J.M. Bailey, E. Latty, and G. Rieger. "A sex difference in the specificity of sexual arousal." Psychol Sci. 15, no. 11 (November 2004): 736–44. doi: 10.1111/j.0956-7976.2004.00750.x.

Christina, Greta. "Atheists Do It Better: Why Leaving Religion Leads to Better Sex." Alternet (May 17, 2011). http://www.alternet.org/story/150978/atheists_do_it_better%3A_why_leaving_religion_leads_to_better_sex.

Clinton, Leah Melby. "Study: 86% of Men Say They Care What Your Underwear Looks Like." *Glamour Fashion* (August 10, 2015). http://www.glamour.com/story/men-like-matching-lingerie.

Cohen, Adam, and Llana J. Tannenbaum. "Lesbian and bisexual women's judgments of the attractiveness of different body types." *The Journal of Sex Research* 38, no. 3 (2001): 226–232. http://www.researchgate.net/publication/247525233_Lesbian_and_bisexual_women's_judgments_of_the_attractiveness_of_different_body_types.

Cohen, A. J. "Ginkgo Biloba for Antidepressant-Induced Sexual Dysfunction." *Journal of Sex and Marital Therapy* (April–June 1998). PubMed. http://www.ncbi.nlm.nih.gov/pubmed/9611963.

Costanza, Justine Ashley. "Why Do Modern Women Love Romance Novels? Call It the 'Fifty Shades of Grey' Syndrome." *IBT Times* (June 30, 2012). http://www.ibtimes.com/why-do-modern-women-love-romance-novels-call-it-fifty-shades-grey-syndrome-720842.

Cromie, William J. "Male Body Image: East doesn't meet West." Harvard University—*Harvard Gazette* Archives (February 10, 2005). http://news.harvard.edu/gazette/2005/02.10/11-bodyimage.html.

Dineen, Cari Wira. "The Hidden Health Benefits of Sex." *Women's Health* (March 12, 2014). http://www.womenshealthmag.com/health/health-benefits-of-sex.

"Does Frequent Ejaculation Help Ward Off Prostate Cancer?" *Prostate Knowledge* (April 2009).http://www.harvardprostateknowledge.org/does-frequent-ejaculation-help-ward-off-prostate-cancer.

Dyer, Geoff. "The Demise of a Blowjob: And the Rise of Cunnilingus." *Esquire* (April 2012): 97.

"Eating Disorders Disrupt Healthy Sexual Function." *Eating Disorders Review* 21, no. 4 (July/August 2010). http://eatingdisordersreview.com/nl/nl_edr_21_4_10.html.

Eaves, Ali. "Why Your Grandparents Are Having Better Sex Than You." *Men's Health* (April 1, 2015). http://www.menshealth.com/sex-women/more-sex-after-50-years.

———. "The 5 Secrets of Long-Term Couples Who Still Have Sex." *Men's Health* (March 7, 2016). http://www.menshealth.com/sex-women/secrets-of-couples-who-still-have-hot-sex.

"8 Sex Habits of Happy Couples." *New York Post* (June 30, 2015). http://nypost.com/2015/06/30/8-sex-habits-of-happy-couples/?utm_campaign=socialflow.

"The 11 Best Sex Toys for Men." *Men's Health* (January 10, 2016). http://www.menshealth.com/sex-women/11-best-sex-toys-for-men/slide/12.

Fisher, Helen E. "Brains Do It: Lust, Attraction, and Attachment." The Dana Foundation (January 1, 2000). http://www.dana.org/Cerebrum/Default.aspx?id=39351.

Frederick, David A. "What Keeps Passion Alive? Sexual Satisfaction Is Associated with Sexual Communication, Mood Setting, Sexual Variety, Oral Sex, Orgasm, and Sex Frequency in a National U.S. Study." PubMed (2016). http://www.ncbi.nlm.nih.gov/m/pubmed/26900897.

Friedman, Richard A. "Infidelity Lurks in Your Genes." *New York Times* (May 22, 2015). http://www.nytimes.com/2015/05/24/opinion/sunday/infidelity-lurks-in-your-genes.html.

"The Future of Onanism: 6 Sex Toys That Redefine Male Masturbation." *GQ* (May 26, 2014). http://www.gq.com/story/the-future-of-Onanism-6-new-sex-toys-that-redefine-male-masturbation.

Goodrich, Terry. "Marital 'Long-Timers' Have a 'Slight Rebound' in Sexual Frequency After 50 Years, Study Finds." Baylor University/Media Communications (February 16, 2015).

Gregorie, Carolyn. "When It Comes to Sexual Fantasies, What's 'Normal?'" *Huffington Post* (November 4, 2014). http://www.huffingtonpost.com/2014/11/03/sexual-fantasies-normal_n_6081746.html.

Gummow, Jodie. "12 Things That Impact Your Sexual Satisfaction." *Alternet* (February 26, 2014). http://www.alternet.org/sex-amp-relationships/12-things-impact-your-sexual-satisfaction.

Hirsch, Kenneth R. "Signs of Low Testosterone in Men." Healthline (September 30, 2014). http://www.healthline.com/health/low-testosterone/signs-men-under-30#Overview1.

"How Can I Get Help for Depression?" *Healthline* (December 12, 2013). http://www.healthline.com/health/depression/help-for-depression#TreatmentFacts1.

Izadi, Elahe. "Yes, Men Gain Weight When They Become Dads, Study Confirms." *Washington Post* (July 21, 2015). https://www.washingtonpost.com/news/to-your-health/wp/2015/07/21/yes-men-gain-weight-when-they-become-dads-study-confirms.

Jones, Chris. "Ladies: You're Not As Good As You Think." *Esquire* (April 2012): 100–101.

Kabat-Zinn, Jon. "Stop Spectatoring: Mindfulness to Enhance Sexual Pleasure." *Psychology Today* (March 29, 2013). https://www.psychologytoday.com/blog/stress-and-sex/201303/stop-spectatoring-mindfulness-enhance-sexual-pleasure.

"Kegel Exercises for Men: Understand the Benefits." Mayo Clinic (August 13, 2015). http://www.mayoclinic.org/healthy-lifestyle/mens-health/in-depth/kegel-exercises-for-men/art-20045074.

Kelley, Kathryn, and Donna Musialowski. "Repeated Exposure to Sexually Explicit Stimuli: Novelty, Sex, and Sexual Attitudes." *Archives of Sexual Behavior* 15, no. 6 (December 1986): 487–498. PubMed. http://www.ncbi.nlm.nih.gov/pubmed/3800639.

Kerner, Ian. "What Do I Do about My Low Sex Drive? Sex Advice from Ian Kerner." *Cosmopolitan* (September 27, 2007). http://www.cosmopolitan.com/sex-love/advice/a587/low-sex-drive.

———. "Let's Talk about Sex . . . Even If It's Not Easy." CNN (February 23, 2012). http://thechart.blogs.cnn.com/2012/02/23/lets-talk-about-sex-even-if-its-not-easy.

———. "Your All-Day Seduction Plan for Better Sex." *Men's Health* (April 1, 2015). http://www.menshealth.com/sex-women/guide-to-seducing-her.

Kim, Meeri. "Men and Women Are Equally Good at Reading Partners' Sexual Satisfaction, Study Finds." *Washington Post* (April 12, 2014). https://www.washingtonpost.com/national/health-science/men-2014/04/12/f6be9072-c254-11e3-bcec-b71ee10e9bc3_story.html.

Kylstra, Carolyn. "12 Sex Secrets Women Wish You Knew." *Men's Health* (April 1, 2015). http://www.menshealth.com/sex-women/sex-secrets-she-wishes-you-knew.

Legenbauer, Tanja, Silja Vocks, Corinna Schafer, Sabine Schutt-Stromel, Wolfgang Hiller, Christof Wagner, and Claus Vogele. "Preference for Attractiveness and Thinness in a Partner: Influence of Internalization of the Thin Ideal and Shape/Weight Dissatisfaction in Heterosexual Woman, Heterosexual Men, Lesbians, and Gay Men." *Body Image* 6, no. 3 (June 2009): 228–234. PubMed. http://www.ncbi.nlm.nih.gov/pubmed/19443281. doi: 10.1016/j.bodyim.2009.04.002.

Lester, Gillian L. L., and Boris B. Gorzalka. "Effect of Novel and Familiar Mating Partners on the Duration of Sexual Receptivity in the Female Hamster." *Behavioral and Neural Biology* 49, no. 3 (May 1988): 398–405. *Science Direct*. http://www.sciencedirect.com/science/article/pii/S0163104788904189. doi:10.1016/S0163–1047(88)90418–9.

Lewis, Andy. "'Fifty Shades of Grey' Sales Hit 100 Million." *Hollywood Reporter* (February 26, 2014). http://www.hollywoodreporter.com/news/fifty-shades-grey-sales-hit-683852.

Lewis, Tanya. "Why Men Love Lingerie: Rat Study Offers Hints." *Live Science* (December 3, 2014). http://www.livescience.com/48980-rats-sexual-attraction-lingerie.html.

Ley, David J. "The Appeal of a Woman among Men." *Psychology Today* (March/April 2015): 10.

Loyola University Health System. "What Falling in Love Does to Your Heart and Brain." *Science Daily* (February 6, 2014). https://www.sciencedaily.com/releases/2014/02/140206155244.htm.

Lumpkin, Jincey. "Do Women Really Hate Porn? An Interview with Carlin Ross." *Huffington Post* (February 16, 2012). http://www.huffingtonpost.com/jincey-lumpkin/carlin-ross_b_1278032.html.

MacMillen, Hayley. "Our 30-Day Masturbation Challenge Is about to Change Your Sex Life (NSFW)." *Refinery 29* (January 4, 2016). www.refinery29.com/2016/01/100343/30-day-masturbation-challenge#slide.

———. "The Painful, Little-Known Condition That Messes with Women's Sex Loves." *Refinery 29* (January 11, 2016). http://www.refinery29.com/2016/01/100972/vestibulodynia-burning-pain-during-sex.

"Major Depression Among Adults." National Institute of Mental Health (2010). http://www.nimh.nih.gov/health/statistics/prevalence/major-depression-among-adults.shtml.

Mandel, Harold. "Orgasms May Enhance Quality Communication between Couples." *EMax Health* (July 7, 2014). http://www.emaxhealth.com/11402/orgasms-may-enhance-communication.

Mann (Berman), Jenn. "Sex after Baby." *Los Angeles Family* (February 2003): Pg 29 and 100.

"Marriage Weight Gain: Reasons You've Gained Weight since the Wedding." *Huffington Post* (February 14, 2013). http://www.huffingtonpost.com/2013/02/14/marriage-weight-gain_n_2688106.html.

Mayer Robinson, Kara. "10 Surprising Health Benefits of Sex." WebMD (2013). http://www.webmd.com/sex-relationships/guide/sex-and-health.

McGraw, Dr. Phil. "Moving Forward After Infidelity." Dr. Phil.com. www.drphil.com/advice/moving-forward-after-infidelity.

McMillen, Matt. "Low Testosterone: How Do You Know When Levels Are Too Low?" WebMD (2012). http://www.webmd.com/men/features/low-testosterone-explained-how-do-you-know-when-levels-are-too-low.

Meltzer, Andrea L., James K. McNulty, and Jon K. Maner. "Women Like Being Valued for Sex, As Long As It Is by a Committed Partner." *Archives of Sexual Behavior* (December 1, 2015): 1–14. http://link.springer.com/article/10.1007/s10508-015-0622–1#/page-1.

Meltzer, Andrea L., James K. McNulty, Sara A. Novak, Emily A. Butler, and Benjamin R. Karney. "Marriage Can Threaten Health: Study Finds Satisfied Newlyweds More Likely to Gain Weight." *Science Daily* (April 3, 2013). http://www.sciencedaily.com/releases/2013/04/130403200416.htm.

Meltzer, Andrea L., Sara A. Novak, James K. McNulty, E. A. Butler, and B. R. Karney. "Marital Satisfaction Predicts Weight Gain in Early Marriage." *Health Psychology* 32, no. 7 (July 2013): 824–827. PubMed (March 11, 2013). http://www.ncbi.nlm.nih.gov/pubmed/23477578. doi: 10. 1037/a0031593.

Michael, Dawn. "The Super Kinky Act Your Man Is Scared to Tell You He's Into." Your Tango (March 12, 2016). http://www.yourtango.com/experts/dawn-michael/what-cuckold-marriage-get-information-la-sex-counselor.

Miller, Korin. "Male Kegel Exercises—They're Real." *Cosmopolitan* (December 12, 2012). http://www.cosmopolitan.com/sex-love/advice/g2541/male-kegel-exercises?

Millikan Humphrey, Shonna. "On Marrying a Survivor of Childhood Sexual Abuse." *The Atlantic* (August 27, 2013). http://www.theatlantic.com/health/archive/2013/08/on-marrying-a-survivor-of-childhood-sexual-abuse/278967.

Orwig, Jessica, and Mike Nudelman. "What Men and Women Fantasize about Has More in Common Than You Think." *Business Insider* (October 19, 2015). http://www.businessinsider.com/10-most-common-sexual-fantasies-2015-10.

Parker-Pope, Tara. "The Science of a Happy Marriage." *New York Times* (May 10, 2010). http://well.blogs.nytimes.com/2010/05/10/tracking-the-science-of-commitment.

Parr Dip, Michael. "Quit Smoking Now to Reduce Your Stress, Explode Your Energy Levels And Increase Your Sexual Performance and Pleasure!" Mobile Smoke Busters (December 10, 2015). http://www.mobilesmokebusters.com.au/better-sex.

Persad, Michelle. "Lingerie Poll Shows Men Prefer Thongs and Push-Up Bras. Surprise, Surprise." *Huffington Post* (July 24, 2015). http://www.huffingtonpost.com/entry/surprise-surprise-when-it-comes-to-lingerie-poll-shows-men-prefer-thongs-and-push-up-bra_us_55afc51ee4b07af29d5717cd.

Persaud, Raj, and Jenny Bivona. "Women's Sexual Fantasies: The Latest Scientific Research." *Psychology Today* (August 28, 2015). https://www.psychologytoday.com/blog/slightly-blighty/201508/womens-sexual-fantasies-the-latest-scientific-research.

Portner, Martin. "The Orgasmic Mind." *Scientific American MIND: The Sexual Brain* (May 3, 2016): 5–9.

Robinson, Jennifer. "Sexual Performance Anxiety." WebMD (2015). http://www.m.webmd.com/sexual-conditions/guide/sexual-performance-anxiety-causes-treatments.

Russell, Eric M. "Gay Men's Bodily Attractiveness: Why a Higher Standard?" *Gay-Straight Relationships* (October 23, 2013). http://gaystraight.com/body-image/gay-mens-body-attractiveness.

Samadi, David. "The Link between Sex and Prostate Cancer" (Op-Ed). *Live Science* (November 21, 2014). http://www.livescience.com/48858-link-between-sex-and-prostate-cancer.html.

Schwyzer, Hugo. "The War against Monogamy Is Bullshit." *Jezebel* (February 8, 2013). http://Jezebel.com/5982801/the-war-against-monogamy-is-bullshit.

"Science: Human Body & Mind—The Science of Love." BBC Home (September 17, 2014). http://www.bbc.co.uk/science/hottopics/love.

"Sex Confession: What Happened When I Introduced Pegging to My Relationship." *Cosmopolitan* (March 26, 2016). http://www.cosmopolitan.com/sex-love/a55855/what-is-pegging/?src=TrueAnth_COSMO.

"6 Reasons Why People Gain Weight after Marriage." *Happy Lifestyle Journal (August 6, 2015).* http://happylifestylejournal.com/6-reasons-why-people-gain-weight-after-marriage.

Smith, Anthony, Anthony Lyons, Jason Ferris, Juliet Richters, Marian Pitts, Julia Shelley, and Judy Simpson. "Sexual and Relationship Satisfaction among Heterosexual Men and Women: The Importance of Desired Frequency of Sex." *Journal of Sex and Marital Therapy (2011).* PubMed. http://www.ncbi.nlm.nih.gov/m/pubmed/21400335.

Stevens, Heidi. "Key to a Satisfying Sex Life after 5, 10, 20 Years? Variety, Says Study." *Chicago Tribune* (February 10, 2016). http://www.chicagotribune.com/lifestyle/Stevens/ct-sex-life-longterm-happiness-balancing-0210-20160210-column.html.

Stills, Sharon. "Health Benefits of Masturbation." Women's Health Network (n.d.). http://www.womenshealthnetwork.com/sexandfertility/health-benefits-of-masturbation.aspx.

Taddeo, Lisa. "Why We Cheat: An Honest Appraisal." *Esquire* (April 2012): 103–105.

"10 Ways More Sex Can Improve Your Health." *Men's Health* (June 17, 2011). http://www.menshealth.com/sex-women/sex-health-benefits.

Thapoung, Kenny. "The Weird Thing That Happens to Guys After They're Married." *Women's Health* (January 21, 2014). http://www.womenshealthmag.com/sex-and-love/men-gain-weight-after-marriage.

Tiger, Caroline. "Happily Ever Fatter? How to Avoid Post-Wedding Weight Gain." *Fitness* (October 2011). http://www.fitnessmagazine.com/weight-loss/tips/avoid-weight-gain-after-marriage.

United Press International. "Romance Novel Fans: Life Imitates Fiction." *Los Angeles Times* (October 28, 1985). http://articles.latimes.com/1985-10-28/news/mn-11910_1_romance-novels.

Van Kirk, Kat, and Jessica O'Reilly. "How Masturbation Affects Your Sex Life." *Great List* (2016). http://greatist.com/live/masturbation-affects-sex-drive.

Vann, Madeline. "1 in 4 Men Over 30 Has Low Testosterone." ABC News (March 23, 2016). www.abcnews.go.com/Health/Healthday/story?id=4508669.

Yelland, Christine, and Marika Tiggermann. "Muscularity and the gay ideal: body dissatisfaction and disordered eating in homosexual men." *Eating Behaviors* 4, no. 2 (August 2003): 107–116.

"Watch Your Spouse Masturbate? 190 Woman and 588 Men Have Answered." *The Marriage Bed* (May 5, 2015). http://site.themarriagebed.com/surveys/watch-your-spouse-masturbate.

WebMD. "Kegel Exercises—Topic Overview." WebMD/Women's Health (September 9, 2014). http://www.webmd.com/women/tc/kegel-exercises-topic-overview.

———. "Sex, Exercise, and Stress Incontinence." WebMD/Women's Health (2007). http://www.webmd.com/women/features/sex-exercise-stress-incontinence?page=3.

Wilcox, Melanie. "Why Romance Novels Turn Women On." *Acculturated* (July 9, 2015). http://acculturated.com/why-romance-novels-turn-women-on.

Williams, Bonnie. "Readers of Romance Novels Have Better Sex Lives." WebSyte (2006). http://ascnetwork.soup.io/post/100808640/Way-To-Get-Ex-Back-Readers-of.

Wilson, Glenn. "The Psychology of Sex: Glenn Wilson on the Coolidge Effect." *The Great Sex Divide*, pp. 41–45. Peter Owen (London) 1989, Scott-Townsend (Washington D.C.) 1992. http://www.heretical.com/wilson/coolidge.html.

Woznicki, Katrina. "Saving Your Sex Life When You're Depressed." WebMD (2013). http://www.m.webmd.com/depression/features/depression-and-sex.

"You Need Help: What's the Deal with Scissoring?" *Autosraddle* (July 1, 2014). http://www.autostraddle.com/you-need-help-whats-the-deal-with-scissoring-242968.

Zamosky, Lisa. "The Science behind Romance." WebMD/Health & Sex (January 15, 2009). http://www.webmd.com/sex-relationships/features/the-science-behind-romance.

Zebroff, Petra. "Worrying about Looking 'Sexy' Enough During Sex?" *Art of Connection* (April 22, 2014). http://artofconnection.org/tips-for-body-spectatoring.

Acknowledgments

Writing is a very solitary activity, but turning the author's words into an actual book takes a village. I am very grateful to my village.

I am eternally grateful to my family. I want to thank my daughters Quincy Berman and Mendez Berman. You have both been so patient and understanding during this writing process. Thank you for encouraging me to get back on my computer to write, entertaining yourselves so I could work, and supporting this ambitious undertaking. Even if we didn't get to do many exciting activities while I was writing, I hope I was at least able to be a good role model to you regarding hard work and dedication. I am so excited to do all the things we planned on the "when the book is done" list! Eric Schiffer: As I mentioned in the dedication, you are my soul mate. I know this was not an easy journey. Thank you so much for your encouragement, support, and for taking the girls on so many fun outings so that I could write. You are my relationship inspiration. Thank you for believing in therapy, believing in me, and, most of all, for believing in us. To my parents, Barry Mann and Cynthia Weil: My relationship expertise would not exist without the education you helped me get, the therapy-positive home you created, and the relationship you two have, flaws and all. Thank you for allowing me to share some of your relationship experiences with my readers. But most of all, thank you for being the most wonderful, supportive nonjudgmental, loving parents anyone could ever have. Thank you for always encouraging me to follow my passion and creative inspiration.

Jennifer Williams, my editing soul mate, I would follow you to the literary ends of the earth. Thank you for always bringing my writing to the next level, honoring my nutty creative process, and providing me with literary therapy, along with great vegan food (and a few drinks!). Working with you is both an honor and a pleasure.

Theresa Thompson and Marilyn Kretzer, thank you for making this book a reality and for your support.

Sari Lampert, Marketing Director for Sterling, your excitement about this project is contagious! Thank you for your enthusiasm and hard work on

The Relationship Fix. Lauren Tambini, thank you for helping get the word out about this book! You are both a joy to work with!

Kudos for this beautiful cover and interior design go to the great Sterling creative team! Jo Obarowski, Elizabeth Lindy, and David Ter-Avanesyan, thank you so much for this stunning cover. It took three books and your great work to get Jennifer Williams to get her way, my face on the cover! Most people don't realize how important the interior design is in a book. Oftentimes, it is the difference between the author's words being read or the book being put back on the shelf. I am grateful to Lorie Pagnozzi, Gavin Motnyk, and Ellen Hudson for making my words look so good!

To take a great photograph requires vision, creativity, and great skill. Thank you Sarah Orbanic for your great photography. I hate having my picture taken, but you made it such a fun experience and it shows in the work. Thank you for your amazing eye and for making me look like the best possible version of myself. Sommer Anzaldo, there is no greater gift than to have a best friend who is so gifted as a makeup artist. I am always in awe of your artistic talent and vision. Thank you for making me look beautiful, doing therapy on me, drying my tears, making me laugh, and always being such a wonderful friend. Also, thank you for helping me with my research and the References chapter. Maggie Schwartz, thank you for being the biggest hair perfectionist on the planet. Thank you for making me look like the natural blonde nature intended me to be! Eric, thank you for the very special shirt I am wearing on the cover. I will never forget the magical weekend when you bought it for me.

Thank you Joe Weiner, my wonderful attorney. Thank you for always having my back and being such a great deal maker. Carole Mann, my agent, thank you so much for making my dream to do another book with Sterling a reality. Maura Teitelbaum, I wanted to give you a long overdue thank-you for the great work you did with *SuperBaby.* My oversight in the last book was not for lack of appreciation or respect for the great work you have done for me over the years; it was purely a sleep-deprived mistake. You have my love and gratitude.

Dr. Sharon O'Conner, thank you for your brilliant insights into relationships and therapy, and your ongoing support. I wouldn't be where I am today if it wasn't for you. Andrea Weiss, thank you for being my dear friend, a fantastic assistant, and a mom role model. Thank you for your help getting books and doing research.

Michele Musso, thank you for tracking down old radio calls, chasing down endorsement quotes with me, and for all your amazing support. Jennifer Ariemma, thank you for helping make my work more LGBT sensitive and for all your support. Lou Paget, thank you for going the extra mile and sharing new information and studies and educating me for the sex chapter!

I want to thank VH1 for allowing me to do VH1 Couples Therapy with Dr. Jenn, a program that shows real couples doing real therapy, and which has brought much healing to many viewers. I am also grateful to all of the couples who have opened their hearts and their lives to our viewers and now to my readers. I am so grateful for the platform and the support you all provide me with. I want to thank those of you I work with and have worked with in the past: Jill Holmes, Fernando Mills, Paula Aranda, Trevor Rose, Chris Delhomme, Michael Fabiani, Susan Levison, Jeff Olde, and Tom Huffman. Thank you for letting me share pieces of *Couples Therapy* with my readers.

I am so grateful to John Irwin of Irwin Entertainment. Thank you for betting on me, supporting me, and believing in me. I am especially grateful to Damian Sullivan for creating *Couples Therapy*. When I auditioned for the show, you made me two promises: (1) that you would never interrupt the therapy for production because you have too much respect for the therapeutic process and (2) that the therapy and well-being of the cast would always come first. Thank you for keeping your promises and for making such a meaningful, soulful show that touches lives in such positive ways. Patrick Sayers, thank you for being the greatest director on the planet and for always offering me all the information I need. I am very lucky to work with you and have you as a friend.

I am grateful to SiriusXM for giving me such a wonderful opportunity to reach so many listeners and help so many people on my call-in advice shows over the years. I want to thank those of you I have worked with over the years: Serena Kodilla, Craig Schwab, Dave Gorab, Megan Kustra, Ashley Wandishin, and Michele Musso. Thank you to John Searles, Kate White, and Joanna Coles for the *Cosmopolitan magazine* support. Thank you to my friends at *Oprah*, especially Erik Logan and Corny Koehl. You have all helped me take my work to the next level. Thank you!

Thank you to my clients, my callers, and to the many brave souls who come on my shows, trust me with your hearts, and share your lives with me. It is my honor and my pleasure to be there for you all.

Index

About the Author

Dr. Jenn Mann is a well-known psychotherapist, author, and television and radio show host. She is the host and therapist for VH1's long-standing hit shows *Couples Therapy with Dr. Jenn* and *Family Therapy with Dr. Jenn*. She has appeared as a guest expert on hundreds of shows, including: *The Today Show, The Early Show, Dr. Oz, Wendy Williams, The Doctors, The Maury Show, Steve Harvey, Access Hollywood, The Insider,* and *Jimmy Kimmel Live.* Dr. Jenn hosts a widely popular call-in advice radio show, and is the author of two bestselling parenting books, *SuperBaby: 12 Ways to Give Your Child a Head Start in the First 3 Years* and *The A to Z Guide to Raising Happy, Confident Kids.* She is also the co-author of a children's book, *Rockin' Babies,* which she co-wrote with her mother, Grammy award-winning songwriter Cynthia Weil. Dr. Jenn is a licensed Marriage, Family, and Child Therapist, and has been in private practice for almost three decades. She lives in Beverly Hills, California, with her family. To learn more about Dr. Jenn, visit DoctorJenn.com or check out Twitter, Instagram, Facebook, and Snapchat @DrJennMann.